CW01500725

ROMANCING TREASON

Romancing Treason

The Literature of the Wars of the Roses

MEGAN G. LEITCH

OXFORD
UNIVERSITY PRESS

OXFORD
UNIVERSITY PRESS

Great Clarendon Street, Oxford, OX2 6DP,
United Kingdom

Oxford University Press is a department of the University of Oxford.
It furthers the University's objective of excellence in research, scholarship,
and education by publishing worldwide. Oxford is a registered trade mark of
Oxford University Press in the UK and in certain other countries

© Megan G. Leitch 2015

The moral rights of the author have been asserted

First Edition Published in 2015

Impression: 1

Published in the United States of America by Oxford University Press
198 Madison Avenue, New York, NY 10016, United States of America

British Library Cataloguing in Publication Data
Data available

Library of Congress Control Number: 2014940460

ISBN 978–0–19–872459–9

Printed and bound by
CPI Group (UK) Ltd, Croydon CR0 4YY

Acknowledgements

Many people have supported me in writing this book, both directly and indirectly, and I am delighted to be able to express my gratitude here. Dan Wakelin and Helen Fulton both gave very valuable suggestions when examining the doctoral version of this book, as did the anonymous readers for Oxford University Press at a later stage. Various other medievalists assisted by kindly proof-reading chapters, offering encouragement, or discussing interesting ideas (both apposite and otherwise) at conferences and in library tea rooms and departmental corridors, including the following: Elizabeth Archibald, Joanna Bellis, Venetia Bridges, Aisling Byrne, Rob Gossedge, Sara Harris, Joni Henry, David Johnson, Amy Kaufman, Jessica Lockhart, Andrew Lynch, Margaret McCarthy, Megan Murton, Carl Phelpstead, Ad Putter, Robert Rouse, Cory Rushton, Corinne Saunders, Danica Summerlin, Kevin Whetter, and Emily Wingfield.

In its dissertation form, the writing of this book benefited from the generous support of the Commonwealth Scholarship Commission, the Cambridge University International Scholarship Scheme, the St John's College Benefactors' Scholarships, and the Social Sciences and Humanities Research Council of Canada. Thanks are also due to the Bibliothèque Nationale, the Bodleian Library, the British Library, and Cambridge University Library for permission to consult their collections of manuscripts and early printed books.

Earlier versions of parts of this book have appeared as 'Speaking (of) Treason in Malory's *Morte Darthur*', *Arthurian Literature*, XXVII (2010), 103–34, and 'Thinking Twice about Treason in Caxton's Prose Romances: Proper Chivalric Conduct and the English Printing Press', *Medium Aevum*, LXXXI.1 (2012), 41–69. I am grateful to the editors of these journals for permission to develop this published material here.

My warmest thanks are due to Siân Echard, for first engaging my interest in this topic when I had the pleasure of taking her undergraduate module on medieval Arthurian literature; and most especially to Helen Cooper, who supervised both my M.Phil. and my Ph.D. with more wisdom, generosity, insight, and encouragement than I could ever have asked for.

Contents

List of Abbreviations

EETS ES	Early English Text Society, Extra Series
EETS OS	Early English Text Society, Original Series
EETS SS	Early English Text Society, Supplementary Series
MÆ	*Medium Ævum*
MED	*The Middle English Dictionary*
NS	*New Series*
N&Q	*Notes and Queries*
OED	*The Oxford English Dictionary*

1

Introduction

Wo hath þat conyng by wysdam or prudence
To know whether his frende be feynt or stable?
Ther ys no creature, I trow, þat hath þat science
To know his ffrende—the world ys so mutable,
And ffrenship ys double and varry disseyvable;
The mowthe seythe ane, þe hert þinketh anoþer;
Allas to say, hit ys full lementable,
Vnneth a man now may truste his owne broþer.[1]

Scrawled in a separate hand at the end of an understudied mid-fifteenth-century vernacular miscellany, this verse critique of treachery addresses ideals of interpersonal conduct through their negation. Subsequent readers, upon reaching the end of the manuscript, endorsed the poem's bleak assessment by responding to it with a manicule and a comment of 'marke this well'. Here, the reader-response poet and commentator both react to, and epitomize, this manuscript's mode of engaging with its sociopolitical context. Those who penned this poem and their agreement with it wrote at a time when English civil strife made the volatility of social bonds an ever-present preoccupation. In the mid- to late fifteenth century, the tensions and conflicts surrounding the Wars of the Roses fostered an atmosphere of anxiety about the breakdown of social order and of traditional loyalties. The poem locates these concerns in horizontal relationships and their betrayal, in the fissures within friendship, family, and faithful alliances. In dealing with doubleness and deceit, it departs from earlier medieval models by eschewing any reference to the refuge of divine providence or the priorities of the next world. It dwells instead on its lament, refusing to disengage from its earthly moment—its 'now', its world 'so mutable'.

---

[1] The manuscript is *c.*1450, and the verse annotation and marginalia are late fifteenth century: Oxford, Bodleian Library, MS Rawlinson D82, f.34r; 'Deceit, III', in *Secular Lyrics of the XIVth and XVth Centuries*, ed. by Rossell Hope Robbins (1952; Oxford: Oxford University Press, 1955), p. 101. Primary sources are cited first in full, and then by page and/or line number in the text. All italics and translations are mine unless otherwise stated.

This is the same historical moment that made one Paston correspondent
urge another to 'remembre the onstabylnesse of thys wold' and in which Sir
Thomas Malory wrote of a Launcelot who 'threwe hys armes abrode, and
sayd, "Alas! Who may truste thys worlde?" '² Like Malory and the Paston
gentry family, these readers-turned-writers belonged to a generation for
whom the confidence and prosperity of Henry V's reign were a distant
memory, and whose pragmatic political consciousness was instead conditioned by the crises occasioned by England's experience of weak kingship,
unrest, and the loss of its continental possessions under Henry VI; and
the resulting divisions, reversals, and rebellions of the Wars of the Roses,
which continued through to the midpoint of Henry VII's reign. This book
takes as its delimiting dates *c*.1437 to *c*.1497, from Henry VI's assump-
tion of majority rule to the last of the Yorkist rebellions against Tudor rule.
These dates are indicative rather than definitive: historical events can be
dated, literary movements are broader, and the dates of individual texts are
often uncertain. This study argues, however, that the relatively neglected
English literature of these six decades can be distinguished and understood
in terms of its intense and admonitory concerns with the breakdown of
social and political faith expressed in the idea of treason.

The Rawlinson D82 reader-response poet and commentators offer contemporary annotations to this miscellany's main texts: the anonymous
mid-fifteenth-century *Siege of Thebes* and *Siege of Troy*, prose romances that
manifest the same markedly secular lamentation of social instability as the
marginalia. These Wars of the Roses romances, and others like them, are
rife with treason. This study argues that such texts dwell upon treason in
a fashion that is characteristic of their literary culture, and that insistently
engages with the problems of contemporary England. In this textual practice, treason—and its disturbing prevalence—is presented in a way that is
disillusioned and anxious, yet not wholly pessimistic. Treason is effectively

---

    ² John Russe to John I (1465), in *Paston Letters and Papers of the Fifteenth Century*,
ed. by Norman Davis, Richard Beadle, and Colin Richmond, EETS SS 20–2, 3 vols
(Oxford: Oxford University Press, 2004–5), II, 688.58; Sir Thomas Malory, *The Works
of Sir Thomas Malory*, ed. by Eugène Vinaver, 3rd edn, rev. by P. J. C. Field, 3 vols
(Oxford: Clarendon Press, 1990), III, 1254.11–12. Launcelot's *gesture* is precedented in the
Stanzaic *Morte Arthur: King Arthur's Death*, ed. by Larry D. Benson (Kalamazoo: Medieval
Institute Publications, 1994), line 3778. However, only Malory's late fifteenth-century
Launcelot speaks these words. Similarly, John Paston II wrote to his mother Margaret
after fighting at Barnet for the losing (Lancastrian) side, reporting from London on 18
April 1471 that 'the worlde, I ensure yow, is ryght qwesye' (*Paston Letters*, I, 261.29–31).
For further laments about 'this world', see the final section of Chapter 2, and the poem
written (its recorder claims) by Anthony Woodville when incarcerated at Pontefract in
1483 (John Rous, *Antiquarii Warwicensis Historia Regum Angliae*, ed. by Thomas Hearne
(Oxford: Fletcher, 1745), p. 214, lines 2–3).

the antithesis of chivalry in this cultural imaginary; therefore, by focusing upon treason, the literature of the Wars of the Roses addresses ideas of proper conduct through their opposites. Here, negative social commentary both claims a dominant position, and is entwined with a didacticism designed to counteract the transgressive behaviour that it laments and critiques. Numerous other texts from this period operate in a similar manner to the prose *Siege*s and their appended poem: poetry from Lydgate's *Fall of Princes* to Hardyng's *Chronicle*, George Ashby's *Active Policy of a Prince*, and the verse *Melusine*; and prose from the *Pseudo-Turpin Chronicle* and Malory's *Morte Darthur* to William Caxton's own romances. All of these 'treat' treachery in both senses of the word, by discussing it and seeking to cure it. Caxton's prologue to *Godeffroy of Boloyne* (1481) encapsulates the didactic strategies of this and other prose romances he printed, and of much contemporary English literature: *Godeffroy*, he writes, is intended 'to moeue and tenflawme the hertes of the Redars and hierers, for *teschewe and flee werkes vycious, dishonnest and vytuperable* / And for tempryse and accomplysshe enterpryses honnestes, and werkes of gloryous meryte.'[3] Here, representations of treason, as 'werkes vycious, dishonnest and vytuperable', carry both a warning and an aspirational hope for better conduct. The secular literature of the Wars of the Roses instructs by both positive and negative reinforcement, with the latter—the mode of paraenesis or admonition—attaining a distinctive primacy. Thus, these texts engage in an ethical discourse; a discourse in which treason receives focused attention as the act most threatening to social cohesion.

This study addresses the scope and significance of the secular English literature of the Wars of the Roses. It analyses mid- to late fifteenth-century English literature of a variety of genres alongside contemporary social and political discourses, arguing that this literary culture is broader and richer than has previously been recognized. Despite the context of decades of civil war, treason is an understudied theme even with regards to the *Morte Darthur*. This book accordingly provides a double contribution to Malory criticism by addressing the *Morte Darthur*'s important and nuanced engagement with the theme of treason, and by reading the *Morte* in the hitherto neglected context of the prose romances and other secular literature written by Malory's English contemporaries. It thus also brings back to light the thematic sophistication of undeservedly neglected texts— such as the prose *Siege of Thebes* and *Siege of Troy*, *Melusine*, the *Squire of Low Degree*, and the romances William Caxton translated from French (especially *Godeffroy of Boloyne, Charles the Grete*, and the *Foure Sonnes of*

---

[3] William Caxton, *Godeffroy of Boloyne*, ed. by Mary Noyes Colvin, EETS ES 64 (London: Paul, Trench, Trübner, 1893), pp. 1.5–8.

Aymon)—by reading them in their own right. An especial focus, recurring across Chapters 3, 4, 5, and 6, concerns this period's contributions to the romance genre, contributions which occur in both manuscript and print, and which, unlike earlier English romances, are predominantly in prose. Thus, while studies of popular romance customarily focus exclusively on verse romances, this book attends to the nature of medieval English prose romance in a way that highlights both what these texts share with earlier verse romances, and what makes them distinctively different. This study argues both that prose romances play a central role in this preoccupation with treason, and that the concentrated yet contested ways in which treason is discussed in fifteenth-century chronicles, correspondence, and political documents, as well as romances, point us to a key word and concept of the time that illuminates literary and non-literary texts alike.

What exactly 'treason' means is important here, and is complicated not only by the fact that the various powerful figures vying for control of the kingdom could—and often did—accuse each other and each other's supporters of treason. Moreover, during the Wars of the Roses, treason had both vertical and lateral dimensions, and these are combined in contemporary literary texts in a distinctive way. The more familiar, hierarchical idea of treason in late medieval England rests in the legal definition of treason as an attempt to harm or kill one's king, master, husband, or prelate. In addition, however, horizontal betrayals of one's neighbour, brother-in-arms, friend, or even foe could be considered treasonous: according to the law of arms that (at least theoretically) regulated the conduct of international conflict; according to non-institutional ideas of betrayal of bonds of affinity or expectations of chivalric conduct; and, especially significantly, according to the concept of the commonweal, which gained political currency from *c.*1450 onwards, and to which ideal contemporaries often accused each other of being treasonous. Thus, treason was antithetical to community, and what community meant was shaped by ideas and accusations of treason as well as the other way around. When Malory's Launcelot defends his honourable reputation by declaring, 'I reporte me to all knyghtes that ever have knowyn me, I fared never wyth no treson, nother I loved never the felyshyp of hym that fared with treson' (1134.16–19), treason is figured as a travelling-companion or fellow, as a tangible subversion of community. The romances of the Wars of the Roses are informed by both hierarchical and horizontal understandings of treason, and they consistently apply the legal lexis of formal accusations of (hierarchical) treason to a broader set of transgressions in a way that intensifies condemnations of such conduct. The ways in which treason and betrayal constitute crucial concerns for Malory and less renowned contemporary writers illuminate their texts' significant thematic and stylistic affinities.

By reading these texts' constructions of treachery, this book reassesses the understudied textual culture and genre of late romance to which the *Morte Darthur* belonged. Thus, by addressing the parameters and permutations of treason in both literary and non-literary texts, this study pursues a wider aim of establishing some characteristics for the literary culture that spanned the late Lancastrian to the early Tudor age.

The literary terrain of the Wars of the Roses has customarily been perceived as sparsely tenanted and incoherent. Criticism has traditionally taken a limited view of the role of the fifteenth century in English literary history even when devoting attention to it.[4] The past two or three decades have indeed seen a surge in studies seeking to recuperate fifteenth-century literature, but these have largely focused on the first part of the century and on poetry, in particular the post-Chaucerian generation of Lydgate and Hoccleve.[5] Recent scholarship has addressed how, during the early fifteenth century, poets engaged in a dialogue with the Lancastrian regime,[6] or has articulated identities for the often-overshadowed Tudor courtly literatures of the early and mid-sixteenth century.[7] Yet the second half of the fifteenth century receives short shrift in medieval and early modern literary studies. James Simpson's innovative *Reform and Cultural Revolution: 1350–1547* argues for a shift from late medieval cultural heterogeneity to Tudor centralization by comparing Ricardian and Lancastrian texts to Tudor ones. As David Wallace points out, 'some account of the differing pockets of time that we might expect to find in the earlier period . . . would happily

---

[4] For instance: Derek Pearsall, *John Lydgate* (London: Routledge, 1970), pp. 14 and 67–70; A. C. Spearing, *Medieval to Renaissance in English Poetry* (Cambridge: Cambridge University Press, 1985). For a more sensitive view, see Helen Cooper, 'Introduction', in *The Long Fifteenth Century*, ed. by Helen Cooper and Sally Mapstone (Oxford: Clarendon Press, 1997), pp. 1–14 (esp. pp. 3–4).

[5] David Lawton, 'Dullness and the Fifteenth Century', *English Literary History*, 54.4 (1987), 761–99; A. S. G. Edwards, 'Tradition and Innovation in Fifteenth-Century Poetry', *Modern Language Quarterly*, 53 (1992), 1–4; *Writing after Chaucer: Essential Readings in Chaucer and the Fifteenth Century*, ed. by Daniel J. Pinti (New York: Garland, 1998).

[6] Maura Nolan, *John Lydgate and the Making of Public Culture*, Cambridge Studies in Medieval Literature, LVIII (Cambridge: Cambridge University Press, 2005); Jenni Nuttall, *The Creation of Lancastrian Kingship: Literature, Language and Politics in Late Medieval England*, Cambridge Studies in Medieval Literature, LXVII (Cambridge: Cambridge University Press, 2007).

[7] *Rethinking the Henrician Era: Essays on Early Tudor Texts and Contexts*, ed. by Peter C. Herman (Chicago: University of Illinois Press, 1994); Mike Pincombe, 'Introduction: Tudor Literature: Drab or Tarnished?', in *The Anatomy of Tudor Literature*, ed. by Mike Pincombe (Aldershot: Ashgate, 2001), pp. 1–8; Mike Pincombe and Cathy Shrank, 'Prologue: The Travails of Tudor Literature', in *The Oxford Handbook of Tudor Literature, 1485–1603*, ed. by Mike Pincombe and Cathy Shrank (Oxford: Oxford University Press, 2009), pp. 1–17; Antony J. Hasler, *Court Poetry in Late Medieval England and Scotland: Allegories of Authority*, Cambridge Studies in Medieval Literature, LXXX (Cambridge: Cambridge University Press, 2011).

augment' Simpson's overarching narrative.[8] Yet in this otherwise promising reassessment of the place of the medieval in literary history, Simpson not only avoids distinguishing the literary character of the mid- to late fifteenth century from other moments, but also follows critical convention in neglecting even to consider most of the secular literature of this period, vaulting from one side of it to the other with only Malory's *Morte Darthur* as a stepping stone in between.[9]

The *Morte Darthur*, written in 1469 and printed in 1485, has, in fact, often been perceived as a solitary landmark in a desolate literary landscape. Studies contextualizing Malory's textual interests and style have focused on (largely continental) Arthurian traditions, earlier English verse romances, and chronicles and gentry correspondence, but have overlooked the prose romances of Malory's English contemporaries, and indeed most contemporary English literature.[10] Larry Benson rejects the notion that the *Morte* can be understood as part of a larger insular genre by summarily dismissing the other fifteenth-century English prose romances, which, he contends, 'hardly established a tradition of English secular prose on which Malory could draw for his style'.[11] While recent and refreshing studies by Paul Strohm on political texts and Daniel Wakelin on humanism are both attentive to some of the secularities of the later fifteenth century, these leave unaddressed other forms of secular literature, notably romance,

---

[8] David Wallace, 'Oxford English Literary History', *Journal of Medieval and Early Modern Studies*, 35.1 (2005), 13–24 (p. 17).

[9] See James Simpson, *Reform and Cultural Revolution: 1350–1547* (Oxford: Oxford University Press, 2002), and, again, Spearing, *Medieval to Renaissance*. Simpson isolates Malory generically as well as chronologically by claiming that the *Morte* is not a romance; see the last section of Chapter 4 in the present work for a rebuttal.

[10] P. J. C. Field, *Romance and Chronicle: A Study of Malory's Prose Style* (London: Barrie & Jenkins, 1971); Larry D. Benson, *Malory's 'Morte Darthur'* (Cambridge, MA: Harvard University Press, 1976); Felicity Riddy, *Sir Thomas Malory* (Leiden: Brill, 1987); Catherine Batt, *Malory's 'Morte Darthur': Remaking Arthurian Tradition* (New York: Palgrave, 2002), esp. pp. 1–35; Raluca L. Radulescu, *The Gentry Context for Malory's 'Morte Darthur'*, Arthurian Studies, LV (Cambridge: Brewer, 2003); Miriam Edlich-Muth, *Malory and his European Contemporaries: Adapting Late Arthurian Romance Collections* (Cambridge: Brewer, 2014). Two exceptions are the reading of Malory alongside William Caxton's *Paris and Vienne* and *Charles the Grete* in Jennifer Goodman's doctoral thesis, *Malory and William Caxton's Prose Romances of 1485* (New York: Garland, 1987); and the more inclusive adumbration of a contemporary literary context for Malory's *Morte* in Helen Cooper, 'Counter-Romance: Civil Strife and Father-Killing in the Prose Romances', in *Long Fifteenth Century*, pp. 141–62. Raluca L. Radulescu, in *Romance and its Contexts in Fifteenth-Century England: Politics, Piety, and Penitence* (Cambridge: Brewer, 2013), productively considers the reception of some romances during the fifteenth century, but focuses on reading earlier, pious romances alongside Malory's *Morte Darthur*.

[11] Benson, *Malory's 'Morte Darthur'*, p. 21. The lesser-known fifteenth-century English prose romances are elsewhere referred to less disparagingly, but no less summarily: Derek Pearsall, 'The English Romance in the Fifteenth Century', *Essays and Studies*, 29 (1976), 56–83 (p. 73);

which, as this book argues, is central to this literary period's identity.[12] This study's examination of the role of treason in identity construction and community formation offers a deeper understanding of the nature and interconnections of the various works of literature produced during the Wars of the Roses, and of this literary culture's relationship to what precedes and follows it.

TRACING TREASON: A TOPOGRAPHY OF FIFTEENTH-CENTURY ENGLISH LITERATURE

This study, then, argues that English literature from *c*.1437 to *c*.1497 concentrates on treason as a source of anxieties about community and identity, and as a way of responding to those concerns within a secular ethical framework. The lens of treason brings a distinct literary culture into focus; a literary culture that both reflects, and reflects upon, the troubles of its time. As stated previously, while necessarily approximate and relative, fluid rather than fixed, this literary moment can be perceived as opening with the start of Henry VI's ineffectual majority in 1437; it continued through the progressive loss of most of England's continental possessions up to 1453, which, combined with the king's weak rule, helped to precipitate the Wars of the Roses; and it can be seen to close with the very last phase of the Wars of the Roses in the capture of the Yorkist impostor Perkin Warbeck in 1497, as political instability was at last superseded by Henry VII's increasingly centralized and firm governance. In the decades between, as recurring dynastic struggles caused cycles of strife and instability, a literary culture poised between medieval and early modern articulated its powerful ideological preoccupations with treason. In order to further clarify why this book focuses on these six decades, the following paragraphs map the differing contours of literary treason in the decades

---

Douglas Gray, *Later Medieval English Literature* (Oxford: Oxford University Press, 2008), p. 180. Mark Lambert mentions a few of them, but only as foils for the *Morte: Malory: Style and Vision in 'Le Morte Darthur'* (New Haven: Yale University Press, 1975).

[12] Paul Strohm, *Politique: Languages of Statecraft between Chaucer and Shakespeare* (Notre Dame: University of Notre Dame Press, 2005); Daniel Wakelin, *Humanism, Reading, and English Literature 1430–1530* (Oxford: Oxford University Press, 2007). Other recent studies productively reconsider the fifteenth century, but periodize very differently, and again largely focus their attention elsewhere than romance: Catherine Nall, *Reading and War in Fifteenth-Century England: From Lydgate to Malory* (Cambridge: Brewer, 2012); *Form and Reform: Reading across the Fifteenth Century*, ed. by Shannon Gayk and Kathleen Tonry (Columbus, OH: Ohio State University Press, 2011); Joanna Summers, *Late-Medieval Prison Writing and the Politics of Autobiography* (Oxford: Oxford University Press, 2004). For William Kuskin's scholarship on Caxton, see Chapter 5.

before, during, and after this period alongside the sociopolitical conditions that inform each era. Their content is summarized in table form in the Appendix at the end of the book.

In contrast to what emerges later in the century, English literature of the first decades of the fifteenth century (and earlier) does not display the same degree or type of interest in treason. Following the security of Henry V's reign (1413–22) and the hopeful efficiency of conciliar rule during Henry VI's minority (1422–37), the effectiveness of central governance diminished; social stability and confidence in authority progressively crumbled.[13] This sociopolitical progression parallels a darkening in the tone of literary treatments of treason. While the triumphs and termination of Henry V's reign generated literature such as Lydgate's *Troy Book* and *Siege of Thebes*, which place faith in providence as the source of redress for treason, the growing instability and lack of effective authority in the late 1430s accompanied Lydgate's darker *Fall of Princes*. Thereafter, political tensions further increased in the late 1440s as the lack of clear royal authority became more apparent, resulting in open strife and a 'breakdown of public order' in the 1450s.[14] This environment in which multiple powers vied for control and accusations of treason were issued in all directions gave rise to heightened concerns about instability that were to recur until the 1490s and that underpinned the treason-focused literary culture addressed here. These concerns were conditioned by a type of sociopolitical stress that lasted for approximately two generations, and involved the politically active—and literate—classes of gentry, aristocracy, and, sometimes, merchants. Landowners were the most affected by this 'prolonged crisis of kingship', since throughout the Wars of the Roses, maintaining public order and settling disputes were usually the responsibility of the gentry and magnates in their localities.[15] The gentry and aristocracy thus

---

[13] B. P. Wolffe argues that the transfer of power to Henry VI marked the end of effective government because Henry was too irrationally wilful to rule properly, while for John Watts, it was because Henry lacked the independent will to do so; however, both agree that the appointment of the new, non-minority council on 9 November 1437 was the point at which it became apparent (at least to the lords) that Henry VI was not capable of rule: B. P. Wolffe, 'The Personal Rule of Henry VI', in *Fifteenth-Century England, 1399–1509: Studies in Politics and Society*, ed. by S. B. Chrimes, C. D. Ross, and R. A. Griffiths (Manchester: Manchester University Press, 1972), pp. 29–48 (pp. 29–30 and 36); John Watts, *Henry VI and the Politics of Kingship* (Cambridge: Cambridge University Press, 1996), pp. 111–12 and 133–5. On Henry VI's lack of 'the capacity to rule', see also R. L. Storey, *The End of the House of Lancaster* (London: Barrie & Rockliff, 1966), pp. 27 and 29–42.

[14] Michael Hicks, *The Wars of the Roses* (New Haven: Yale University Press, 2010), p. 40; Storey, *The End of the House of Lancaster*, esp. pp. 5–9.

[15] Christine Carpenter, *The Wars of the Roses: Politics and the Constitution in England, c. 1437–1509* (Cambridge: Cambridge University Press, 1997), pp. 262–3; C. D. Ross, 'The Reign of Edward IV', in *Fifteenth-Century England*, pp. 49–66 (p. 62), and *Edward IV*

had to rely upon horizontal networks and friendships as well as hierarchical loyalties in order to maintain social order. This local and lateral responsibility expanded in periods of increased disorder such as the first decade of Edward IV's rule (1461–71), as dynastic changes and rebellions weakened royal control of many parts of the kingdom. Therefore, for these social classes, who regulated regional disputes 'through networks of neighbourhood, family, friends and lordship',[16] social cohesion and its antithesis, treason, were of pressing concern, and the literary culture of the Wars of the Roses engaged with these concerns of the literate classes. Of course, the disorder and despair of England during the Wars of the Roses were not as dire as Tudor portrayals would claim;[17] however, in this sociopolitical climate, the danger of committing or being affected by *horizontal* betrayal was at least as significant and politically charged as the danger of hierarchical betrayal, and, as we shall see, both were great enough to preoccupy contemporary readers and writers.

Accompanying this particular lateral concern in mid- to late fifteenth-century literature is an equally distinctive secularity. During the Wars of the Roses, many literary writers eschewed expressing faith in providence and instead expressed a heightened degree of pragmatism and insistent focus on human affairs. The middle decades of the century saw the production of a number of romances strongly interested in treason and in seeking to counteract it through worldly initiative, such as the anonymous *Siege of Thebes* and *Siege of Troy, King Ponthus and the Fair Sidone*, the prose *Life of Alexander*, and the Middle English *Pseudo-Turpin Chronicle*. There were further power struggles, battles, accusations, and attainders leading up to the regime change in 1461, which also generated occasional literature with an emphasis on treason, such as the Lancastrian *Somnium Vigilantis* and an array of Yorkist verses. Edward IV's first reign (1461–70) was briefly peaceful and stable at its midpoint, but it was characterized by discord and rebellions in both its early and late years, and culminated in the Lancastrian readeption in 1470–1; it is perhaps no coincidence that the later years of this decade produced some of the most focused literary engagements with treason: George Ashby's partisan poetry and Malory's

(1974; New Haven: Yale University Press, 1997), pp. 41 and 119; G. L. Harriss, 'Political Society and the Growth of Government in Late Medieval England', *Past and Present*, 138 (1993), 28–57 (pp. 52–3); Carpenter, *Locality and Polity: A Study of Warwickshire Landed Society, 1401–1499* (Cambridge: Cambridge University Press, 1992), pp. 281–5; Hicks, *Wars of the Roses*, pp. 27–8.

[16] Harriss, 'Political Society and the Growth of Government', p. 51; J. R. Lander, *Government and Community: England 1450–1509* (London: Arnold, 1980), pp. 42–7.

[17] Charles Ross, *The Wars of the Roses: A Concise History* (London: Thames and Hudson, 1976), p. 151; Hicks, *Wars of the Roses*, pp. x and 12.

Morte Darthur. These decades were not, however, uniformly infused with a sense of disaster and strife. Edward IV's primarily peaceful second reign (1471–83), with no viable contenders for the throne, did not contribute as much to this type of literature as the more troubled decades to either side. However, even in the 1470s there was 'a disturbing incidence of outrageous crime and sustained defiance of the government's authority',[18] and the table in the Appendix shows some relevant texts produced during this time. The strife between Edward IV's death in 1483 and Richard III's defeat in 1485, and the rebellions and uncertainties of Henry VII's early reign, saw the printing of the half-dozen of Caxton's prose romances and chivalric tracts most focused on treason, the 'translation' of the prose and verse *Melusine* romances with increased attention to treason, and perhaps the composition of the treason-focused *Squire of Low Degree*. This literature is innovative in the ways in which it elides or interrogates a providential framework in connection with treason. As when the Rawlinson D82 reader-response poem refuses to disengage from its earthly moment by resisting any reference to providence or the justice of the next world, mid- to late fifteenth-century texts expand the scope available for secular pragmatism, for responding constructively or correctively to treason. However, the elision of a providential framework also shows the way in which treason cannot be written out of these texts. Encoded in the definition and discussion of treason are ineradicable anxieties; we see this pervasive sense of unease concerning the way in which treason is both expected and unpredictable when the reader-response poet asks, 'Wo hath þat conyng by wysdam or prudence / To know whether his frende be feynt or stable?' In part through a recognition of these secular and interrogative strains in the literature of the Wars of the Roses, this book contributes more broadly to the emerging and ongoing scholarly interest in reconsidering the relationship between medieval and early modern literary culture. It focuses on a comparatively neglected sixty-year interval—the interval that is customarily the dividing line, the 'no man's land', between well- but separately studied periods in English literary studies.

There was a decrease in the production of these treason-focused texts around or shortly before the beginning of the sixteenth century, which accompanies mutually informative changes in the extent and nature of civil strife, and in sociopolitical relationships. As Henry VII strengthened his hold on the crown, fewer new texts dwelt upon treason in the interrogative and horizontal ways characteristic of the literary culture of the previous decades. While contemporaries could not know that there

---

[18] Ross, 'The Reign of Edward IV', p. 61.

would be no further regime changes or civil wars for two generations, the likelihood of such divisions faded, not with the Battle of Bosworth in 1485 but a dozen years later.[19] Treasonous plots and conspiracies did recur throughout Henry VII's reign (1485–1509), but the nature and degree of threat they presented changed after 1497. Henry faced dynastic threats from unreconciled Yorkists and two successive would-be usurpers who posed as Yorkist scions and won international support for invasions of England: Lambert Simnel pretending to be Edward IV's nephew (1487), and the more threatening Perkin Warbeck impersonating Edward IV's younger son (1491–7). However, Henry defeated these challengers, and after the capture and uncloaking of Warbeck in 1497, there were no strong contenders for, or viable attempts to claim, the throne.[20] Unrest under the Tudors thereafter came more in the form of specific rebellions than the longstanding divisions between equal powers that had previously encouraged aristocracy, gentry, and merchants to take sides, or to worry about which side had sufficient right and/or might to prevail. Accordingly, as the earlier forms of unrest and instability began to fade from public memory, anxieties regarding treason were not as great. Moreover, while Edward IV and Henry VII both intervened in localities, Edward IV relied more on trust, and thus gentry self-governance, than did Henry VII's policy of more authoritative interventionism which 'came into its own in [Henry's] last dozen years' (1498–1509).[21] The behavioural binary of troth and treason, and the horizontal friendships and peer regulation that gentry self-governance required, were thus more important before the end of the fifteenth century, when they figured more centrally in romances. As the Postscript addresses, not only do romances after *c*.1497 reflect a narrower—and more providentially contained—idea of treason, but romance also becomes more intellectually marginalized and trivialized in the early to mid-sixteenth century, when disparaged by early modern humanists. The romances of *c*.1437–*c*. 1497, then, especially in their questioning of

[19] Anthony Goodman, *The Wars of the Roses: Military Activity and English Society, 1452–97* (London: Routledge, 1981), p. 8; Hicks, *Wars of the Roses*, pp. 6 and 233–7.

[20] S. B. Chrimes, *Henry VII* (1972; London: Methuen, 1977), pp. 68–94; Sean Cunningham, *Henry VII* (London: Routledge, 2007), pp. 97–8; John Watts, *The Making of Polities: Europe, 1300–1500* (Cambridge: Cambridge University Press, 2009), p. 346; P. R. Cavill, *The English Parliaments of Henry VII, 1485–1504* (Oxford: Oxford University Press, 2009), pp. 15–17 and 33–43. Warbeck was executed in 1499, but posed no real threat after his submission and exposure in 1497.

[21] Steven Gunn, *Early Tudor Government, 1485–1558* (Basingstoke: Macmillan, 1995), pp. 28–33 and 204–5, and 'Chivalry and the Politics of the Early Tudor Court', in *Chivalry in the Renaissance*, ed. by Sydney Anglo (Woodbridge: Boydell, 1990), pp. 107–28 (p. 122); Carpenter, *Locality and Polity*, pp. 9 and 633–8, and *Wars of the Roses*, p. 236; Michael Hicks, *Edward IV* (London: Arnold, 2004), p. 150; Cunningham, *Henry VII*, pp. 63 and 192.

divine intervention through representations of treason, made the genre interrogative in a way that it had not been either before or after these decades.

Given this book's focus on a specific literary period and on reading literary texts in relation to their historical moment, two methodological matters are worth addressing here: the dating of texts, and the approach to reading different types of texts alongside each other. Attempting to determine precise dates for the production or copying of mid- to late fifteenth-century texts can be a tricky business because we often have only their handwriting to draw upon as evidence of their rough dating, but both their probable dates of composition and their copying demonstrate their relation to contemporary events and attitudes. Some, due to internal evidence or inscriptions, can be firmly dated, such as Malory's *Morte Darthur* (1469), the second edition of Hardyng's *Chronicle* (early 1460s), and Caxton's prose romances (many are precisely dateable, and all fall between 1475 and 1490); some can be dated due to their topicality, such as the *Somnium Vigilantis* (treating the 1459 attainder of the Yorkist lords); for others, the paleographical evidence is less exact. Yet exact dates are not necessary; while these texts can sometimes only be pinpointed to within a decade or two, all of those contributing to the cultural preoccupation with treason addressed here were produced after the first few decades of the fifteenth century and prior to the century's end, with a probable concentration from mid-century until 1490 or so. The Appendix gives some indication of the coincidence of texts and events. We know, for instance, that the prose *Siege of Thebes* and *Siege of Troy* were written after their Lydgatean sources were finished between 1420 and 1422; the prose *Siege*s are extant only in a mid-fifteenth-century manuscript, and they differ from Lydgate's works in their increased focus on treason and pragmatic admonition instead of divine retribution.[22] Romances such as the prose *Siege*s, *King Ponthus*, and *Melusine* are addressed in the following chapters with reference to paleographic approximations of their dates of composition, but it should be borne in mind that even despite any remaining ambiguities, these texts are reliably dateable to *somewhere* within the decades surveyed here, and this is what is important for the argument this book makes.

---

[22] Thematic fit is, of course, never used on its own here to suggest a date, but it is worth noting that certain texts' thematic peculiarities gain wider significance if their existing tentative dates do indeed indicate when they were written. A pertinent example is the *N-Town Play*, the extant manuscript of which carries an inscription of the year 1468: as discussed in Chapter 3, *N-Town* contains a much stronger focus on treason than other extant cycle plays which do not have an association with the mid- to late fifteenth century.

Moreover, when drawing attention to the contemporaneity of texts and events as this section of the Introduction has done, it should be mentioned that this study does not always approach texts and events as separate forms of evidence. In some ways, texts *are* events; they are interventions into the discourses and debates about treason and governance that preoccupied contemporaries of the Wars of the Roses. Nor does this study approach literary and non-literary texts as entirely distinct categories. Historians and literary scholars alike have observed how fifteenth-century 'kings, magnates, gentry and commoners...felt the need to "draw attention to the ideas and principles which underpinned their actions", at a time when "disorderly political events...were accompanied by a rich debate over the rights and duties of rulers and subjects" '.[23] A further appreciation of *how* attention was drawn to such ideas and principles will add to our under-standing of them, and here the literary mode of expression offers evidence that both resonates with and reaches beyond non-literary documents. Treason, as the opposite of ideal social conduct, was a concept central to the definition of exemplary behaviour, and it is perhaps unsurprising that failures received greater textual attention than exemplary successes in an era of unprecedented civil strife and uncertainty. Texts whose primary mode of reference to contemporary England is direct or occasional are treated in Chapter 2, while literary texts with more distant settings are treated in the subsequent chapters. The interconnections between these sets of material are, however, highlighted throughout. Indeed, treason-focused literary texts sometimes share their manuscript context with non-literary ones, as is the case, for example, with the *Serpent of Division*. Lydgate's only prose work, the *Serpent* narrates the disintegration of the First Roman Triumvirate as a warning about the dangers of discord. John Vale's book, which, as discussed in Chapter 2, records the era's treason-focused letters, proclamations, and petitions, includes a copy of the *Serpent*. The repeated copying of the *Serpent* in the mid- to late fifteenth century (when all four of its extant manuscripts were produced) shows that it was considered relevant to current crises and fears of treason and division. It was also included in 'Grete Bokes'—anthologies of chivalric and governmental material—compiled for knights in the mid- to late fifteenth century, and is found alongside Hoccleve's *Regiment of Princes* and other regiminal texts.[24]

---

[23] Radulescu, *Gentry Context*, p. 5; quoting Watts, 'Ideas, Principles, and Politics', in *The Wars of the Roses*, ed. by A. J. Pollard (Basingstoke: Macmillan, 1995), pp. 110–33 (p. 111).

[24] Radulescu, *Gentry Context*, pp. 39–50, and '*John Vale's Book* and Sir Thomas Malory's *Le Morte Darthur*: A Political Agenda', *Arthuriana*, 9.4 (1999), 69–80; Nigel Mortimer, *John Lydgate's 'Fall of Princes': Narrative Tragedy in its Literary and Political Contexts* (Oxford: Oxford University Press, 2005), pp. 89–90. Various dates between 1400 and the late 1430s have been proposed for the *Serpent*, but the most likely date of

Thus, while some of the insights of this study are gained through attention to differences of genre, others are produced by reading across genres and across both literary and non-literary texts, recognizing that the Wars of the Roses discourse of treason transcends such divisions.

THE LITERATURE OF THE WARS
OF THE ROSES

This study proposes neither one-to-one correspondence between text and event nor points of strict political allegory, but rather examines a broader and looser, yet no less urgent, mode of topical engagement and didactic response. Chapter 2 assesses what treason meant to fifteenth-century English people, and argues that treason is worth our attention for the ways in which it received a significant share of theirs. Beginning with an analysis of the legal parameters of treason, and the contested ideas of allegiance circulating in this period, this chapter both lays the groundwork for the ensuing analyses of literary texts and considers the cultural work of a diffuse set of texts in their own right. Drawing upon theories of political discourse and interpellation, of the power of language to shape social identities, this chapter argues that, in this textual culture, treason shapes contemporary mentalities as both a source of anxieties about community and identity, and a way of responding to those concerns. In the correspondence, chronicles, proclamations, petitions, treatises, and literary texts of these years, treason is often represented as an act that injures the commonweal in particular, with implications for how contemporaries understood, and sought to shape, their community. The final sections of this chapter address the way in which non-literary texts manifest an apprehensive and/or persuasive rhetoric concerning treason, a rhetoric that demonstrates not only a fixation on a certain lexicon and concerns about treason, but also anxieties about the instability surrounding what could be construed as treason.

In order to demonstrate the distinctiveness of the literature of the Wars of the Roses, and particularly its romances, Chapter 3 begins

composition is 1422: see Henry Noble MacCracken, ed., *John Lydgate's Serpent of Division* (London: Oxford University Press, 1911), pp. 1–4; Derek Pearsall, *John Lydgate (1371–1449): A Bio-bibliography* (Victoria: University of Victoria, 1997), p. 24; Maura Nolan, *John Lydgate and the Making of Public Culture* (Cambridge: Cambridge University Press, 2005), p. 2; Mortimer, *Lydgate's 'Fall of Princes'*, p. 82. For alternative dates, see Eleanor Prescott Hammond, *English Verse between Chaucer and Surrey* (Durham, NC: Duke University Press, 1927), p. 177; Anne F. Sutton and Livia Visser-Fuchs, 'The Provenance of the Manuscript: The Lives and Archive of Sir Thomas Cook and His Man of Affairs, John Vale', in *The Politics of Fifteenth-Century England: John Vale's Book*, ed. by Margaret Lucille Kekewich and others (Stroud: Sutton, 1995), pp. 73–123 (p. 117).

by comparing the treason treatments of mid- to late fifteenth-century romances with contemporary poetry and drama, and by contrasting them with thirteenth- and fourteenth-century English romances. The romances of the Wars of the Roses create a broadly conceived and coherent system of obligations, ideals, and prohibitions that can be applied to all relationships—at least between people of chivalric or respectable status. It is significant both that these romances pointedly employ the same *language* of treason as that for the historical crime, and that they apply it to a wider set of betrayals, especially including horizontal ones. This chapter establishes the mode of ethical narrative that distinguishes Wars of the Roses literature by reading the prose *Siege of Thebes* and *Siege of Troy* in their manuscript context, and by contrasting them with their Lydgatean sources. The prose romances elide a providential framework and dwell upon treason performatively, deploying speech acts and textual utterances to construe and attempt to confine treason. The chapter concludes with a parallel reading of the late fifteenth-century English Melusine romances against their French sources to reveal further aspects of the cultural and linguistic specificity of treason in Wars of the Roses romances.

Chapter 4 both examines the way in which Malory's *Morte Darthur* employs a narrowed and emphatic lexicon of treason that affects the understanding of the text in itself, and demonstrates the hitherto unrecognized degree to which the *Morte* forms part of a wider English generic and cultural movement. In so doing, this chapter is able to offer a more nuanced view of some of the ways in which Malory's work is both typical and exceptional. The first half of this chapter demonstrates how treason, like fellowship, receives greater textual attention in Malory than it does in his sources, even though Malory condenses his source materials much as the author of the prose *Thebes* and *Troy* condenses his. While Malorian strategies of treating treason and betrayal are sometimes more sophisticated than those of the prose *Thebes* and *Troy* and other literature of the Wars of the Roses, the ways in which the former nonetheless resonate with the latter are explored in the second half of this chapter. These texts' genre inhabits yet transforms the space of traditional romance to generate its divergent meanings and implications. Moreover, as addressed at the end of this chapter and, more fully, in the Postscript, the *Morte* and contemporary texts, such as the *Somnium Vigilantis* and John Hardyng's *Chronicle*, pursue a mode of secular pragmatism that interrogates divine providence, placing late fifteenth-century literature in a closer relation to early modern literature.

While the continental influences on Caxton's prints have been well documented, scant attention has been paid to their English antecedents and resonance; Chapter 5 seeks to fill part of that gap by focusing on a close reading of his romances, and on the fused chivalric and civic ideology of secular loyalties they manifest. To address what Caxton's prose romances were 'doing' in England (in terms of both provenance and cultural work), the reading of their cultural significance pursued here is informed not only by these texts' origins, print production, and broader readership, but also by their generic and thematic affinities with Malory's *Morte Darthur* (which Caxton printed in 1485) and other recent English literature. This chapter concentrates upon *Godeffroy of Boloyne* (1481), *Charles the Grete* (1485), and *The Foure Sonnes of Aymon* (1488) as the three of Caxton's prose romances most centrally concerned with treason, and also considers non-romance tracts in Caxton's oeuvre that promulgate similar attitudes towards treason. This chapter analyses these works' pervasive condemnations of treason as a crime with both hierarchical and horizontal dimensions, and one that can be committed between affinity groups, polities, and faiths, in order to establish the extent to which Caxton's romances and related chivalric tracts are cognate with other texts produced in and for mid- to late fifteenth-century England. The *Morte Darthur* is by no means the sole English touchstone for Caxton's romances; like the *Morte Darthur*, Caxton's prose romances parallel the other English romances, poems, chronicles, and correspondence addressed in earlier chapters. Moreover, in the English print culture of the 1480s, the presence of treason is especially intertwined with the significance of the commonweal, in ways that speak to strong connections between these tracts and their broader readerships. Paying heed to the role of treason in each text both permits a deeper understanding of how these texts reimagine and seek to regulate their society, and allows a reconsideration of the relationships between Caxton's canon of (printed) prose romances and contemporary English (manuscript) romances.

The final chapter, or Postscript, addresses the decrease in the production of these treason-focused texts around or shortly before the beginning of the sixteenth century by focusing on the literary output of the early sixteenth-century printer Wynkyn de Worde and his contemporaries. While de Worde, operating Caxton's printing press after the latter's death, did continue to print romances, he did not focus on producing the same *kind* of romances on thematic and ethical criteria (as opposed to criteria of form or superficial 'subject' matter). Other romances written during the early sixteenth century, such as Stephen Hawes' allegorical romances, indicate a marked reversion to the moral model of divine restoration that operated in romances before 1437; they eschew both the mid- to late fifteenth-century romances' secularized preoccupation with horizontal treason and their possibilities as literary models. This short concluding chapter corroborates the notion that the dwindling of the production of such literature after 1497, like the relative lack of such literature before 1437, indicates grounds on which the intervening decades can profitably be distinguished.

The mid- to late fifteenth century, often disregarded by both medievalists and early modernists, has been perceived as a rupture or a poetically infertile pause between the achievements of Chaucer (and his immediate successors) and the 'developments' of sixteenth-century literature; this study, however, advances recent criticism that reassesses, and advocates further nuancing of, such received ideas of progression from medieval to early modern literature.[25] The challenges confronting a reassessment of Wars of the Roses literature include both prevalent periodizing value judgements and scholarly neglect, with the former contributing to the latter. In seeking to give unprejudiced consideration to the literature of the Wars of the Roses, we must remember that the label is itself anachronistic. Shakespeare and earlier Tudor propagandists such as Stephen Hawes and John Skelton (writing for Henry VII and VIII respectively) deployed the symbolism of red and white roses (and the union of the two with Henry VII's marriage to Elizabeth of York) to portray the Tudors as 'rescuing' England from the turmoil of civil war, and the phrase 'Wars of the Roses' was first printed in the eighteenth century.[26] However, it is still a term worth using, not least because historiography relies upon it; moreover, contemporaries, from the relative hindsight of Henry VII's reign, did accept the conceptual instrumentality of the Roses. It captures now a sense of the fear of social instability informing the secular literature that is centred on, if not entirely contained by, the Wars of the Roses. Viewing Tudor judgements of the *history* of the preceding century for what they are, we can also separate Tudor value judgements of the *literature* of the same period from our own views. Without disregarding the perils of overemphasizing temporal boundaries at the expense of continuities, this study highlights the extent to which the possibilities of treason, as an idea and a problem,

---

[25] Simpson, *Reform and Cultural Revolution*, esp. pp. 44–9; David Wallace, *Premodern Places: Calais to Surinam, Chaucer to Aphra Behn* (Oxford: Blackwell, 2004); Brian Cummings and James Simpson, 'Introduction', in *Cultural Reformations: Medieval and Renaissance in Literary History*, ed. by Brian Cummings and James Simpson (Oxford: Oxford University Press, 2010), pp. 1–9; Helen Cooper, *Shakespeare and the Medieval World* (London: Methuen Drama, 2010).

[26] Although the white rose was a badge used by the House of York, it was only one among several (for instance, Richard III's primary heraldic signifier was a white boar). Henry VI did not use the red rose at all; it became a rival to the white only retrospectively, when Henry VII revived it as his principal badge after his accession in 1485: Ross, *Wars of the Roses*, pp. 11–15; S. B. Chrimes, *Lancastrians, Yorkists and Henry VII* (1964; London: Macmillan, 1967), pp. xii–xiv; Hicks, *Wars of the Roses*, pp. 12–13.

presented themselves particularly to mid- to late fifteenth-century writers. Isolating this literary culture also shows its continuities, as its complex engagements between form, content, theme, and historical moment—its strategies of refashioning its literary heritage to inhabit new spaces in new shapes—situate it firmly within the innovative tradition of English literature. Although these convergences on treason are important ones for the decades in question, it would be specious to argue that they are the only terms through which this literary culture might articulate itself to us; if this study fosters further discussion of the understudied secular English literature of the mid- to late fifteenth century, it will have accomplished another of its aims.

2

'that horrible and falsly forsworne traitor N'

Discourses and Mentalities of Treason, *c*.1437–*c*.1497

On 28 January 1460, William Paston II sent his brother John I some 'tydyngys':

> my Lord Ryuers was brought to Caleys and by-for the lordys wyth viijxx torches, and there my lord of Salesbury reheted hym, callyng hym knaves son that he schuld be so rude to calle hym and these oþer lordys traytours, for they schull be found the Kyngys treue liege men whan he schuld be found a traytour, &c. And my lord of Warrewyk reheted hym and seyd that his fader was but a squyer... and that it was not his parte to have *swyche langage* of lordys beyng of the Kyngys blood. And my lord of Marche reheted hym jn lyke wyse, and Ser Antony was reheted *for his langage* of all iij lordys jn lyke wyse.[1]

In this reported encounter, countervailing accusations of treason are flung between a captured Lancastrian and the Yorkist lords who have fled to Calais after defying Henry VI. Accusations of treason are dangerous; both sides recognize that 'swyche langage' is a weapon, one that they seek to deploy on their enemies and to deflect from themselves. Moreover, talk of treason becomes the subject of discussion in its turn, as, in order to keep each other informed of the events shaping their political world, the Paston correspondents create an inventory of how these lords 'call' and 'rehete' (rebuke) each other. In moments such as these—when rival magnates accuse each other of treason, and when one gentleman reports these events to another—the outcomes are uncertain. Each denunciation is fervent, and each party protests its loyal adherence to the king, but the question of whose voice will prevail—of who will be 'found' a traitor and who will be

---

[1] *Paston Letters*, I, 88.92–102.

'found' true—can only be answered with a degree of hindsight denied to the participants in these exchanges. The 'langage' of an accusation of treason, then, cannot effect its implications in itself; it must be sustained by a combination of force and law in order to definitively transform the status of the accused into that of a traitor. However, such accusations cannot—and could not—be dismissed as insignificant. The act of calling someone a traitor rendered the recipient of the label vulnerable. It created the possibility of ruinous retribution, a possibility that the accused could only avoid by outrunning or overpowering it. Queen Elizabeth I's godson John Harington (1560–1612) seems to have recognized this when he composed the epigram 'Treason doth never prosper, what's the reason? / For if it prosper, none dare call it Treason.'[2] Although penned a century later, this epigram's explicit concern with (lack of) hindsight aptly underscores the perilous subtleties of both treason and accusations of treason in the sociopolitical climate of the mid- to late fifteenth century.

In the dynastic struggles of the Wars of the Roses, the throne was sought after and occupied by multiple contenders, sometimes in rotation. Magnates swore loyalty to the current king, but afterwards supported another contender or attempted to usurp the throne themselves. Lesser nobles and the gentry likewise traded allegiances and betrayed, and/or worried that they would be betrayed by, not only their superiors, but also each other. If their side succeeded, turncoats were unlikely to be called to account, at least officially, for their perjury or treason; Warwick and March, for instance, who as quoted above claimed in 1460 to be 'the Kyngys treue liege men', ensured the truth of their words by replacing the King Henry of whom they spoke with March himself in 1461. Yet during these upheavals and confrontations, no one could be certain who would prosper, and thus there was often troubling uncertainty regarding to whom a lack of loyalty was treasonous. Treason, that is, was talked about, and worried about, a great deal. Stuck in a continuous present, lacking finality, many people ventured to call the actions of others treason, and feared both that they might be the victims of treason and that their own doings or accusations might be called treasonous.

The concentrated yet contested role of treason in contemporary affairs points us to a key word and concept. This chapter argues that, in the fraught, fragile political environment from c.1437 to c.1497, treason weighed heavily on people's minds, impacting on discourses and mentalities as powerfully as it destabilized authority and social stability.[3] Accordingly,

---

[2] John Harington, *Epigrams 1618* (London: Scholar Press, 1970), f.K4v.
[3] The implications of understanding utterances concerning treason as part of a discursive practice, and as contributing to *mentalités*, or collective mental attitudes, are discussed more fully in the final section of this chapter.

this chapter both lays the groundwork for the ensuing analyses of treason in literary texts, and considers the cultural work of correspondence, chronicles, petitions, and political verses in their own right. In order to contextualize these occasional genres, the first two sections of this chapter analyse, respectively, the legal parameters and complex definitions of treason; and ideas of allegiance to king and commonweal. The final section of this chapter addresses the way in which circulatory and record-keeping texts such as letters, chronicles, and verses manifest an apprehensive and persuasive rhetoric concerning treason that gives further insight into the contemporary mentalities and political and social discourses of which the literary texts also formed a part.

LAWS AND TREASON

What exactly did 'treason' mean to contemporaries of the Wars of the Roses? Although, as the 1460 Calais encounter between Rivers and the Yorkists shows, determining *who* was a traitor was a contentious matter, adversaries usually agreed on the *nature* of the crime. In fifteenth-century England, treason was understood and regulated through intersecting national, personal, and international frameworks; the first of these was most important in law and enforcement. A consistent institutional understanding of treason had prevailed in late medieval England since the 1352 Statute of Treason clarified and limited the relevant crimes, articulating definitions for both high and petty treason.[4] Acting contrary to the king's interests constituted high treason if

> a Man doth compass or imagine the Death of our Lord the King, or of our Lady his Queen or of their eldest Son and Heir; or if a Man do violate the King's Companion, or the King's eldest daughter unmarried, or the Wife of the King's eldest Son and Heir; or if a Man do levy War against our Lord the King in his Realm, or be adherent to the King's Enemies in his Realm.[5]

Not only physical actions, but also thoughts, could establish someone as a traitor, since the 1352 statute stipulated 'compassing or *imagining*' the death of the king as treason: intent was central to, and was all that was required to constitute, the crime. Such intention could, after Henry IV, be

---

[4] J. G. Bellamy, *The Law of Treason in England in the Later Middle Ages* (Cambridge: Cambridge University Press, 1970), p. 93.

[5] Edward III, Statute 5 (January 1352); translation (and original French) in *Statutes of the Realm*, ed. by A. Luders and others (London: Record Commission, 1810–28), I, 319–20. Other high treasons included counterfeiting the king's seal or currency, and killing the king's chancellor, treasurer, or justices when they were performing their offices.

proven by words spoken against the king, though this was not always easy
to prosecute.[6] Proof of 'levying war' against the king, the most common
high treason during the Wars of the Roses, was more easily established from
acts such as displaying banners or firing cannon at a siege.[7] The additional
category of petty treason protected certain men from those deemed their
subordinates: 'when a Servant slayeth his Master, or a Wife her Husband,
or when a Man secular or Religious slayeth his Prelate, to whom he oweth
Faith and Obedience', the act was considered not just homicide but treason.[8] Most of the subsequent legislative additions to the 1352 statute were
repealed before Henry VI's reign, with the notable exception of Henry V's
1414 statute, decreeing that injuring those shielded by royal safe-conducts
or truces constituted treason, since harming someone under the king's
protection constituted a denial of the king's authority.[9] Thus, in English
law, treason meant the breach or intended breach of a strictly hierarchical
loyalty, with intent to effect critical harm.

These vertical treasons were policed through codified procedures for
accusation, trial, and punishment. The 1352 statute specified two possible
modes of accusation for treason: an oral appeal or a written indictment.
By the second half of the fifteenth century, indictments were much more
common, but appeals still occurred.[10] Trial by battle was on the decline,
customarily restricted to cases where appeals of treason had been initiated
by 'approvers', complicit individuals who accused fellow criminals to try to
save their own lives through judicial combat. However, fifteenth-century
English people still encountered trials by battle for treason in reality as
well as in romances.[11] More commonly, trials for treason employed ver-
bal testimony by which the accused was 'attainted of open Deed by the
People of their Condition',[12] but trials for treason involving the use of

---

[6] Bellamy, *Law of Treason*, p. 116; Edward Powell, 'The Strange Death of Sir John
Mortimer: Politics and the Law of Treason in Lancastrian England', in *Rulers and Ruled in
Late Medieval England*, ed. by Rowena E. Archer and Simon Walker (London: Hambledon,
1995), pp. 83–97 (pp. 94–7).
    [7] M. H. Keen, 'Treason Trials under the Law of Arms', *Transactions of the Royal Historical
Society*, Fifth Series, 12 (1962), 85–103 (p. 96).
    [8] *Statutes of the Realm*, I, 320.   [9] Bellamy, *Law of Treason*, pp. 128–9.
    [10] John H. Baker, *An Introduction to English Legal History*, 3rd edn (1971;
London: Butterworths, 1990), p. 505; Bellamy, *Law of Treason*, p. 141.
    [11] Baker, *English Legal History*, p. 507; Bellamy, *Law of Treason*, p. 145. For exam-
ple, one London chronicle records a 1447 trial by combat for high treason in which an
armourer's servant appeals and kills his master, whose head is set on London Bridge; another
such chronicle records a 1455 trial by battle for treason, in this case initiated by a (false)
approver: 'Robert Bale's Commonplace Book', in *Six Town Chronicles of England*, ed. by
Ralph Flenley (Oxford: Clarendon Press, 1911), pp. 120–1; 'Gregory's Chronicle', in
Historical Collections of a Citizen of London in the Fifteenth Century, ed. by James Gairdner,
Camden Society, NS, 17 (London: Nichols, 1876), p. 201.
    [12] *Statutes of the Realm*, I, 320.

arms, of which there were many during the Wars of the Roses, took place not under the common law but rather belonged to the jurisdiction of the constable and the marshal, who oversaw the Court of Chivalry. Moreover, since responding to military crimes during civil war required efficiency, summary trials in the field became regular during the second half of the fifteenth century.[13] If the accused were a knight, he could be degraded before execution. Men were usually hanged, drawn, and/or quartered, and sometimes their entrails were burnt; women were burnt at the stake.[14] Descendants were affected too, since the perpetrator's goods were forfeit to the king in cases of high treason, and to the perpetrator's overlord in cases of petty treason. The harshness of these punishments, and the practice of impaling executed traitors' heads and limbs on city gates as a warning to others, bear witness to perceptions of the abhorrent nature of treason and the serious threat it could pose.

The disparities between French and English laws of treason offer further insight into the distinctive way in which English contemporaries of the Wars of the Roses would interpret both real and literary instances of treason. The sorts of crimes that the English termed high treason (seeking the death of, or declaring war on, the king; sleeping with members of the royal family crucial to the succession) were, in France, usually defined as *lèse-majesté*, while 'trahison/traison' was applied only to the betrayal of a non-monarchical lord by his vassal. Accordingly, in French trial proceedings, '*trahison*, the French word etymologically closest to the English "treason" ', usually did not appear;[15] 'trahison' did not carry the same legal force as did 'treason' on the other side of the channel. Moreover, in France, to betray or harm another of the king's subjects—such as through 'pillaging, robberies, larceny, murders, rapes, spoliations of churches... ransoming of people, arson', or waging private war—was again considered *lèse-majesté*: an offence against the king, rather than against the directly injured party.[16] English law did not define private war (overt or covert), robbery, or murder as treason either; however, by treating these offences as felony or trespass, the effect, in contrast to French law, was to entitle the victim to legal redress on his or her own behalf: it made such crimes horizontal, rather than hierarchical.[17] Late medieval England was thus more attuned to viewing crimes detrimental to social stability as lateral, as well

---

[13] Keen, 'Treason Trials under the Law of Arms', pp. 86 and 99–101.

[14] S. H. Cuttler, *The Law of Treason Trials in Later Medieval France* (Cambridge: Cambridge University Press, 1981), p. 116; for example, a London woman was burnt at the stake for petty treason in 1443: 'Gregory's Chronicle', p. 184.

[15] Cuttler, *Treason Trials*, pp. 2 and 21.   [16] Cuttler, *Treason Trials*, p. 33.

[17] *Statutes of the Realm*, I, 320.

as being conditioned to perceive 'treason' as the most serious offence—and not only in institutional interpretations.

For contemporaries of the Wars of the Roses, treason, in both literature and life, had horizontal dimensions. An idea of treason as the betrayal of a personal trust, such as within a family or another affinity group where (mutual) loyalty could be expected, survived in the popular mind from earlier in the middle ages, though without legal force, as a sort of folk-law.[18] Moreover, the persistence of principles propounded by Roman law and reshaped by medieval 'customary usage' had produced a law of arms that, from the mid-fourteenth century onward, applied to combatants in any war.[19] This law focused on breaches of the expected code of conduct between individual soldiers rather than on the polities on whose behalf the soldiers might be fighting. This 'international' military law allowed plaintiffs to seek redress against, for instance, former captives who trea-sonously reneged on promised ransom payments. The law of arms also applied to those fighting on the same side: a knight could be accused of treason to a brother in arms, or to knighthood, if he did not fulfil an oath; faithful conduct was expected between soldiers, and between soldiers and their captains.[20] Justice could be sought in the courts of the wrongdoer's overlord, even if the plaintiff belonged to a different polity; military tri-bunals, army captains, and courts such as the English Court of Chivalry and its French equivalents conducted trials of soldiers from their own and enemy polities in periods of hostility, such as during the Hundred Years' War. Here, as in national frameworks, trial could proceed by ordinary legal process (summary or formal) or by judicial duel.[21]

These horizontal ideas of treason, combined with the cross-channel legal differences, attest to the cultural specificity of the strongly legal and universal force that accusations of treason would have carried when occurring in English texts for English readerships. The correspondences between mid- to late fifteenth-century English literary and non-literary treatments of treason are semantic, in the most significant sense: both deploy, and place a great deal of weight on, the same specific vocabulary of treason. Different types of texts apply the keywords 'treason' and 'traitor',

---

[18] Richard Firth Green, *A Crisis of Truth: Literature and Law in Ricardian England* (Philadelphia: University of Pennsylvania Press, 1999), pp. xiv and 214.

[19] M. H. Keen, *The Laws of War in the Late Middle Ages* (London: Routledge, 1965), pp. 16–17 and 2; Antony Black, *Political Thought in Europe, 1250–1450* (Cambridge: Cambridge University Press, 1992), pp. 14–15 and 89–90.

[20] Keen, *Laws of War*, p. 54; N. A. R. Wright, 'The *Tree of Battles* of Honoré Bouvet and the Laws of War', in *War, Literature, and Politics in the Late Middle Ages*, ed. by C. T. Allmand (Liverpool: Liverpool University Press, 1976), pp. 12–31 (pp. 19–21).

[21] Keen, *Laws of War*, pp. 1–53; Richard W. Kaeuper, *Chivalry and Violence in Medieval Europe* (Oxford: Oxford University Press, 1999), p. 186.

sometimes to different transgressions, but with a shared sense of gravity and intention to incriminate and warn. In parliamentary attainders from the majority of Henry VI through to the midpoint of Henry VII's reign, accusations of treason are vested in the formulaic application of this specific vocabulary to each denounced act of the accused. For instance, the bill impeaching Suffolk that the commons submitted to parliament on 7 February 1450 argues that Suffolk 'falsely and *traiterously* hath ymagined, compassed... and committed dyvers high, grete, heynous and horrible treasons, ayenst your moost roiall persone'.[22] Each of Suffolk's further incriminating acts is condemned here through the terms 'falsely and traiterously' six times (XII.95–7), 'deceyvably and traiterously' (XII.97), and 'traiterously' twice (XII.95; 98). The bill of attainder makes further mention of Suffolk's 'treason and falsehode' (XII.97), his 'fals, fraudulent, traiterous werkes, dedes, and deceyvable ymaginations' (XII.97), and his 'treason' (XII.97). Here, the terms 'treason' and 'traitorously' sometimes stand alone, and are sometimes accompanied by other qualifiers (particularly 'falsehood', 'false', and 'falsely'), but are not themselves replaced or omitted. The vocabulary of treason is the common denominator in these accusations, conveying the resonance and legal force of the condemnation. We find the same vocabulary and structures of accusation throughout the parliamentary attainders of treason during the Wars of the Roses, regardless of who is king, who is being denounced, or who is doing the denouncing.[23] At their conclusion, the parliamentary attainders specify conviction for treason: for instance, when Henry VI's 1459 parliament has the Yorkist lords 'atteynted of high treson' (XII.460–1), or when Edward IV's 1461 parliament has Henry VI 'convicted and atteinted of high treason' (XIII.46). The parliamentary records further focus on proclaiming

---

[22] *The Parliament Rolls of Medieval England*, ed. by Chris Given-Wilson and others, 16 vols (Woodbridge: Boydell, 2005), XII, 95.

[23] For instance, in the next parliament (still 1450), the commons presented a bill of attainder indicting Jack Cade for acting 'falsely and traiterously' (XII.202–3, thrice), the same language in which Suffolk had been denounced. Among the many further instances of this language in attainders spanning the Wars of the Roses, see parliaments: March 1453–February 1454, indicting Jack Cade (again) and York's affiliate Sir William Oldhall (XII.307); November–December 1459, Henry VI indicting the Yorkist lords (XII.456–60); April 1463–March 1465, Edward IV indicting Sir William Stok and squire Robert Myrfyn (XIII.124); January–February 1484, Richard III indicting Buckingham and others (XV.24); November 1485–March 1486, Henry VII indicting Richard III and others (XV.107–8); and Henry VII's further attainders in 1487 (XV.361–3), 1491–2 (XVI.121–5), and 1495 (XVI. 229–31). In Henry VII's next and last parliament (1504), the same language of attainder is employed (XVI.379–81), but more sparingly: most of those who had rebelled in 1497 in Cornwall or in support of Perkin Warbeck were *not* attainted here, because those rebellions had become a non-issue (editor's note, XVI.316); by 1504, Henry VII's more secure hold on the throne dampened the discourses of treason that characterized the Wars of the Roses.

the (name and) status of a traitor, as in appelations such as 'the fals traytour John Cade', and the decree that Cade 'be called within youre seid reame fals traitour for evermore'.[24] Similarly, in its entry for 1463, one of the London chronicles treats the turncoat Somerset by referring to him as 'that fals traytur thee Duke of Somersett'.[25]

These particularly English formulaic constructions are also emphasized in contemporary English *literary* texts, which tend to use words of treason more frequently than their (French) sources, and more frequently than less legalistic words such as 'betray' and 'treachery'.[26] For instance, whereas in one of Malory's sources, the *Roman de Tristan*, Berluse accuses Mark of a heinous crime, saying 'Vous ocheïstes en Cornuaille mon pere, assés vilainnement et desloiaument' ('You slew my father in Cornwall, very cowardlily and disloyally'),[27] the equivalent accusation in Malory is 'ye slew my fader *traytourly* and cowardly' (582.27). Furthermore, again in contrast to the French *Tristan*, where characters often challenge others to combat only by name or some other descriptor even if betrayal is involved, Malory instead peppers his narrative with the likes of Bleoberis' challenge: 'Make redy, thou *false traytoure knyght*, sir Brewnys Saunze Pité!' (684.27–8). Since the French romances' word 'desloiaus', 'disloyal', is not used much (if at all) in English before Caxton's translations in the 1470s and 1480s, English romance writers or translators such as Malory, Caxton, and the authors of the English prose and verse *Melusine*s had to find an English word with which to replace it; however, their translation habits— alongside the broader use of the rhetoric of treason in the textual culture of the Wars of the Roses—show that while 'false' is employed as a cognate for 'desloiaus', to use 'traytourly' or 'treson' is to intensify and shift meaning.[28]

To give just a few more examples of the status of words of treason as culturally specific and resonant keywords, particularly illuminating here are a military treatise and two Latin chronicles. *Knyghthode and Bataile*, a partisan verse tract translated in 1460 by a Lancastrian clerk from Vegetius' late fourth-century prose *De re militari*, periodically diverges from its source in order to comment upon the current political situation.[29] Offering military

---

[24] *Parliament Rolls*, XII.202–3.

[25] 'Gregory's Chronicle', p. 221; repeated, with respect to Somerset and his men, at pp. 223–4.

[26] See Chapters 3 and 4.

[27] *Le Roman de Tristan en Prose*, ed. by Philippe Ménard and others, 9 vols (Genève: Droz, 1987–97), IV, 102.

[28] See Chapter 5, note 31.

[29] Daniel Wakelin, 'The Occasion, Author and Readers of *Knyghthode and Bataile*', *MÆ*, 73.2 (2004), 260–72; Diane Bornstein, 'Military Manuals in Fifteenth-Century England', *Mediaeval Studies*, 37 (1975), 469–77 (pp. 472–3); Nall, *Reading and War in Fifteenth-Century England*, pp. 17–20 and 114–38.

advice to Henry VI against his rebels, *Knyghthode and Bataile* discusses the danger of sub-par soldiers, warning that if a knight is a 'traitour or a coward', he would be a liability to his army. Here, the fourth-century Latin source mentions cowards, but *not* traitors.[30] Interestingly, the late fifteenth-century *Compilatio de gestis Britonum et Anglorum* twice switches to English from its Latin account of the 1459 parliament in order to inscribe 'ateyntid traytours' in the vernacular:

> convocato parliamento apud Coventre, indicati sunt ibidem dicti Dux et tres Comites cum aliis multis militibus et magnatibus super grandi prodicione et declarati pro *ateyntid traytowrs* per dominos illius parliamenti;...publice proclamati sunt pro *ateyntid traytours.*
>
> (parliament having been summoned at Coventry, that said duke [of York] and three earls [of Warwick, Salisbury, and March] with many other knights and lords were indicted of high treason and were declared as *attainted traitors* by the lords of that parliament;... [and they were] publicly proclaimed as *attainted traitors.*)[31]

Similarly, John Rous' chronicle of England, written *c.*1489–91, interrupts its Latin narrative to record Richard III's accusatory lament about treason at Bosworth in English: 'saepius se proditum clamans & dicens, Treson, Treson, Treson, & sic gustans quod aliis saepius propinaverat miserrime vitam finavit' ('repeatedly lamenting that he was betrayed and saying, "Treason, Treason, Treason", and so tasting what he had frequently given to others, he finished his life miserably').[32] Thus, the specific *English* rhetoric of treason was resonant enough to be vital not only to vernacular writers, but also to (some) English people writing in Latin. Deploying the language of treason was a recognized, and essential, element of performative political discourse.

While the polyvalent political milieu of the Wars of the Roses has been characterized in terms of its discourses, operating on 'accepted principles' and through the deployment of certain 'buzz words', the contrary but integral role that 'treason' and 'traitor' play as keywords in these discourses has not been adequately addressed. Critics have recognized the innovativeness of the mid- to late fifteenth-century political environment in its 'emergent political language' and its 'sense of a common discursive space', with a 'treasury—or perhaps an emporium—of acceptable language' that

---

[30] *Knyghthode and Bataile*, ed. by R. Dyboski and Z. M. Arend, EETS OS 201 (London: Oxford University Press, 1935), line 278; compare Flavius Vegetius Renatus, *Epitoma rei militaris*, ed. and trans. by Leo F. Stelten (New York: Lang, 1990), p. 20.

[31] 'A Brief Latin Chronicle', in *Three Fifteenth-Century Chronicles*, ed. by James Gairdner, Camden Society, NS, 18 (London: Nichols, 1880), p. 169; emphasis editorial; translation mine.

[32] Rous, *Historia regum Angliae*, p. 218; translation mine.

individuals and groups could use to represent their policies.[33] Political or ideological concepts were deployable by whoever could claim and employ the relevant language successfully;[34] treason had 'become a mobile signifier, available for application and use by either party',[35] and, we might add, by those who did not, or did not wish to, belong to a party. But how did 'treason' in fact operate within this milieu? While conceptual shifts are often both heralded and prompted by 'a new vocabulary',[36] in the case of fifteenth-century treason, we do not find a 'new' vocabulary being used: the words 'treason' and 'traitor' already had centuries' worth of history in England.[37] However, in this period we do find a particular and precise vocabulary of treason (as this section has shown), and we find it being used in new ways: that is, more frequently, by new actors, and with both more urgency and more uncertainty. Watts argues that political texts and speeches sought to 'harness the "accepted principles" of their polity', with their ability to do so determining their effectiveness.[38] Yet treason was not, of course, a principle; we can profitably understand it as constituting the antithesis of principles of virtuous conduct and loyalty to king, lord, kin, and community. Since treason was a concept and a charge that political actors sought to harness and to attach to their opponents as a means of gaining or maintaining power for themselves—since, that is, much of

[33] Strohm, *Politique*, p. 12; Watts, 'The Pressure of the Public on Later Medieval Politics', in *Political Culture in Late Medieval Britain*, ed. by Linda Clark and Christine Carpenter (Woodbridge: Boydell, 2004), pp. 159–80.

[34] Strohm, *Politique*, p. 11. See also Watts on the importance of 'soundbites, buzz-words, strings of interrelated terms and pre-packaged sections of argument' to our understanding of late fifteenth-century political ideas: '*The Policie in Christen Remes*: Bishop Russell's Parliamentary Sermons of 1483–84', in *Authority and Consent in Tudor England*, ed. by G. W. Bernard and S. J. Gunn (Aldershot: Ashgate, 2002), pp. 33–59 (p. 43). Michel Foucault's elucidation of the power of discourses underlies much of this work: *The Archaeology of Knowledge*, trans. by A. M. Sheridan Smith (1969; London: Routledge, 2002), p. 121.

[35] Strohm, *Politique*, p. 188; for Strohm, the list of fifteenth-century keywords also includes tainted lineage, perjury, oppression, exile, heresy, community, and true commons (pp. 182–90). Wendy Scase has also commented on treason, writing that, in this period, '*traitor* has become a floating signifier': '"Strange and Wonderful Bills": Bill-Casting and Political Discourse in Late-Medieval England", *New Medieval Literatures*, 2 (1998), 225–47 (p. 235). However, neither Strohm nor Scase addresses discourses of treason at any length; nor is there a published precedent for my argument that many *literary* texts also engage with contemporary concerns and discourses in their representations of treason.

[36] Quentin Skinner, *The Foundations of Modern Political Thought*, 2 vols (Cambridge: Cambridge University Press, 1978), I, x; Strohm, *Politique*, pp. 6–7. See also Paul Chilton, *Analysing Political Discourse: Theory and Practice* (London: Routledge, 2004), pp. 4–16.

[37] The *MED* and *OED* cite the early thirteenth-century *Ancrene Wisse* as the earliest instance of the words 'treason' and 'traitor', and attest to the continuous use of these words in English thenceforth.

[38] John L. Watts, 'Polemic and Politics in the 1450s', in *Vale's Book*, pp. 3–42 (p. 6).

the debate seems to have occurred through discussion not of the 'positive' principles, but through accusations of these principles' negation—I suggest that we think of treason as an accepted anti-principle, a recognized component of most mid- to late fifteenth-century English political smear campaigns.

What the formulation of treason as an 'accepted anti-principle' recognizes is that claims to legitimacy and validity in this political culture are often built upon a particular sort of nullification. While all utterances inherently make 'validity claims', such as to sincerity and propositional truth,[39] utterances about matters of identity, such as treason, make such claims in a more active and explicit sense. To make an accusation of treason is not only to seek to delegitimize the opposition; it is also, inherently, to lay claim to legitimacy oneself *by means of* the expressed negation of another's legitimacy. One must claim to be speaking or writing as, or on behalf of, central authority when making such accusations in order to expect credence from hearers or readers.[40] This way in which treason is crucial to the Wars of the Roses discourse of dynastic (de)legitimization is addressed further in the final section of this chapter, which analyses the implications of communicating about treason. Treason's nature as an accepted anti-principle is telling in another sense, too: it is 'accepted' in that it is understood, expected, and therefore, in some senses, ineradicable from the horizons of possibility. As has been argued here, to fifteenth-century English people, particularly because they were currently embroiled in internecine strife, treason was recognizably and resonantly a horizontal concept as well as a hierarchical one. In this broad-based and urgent form, treason moulded contemporaries' world views, or mentalities, by conditioning both their ideologies or values, and their ways of thinking about and articulating those values.[41]

LOYALTIES AND TREASON

Despite the law of treason's connection to the king, even institutional treason during the Wars of the Roses had a horizontal dimension due to the expanding yet ambiguous role of the commonweal. In the proclamations,

---

[39] Chilton, *Analysing Political Discourse*, p. 43.
[40] Chilton, *Analysing Political Discourse*, pp. 46–7.
[41] This study understands ideology 'not as a set of inherently false and deliberately distortive beliefs, but more neutrally as the entire set of socially imagined ideas by which people explain their lives and places in a material order': see Paul Strohm's methodology in *Hochon's Arrow: The Social Imagination of Fourteenth-Century Texts* (Princeton: Princeton University Press, 1992), p. 6.

bills, letters, and literary texts of these decades, treason is often construed as an act that harms the commonweal in particular, offering intriguing insight into how contemporaries subscribed to, and sought to shape, political community. In late medieval England, the king was expected to listen to his magnates as his natural advisors, but ultimately the king's will and absolute authority were understood to constitute the common interest; problems with this circularity arose only when the king was not competent.[42] Edward IV articulates this perceived conceptual unity between king and common interest by specifying, in a letter soliciting benevolences from his subjects, that for anyone to 'rebell ageinst us their soveraigne lord...is the dedly siknes of every comune wele and the most likly destruccion of kinges and realmes'.[43] Here, the king ensures the commonweal; thus, to act against the king is to act against the commonweal, and vice versa. While the political objective of the common good existed in fourteenth-century formulations of 'common profit', it gained new force and significance from *c*.1450, when the slogan of the 'commonweal' was inaugurated in English political rhetoric as a rationale for seeking governmental change in the interests of the community.[44] Ordinarily, it was not only the king, but also the aristocracy, gentry, citizens, and commons who equated king and commonweal; however, such normative ideas of authority and community were put under pressure during the Wars of the Roses by contenders' claims to be acting in the interest of the commonweal, sometimes without reference to the king, and by their definition of the opposition as traitorous *to the commonweal*. The conceptual horizontality, or at least mutuality, of the idea of the commonweal was deployed to wrest control over discourses of treason from the king, producing more multi-directional, unsecured accusations of treason. Thus, while the term 'commonweal' promoted broad-based ideals of loyalty and community attractive to gentry and burgesses, it also both encapsulated and intensified their fears (and royal fears) about treason and social instability.

The way in which both Edward IV and those who rebelled against him in 1469–70 sought to deploy the word 'commonweal' to justify their actions shows the slipperiness of the concept. In 1469, Yorkshire rebels,

---

[42] Watts, *Henry VI*, pp. 51–7; Watts, 'Polemic and Politics in the 1450s', p. 6.

[43] *Vale's Book*, p. 146.

[44] Strohm, *Politique*, p. 244, note 11; Carpenter, *Wars of the Roses*, p. 120; Black, *Political Thought in Europe*, pp. 24–8; Watts, 'Public or Plebs: The Changing Meaning of "The Commons", 1381–1549', in *Power and Identity in the Middle Ages*, ed. by Huw Pryce and John Watts (Oxford: Oxford University Press, 2007), pp. 242–60 (p. 257); David Rollison, *A Commonwealth of the People: Popular Politics and England's Long Social Revolution, 1066–1649* (Cambridge: Cambridge University Press, 2010), pp. 13–14; see also Wakelin, *Humanism, Reading, and English Literature*, pp. 20 and 115. The *MED*'s earliest instances of 'commune wele' meaning 'common good' are mid-fifteenth century.

incited by Warwick's grievances, alleged that their challenge to Edward's authority was an attempt to check upstart royal advisors who 'toke no respecte ne consideracion to the weele of the seid prince, ne to the *commone weele* of this lande, but oonly to … enricheyng of hem selfe'.[45] These rebels distanced themselves from treason and aligned themselves with justice by stressing that 'we entende but oonly for weele and suretie of *the king oure soveraigne lorde and the commune wele* of this lande'.[46] The concept of the commonweal was deployed *against* rebels such as these in the *Chronicle of the Rebellion in Lincolnshire*, which reports the discovery of letters incriminating Warwick and Clarence: letters, that is, 'conteining matter of the grete seduccion, and the verrey subversion of *the king and the common wele* of alle this lande, with the most abhominable treason that ever were seen'.[47] In such texts, ideas of loyalty to king and commonweal are rhetorically and conceptually woven together, but are deployed by conflicting parties, and are sometimes detached from the king's interests.

However, others go even further, opposing king and commonweal to support their position. Henry VI's councillors had previously justified their actions by attributing them to the king's personal authority even if their decisions were not in fact backed by active kingship. However, malcontents such as York and Jack Cade's rebels justified their opposition to government policy in 1450 not through the standard medieval critique of bad councillors impairing royal judgement, but by positing an opposition between the interests of the commonweal and the king's will (an outgrowth of the risky suggestion that the king, in his mortal body as distinct from his immortal crowned body, was not capable of ruling properly).[48] One instance of this separation occurred when Suffolk was exiled as scapegoat for the failures of government in 1450. Suffolk's ship was intercepted by rebels who beheaded him in contempt of the royal safe conduct he had been issued, declaring 'they did not know the said king, but they well knew the crown of England', and that 'the aforesaid crown was the community of the said realm and that the community of the realm was the crown of that realm'.[49] While previously the commonweal had been necessarily at one with the king's will, here we see a dialectic between the two, with the floating signifier of the 'crown' unmoored

[45] *Vale's Book*, p. 213.   [46] *Vale's Book*, p. 214.

[47] 'Chronicle of the Rebellion in Lincolnshire 1470', in *Three Chronicles of the Reign of Edward IV*, ed. by Keith Dockray (Gloucester: Sutton, 1988), p. 10.

[48] Ernst H. Kantorowicz, *The King's Two Bodies: A Study in Mediaeval Political Theology* (Princeton: Princeton University Press, 1957), pp. 402–3; Black, *Political Thought in Europe*, pp. 189–90.

[49] Roger Virgoe, 'The Death of William de la Pole, Duke of Suffolk', *Bulletin of the John Rylands Library*, 47.2 (1964–5), 489–502 (p. 499).

between them. This was the dialectic upon which York's articulation of his position and reformist aims in the 1450s sought to capitalize.[50] York sought to defend his dissension from the king's will on the grounds that he acted for the sake of the commonweal, but his enemies did not agree that the latter, when opposed to the former, could be the aim of government. This conflict surfaces in the *Somnium vigilantis*, a dream vision that supports the 1459 parliamentary attainder of the Yorkist lords through a debate about the merits of York's commonweal platform.[51] The Yorkist speaker argues that although York and his adherents rose above their station, their actions 'oght not to be interpreted in the wars partie' because 'thay entende the commen welthe of alle the royame'.[52] However, the Lancastrian speaker counters him by subordinating the commonweal to the king, thereby denouncing York and his adherents as traitors.[53] Yet this concern to refute York's position and articulate a different role for the commonweal indicates that it was not only York, but also his ideas, which threatened Henry VI.

While York abandoned his commonweal platform and, in 1460, made a bid for the throne,[54] the commonweal underpinned the platforms of other (would-be) usurpers. When opposing Henry VI in 1459, Warwick declared that he and the Yorkist lords acted out of 'the tendre love that we bere unto the commene wele and prosperite of this reaume *and secondly* to the kinges estate'.[55] A decade after this subordination of king to commonweal in support of York, in 1470, Warwick and Clarence rebelled against Edward IV and directed a letter to the commons of England expressing similar principles, but for different motives: they assert that they bear 'feithefully toward the seid croune and commen weele of Englonde as fervente zeele, love and affeccion as evur we had'.[56] Here, loyalty to the crown as well as to the commonweal is mentioned, but there are no assurances that the 'crown' means the same thing as the 'king'; this 'crown' instead seems an empty signifier substituting for whomever Warwick, the 'kingmaker', would bestow it upon this time.[57]

[50] Watts, 'Polemic and Politics in the 1450s', pp. 3, 21, and 27.

[51] Margaret Kekewich, 'The Attainder of the Yorkists in 1459: Two Contemporary Accounts', *Bulletin of the Institute of Historical Research*, 55.1 (1982), 25–34.

[52] J. P. Gilson, ed., 'A Defense of the Proscription of the Yorkists in 1459', *English Historical Review*, 26 (1911), 512–25 (p. 515).

[53] 'Proscription of the Yorkists', p. 520.   [54] Watts, *Henry VI*, pp. 44–5.

[55] *Vale's Book*, p. 209.   [56] *Vale's Book*, p. 219.

[57] 'Crown' meant primarily the object itself, and, secondarily, royal authority, but did not metonymically imply the king's person until the sixteenth century (*MED* and *OED*). As Strohm observes, in late medieval England the crown stood for the royal office, for kingly authority but not the king's mortal body: *England's Empty Throne: Usurpation and the Language of Legitimation,* 1399–1422 (New Haven: Yale University Press, 1998), pp. 203 and 207. A refrain written during the reign of Henry V and relevant during the Wars of the Roses illustrates this: in the lines 'Stonde wiþ þe kyng, mayntene þe croun' or 'saue þe kyng, and kepe þe crowne', while king and crown are associated, they are clearly distinct ('God

The protean power of the commonweal is also shown by its appearances in parliamentary attainders. Whereas the attainders of Henry VI and Edward IV do not tend to mention the commonweal per se (though they do sometimes specify that the traitor has harmed the king's subjects as well as the king), the attainders produced during the instability of Richard III's and Henry VII's early reigns denounce traitors' contravention of the commonweal. In his first parliament (January–February 1484) Richard III indicted his enemies in part for their 'subversion of this his said reame of Englond and the *comen wele*' (XV.23); likewise in his first parliament (November 1485–March 1486), Henry VII accused Richard and his supporters for their 'subversion of this roialme, and *comen wele* of the same' (XV.108). It is telling that such foregrounding of the commonweal occurs when these two kings were only barely beyond paralleling reformers or would-be usurpers such as Warwick and Clarence who also sought to buttress their position with the commonweal. Thus, to speak of the commonweal was often to seek legitimacy from a position of opposition. The commonweal was used to reconfigure the nature of authority and governance, but, accordingly, often added to the complexities and uncertainties of community and loyalty for landowners and citizens alike.

The commonweal, as an anchor for a conception of ideal governance and loyalty both hierarchical and horizontal, was a potent idea for the members of these social classes concerned with justice and governance in practice as well as in theory. The gentry's and citizens' attitudes towards governance and the fabric of society were influenced not only by the magnates' debates and struggles over authority, but also by the praxis of their own attempts to effect or affect social cohesion, in which they relied upon and worried about a network of personal relationships. On the one hand, hierarchical 'service'—the personal and mutually beneficial relationship between lord and man—was a 'dominant ethic' of late medieval politics.[58] Service was expected to be a long-standing arrangement viable in both peace and war, and it was common for men to act for more than one lord without expecting irresolvable conflicts of loyalty to arise, though of course they did during the Wars of the Roses.[59] On the other hand, horizontal loyalties and trust were equally important. Private regional networks were integral to public power and stability: as mentioned in the Introduction,

kepe oure kyng and saue the croune', in *The Digby Poems: A New Edition of the Lyrics*, ed. by Helen Barr (Exeter: University of Exeter Press, 2009), pp. 192–201 (lines 8 and 24)).

[58] Rosemary Horrox, 'Service', in *Fifteenth-Century Attitudes: Perceptions of Society in Late Medieval England*, ed. by Rosemary Horrox (Cambridge: Cambridge University Press, 1994), pp. 61–78 (p. 61), and *Richard III: A Study of Service* (Cambridge: Cambridge University Press, 1989), pp. 7–25.

[59] Horrox, 'Service', p. 72.

in order to maintain order and settle disputes in their localities, the gentry had to rely upon themselves and each other as well as the local lord.[60] That not only obedience to mayor and guild leaders, but also lateral fellowship, was important to merchants too is clear in the way in which (London) civic writing focused on the 'over-arching civic virtue of concord, achieved through triumph over discord, or factionalism'.[61] Recognizing that both hierarchical and horizontal relationships were fundamental to, yet often insufficiently stable to ensure, social cohesion for Wars of the Roses aristocracy, gentry, and citizens allows a greater appreciation of the anxieties expressed in their own writings (as addressed in the following section), and of the resonance of the analogous relationships and ideals of fellowship or commonweal with which contemporary romances and chivalric tracts are concerned (as addressed in the following chapters).

COMMUNICATING TREASON: LETTERS, CHRONICLES, AND POLITICAL VERSES

How public were these discourses of treason and the debates about power, law, and loyalty to which they contributed? The central protagonists of the Wars of the Roses and their supporters wished to reach as broad an audience as possible, and evidence suggests that their polemical documents were read by (and copied for) both citizens and landed gentry. Many documents—such as York's 1450 bills and the royal replies, and Warwick's and Clarence's letter directed to the commons of England in 1470—were originally posted up in London and other towns on church doors and in central streets.[62] Royal proclamations from 1450 onward forbade the publishing or reading of bills, but the fact that transmission continued, and that such documents were often removed, demonstrates that bill-posting in public places was a potentially effective method of attracting a readership for a contentious political statement.[63] In part through means such as these, a broad swath of English society was exposed to the ongoing debates

---

[60] Watts, *Henry VI*, pp. 91–3; Philippa Maddern, '"Best Trusted Friends": Concepts and Practices of Friendship among Fifteenth-Century Norfolk Gentry', in *England in the Fifteenth Century: Proceedings of the 1992 Harlaxton Symposium*, ed. by Nicholas Rogers (Stamford: Watkins, 1994), pp. 100–17 (p. 100); see also Introduction, notes 15 and 16.

[61] Sarah Rees Jones, 'Thomas More's *Utopia* and Medieval London', in *Pragmatic Utopias: Ideals and Communities, 1200–1630*, ed. by Rosemary Horrox and Sarah Rees Jones (Cambridge: Cambridge University Press, 2001), pp. 117–35 (p. 123).

[62] Sutton and Visser-Fuchs, 'Provenance of the Manuscript', pp. 92 and 122.

[63] Wendy Scase, *Literature and Complaint in England, 1272–1553* (Oxford: Oxford University Press, 2007), pp. 114 and 133–8; Scase, 'Bill-Casting and Political Discourse', pp. 228–9.

about community and authority. Moreover, as the following examination of letters, chronicles, and political poems illustrates, burghers, gentry, and magnates were profoundly affected by, and interested in discussing, the political upheavals and uncertainties of their time.

Treason's communicative role in this textual culture can be better understood through further attention to the nature of discourses. Foucault defines a 'discursive practice' as 'a body of anonymous, historical rules, always determined in the time and space that have defined a given period, and for a given social, economic, geographical area, the conditions of operation of the enunciative function'.[64] Textual utterances can, of course, be understood as part of the 'enunciative function', as Tony Bex observes:

> Written texts are interventions... [that] contribute to, and are shaped by, the broad ways in which society speaks to itself (i.e. its discursive practices)... As specific interventions they have their own particular shape, but they also have to conform to the norms of the group to which they are directed.[65]

Accordingly, following this Foucauldian definition of the ways in which a given milieu exerts pressures upon the use and interpretation of language, we can recognize the implications of conditions shaping utterances about treason in Wars of the Roses texts. Because political power was often divided, contested, or uncertain in this milieu, control over discourses was also less fixed, such that the use and direction of accusations of treason lacked the limitations normally placed upon them by centralized authority. As discussed earlier, treason operated as an accepted anti-principle; as addressed below, the conditions under which it operated meant that this anti-principle was available for appropriation by greater numbers of people, with greater potential for confusion, conflict, and anxiety. In such an uncertain environment, to communicate about treason was to participate in the struggles to define, denounce, and/or eradicate it. This section focuses on how letters, bills, chronicles, and occasional verses about treason support (or deny) treason accusations by reproducing them; it views these texts as interventions that make factual claims, seek to persuade, and often register misgivings and desires for stability, in ways that bear witness to contemporary mentalities of treason.

It was not only once there were multiple claimants to the throne (at the end of the 1450s) that the anxiety-producing conditions of the Wars of the Roses were established; an assortment of letters and bills produced in

---

[64] Foucault, *The Archaeology of Knowledge*, p. 117.
[65] Tony Bex, *Variety in Written English: Texts in Society: Societies in Text* (London: Routledge, 1996), pp. 66–7.

1450–1 show that an active discourse and strong sense of disquiet about treason were already present then (as is also demonstrated in Chapter 3 by the treason-focused literary texts produced around mid-century). While accusations of treason had been traditionally issued from those 'in secure possession of the mechanisms of the household judiciary' and law courts against those on the margins, by contrast, as central authority fractured from 1450 onward, 'each party arrogat[ed] the language of treason in its accusation of the other'.[66] Further confusion and anxiety arose from the fact that there were more than two parties in this exchange of accusations. The growing political tensions produced conflicting accusations of treason, which produced anxiety in their turn. In June 1450, Cade's Kentish rebels submitted a bill of decried injustices and desired reforms, including a request for 'punysshmente upon the fals traytors the whiche contreved and imagened the detthe of the highe and mightefull excellent prince, the duc of Glowcester', who had died when arrested for treason in 1447; the rebels allege here that he was unjustly 'proclamed as traytor'.[67] In this petition, then, certain people are called traitors for having apprehended another as a traitor. These criss-crossing denouncements soon became even more tangled, as the king responded with a document indicting the rebels for their accusations and uprising, calling Cade 'a fals traytour' in turn.[68] This accusation, because anchored to the king's will, effectively nullified Cade's own in a way that testifies to some of the anxieties engendered by the uncertainties of who could/would be a traitor, and who could successfully label another as a traitor—as articulated in one of the rebels' 1450 proclamations:

> they say that whom the kyng woll shall be traytur and whom he woll shall be non, and that apperyth hederto, for yf eny of the traytours about hym wolde malygne ageynst eny person, hyghe or low, they wolde fynd fals menys that he shuld dy a traytor.[69]

While this complaint registers the perceived injustice and irrationality of accusations issuing from the king's circle, the subjective nature of accusations of treason soon increased further.

Although, in 1450, Henry VI was undisputedly king, the weakness of his rule meant that authority was sometimes partially appropriated by powerful figures such as York or by (other) rebels, and hence accusations of treason began to be made without deference to the king's will. Gentry

---

[66] Strohm, *Politique*, pp. 187–8.   [67] *Vale's Book*, p. 206.
[68] *Vale's Book*, pp. 207–8.
[69] Copied by John Stow and edited as 'A proclamation made by Jacke Cade, Capytayn of the Rebelles in Kent', in *Three Fifteenth-Century Chronicles*, pp. 94–9 (p. 96).

and citizens viewed these debates and divisions as matters of vital concern. For instance, in his letter to John Paston I on 5 May 1450 concerning the recent death of the Duke of Suffolk, William Lomnor registers the personal significance of the event he reports, writing that he is 'right sory of that I shalle sey, and haue soo wesshe this litel bille with sorwfulle terys that on-ethes ye shulle reede it'.[70] Exiled by the king after parliamentary impeachment, Suffolk was on his way to France when his ship was intercepted near Dover by a rebel vessel. These interceptors required Suffolk to board their ship, wrote Lomnor,

> and whanne he come the mastere badde hym, 'Wolcom, *traitour*', *as men sey*;...And yn the syght of all his men...oon of the lewdeste of the shippe badde hym ley down...and toke a rusty swerd and smotte of his hedde withyn halfe a doseyn strokes.[71]

The 'men' who 'sey' that Suffolk is a traitor evidently were not authorized by the king or parliament; public voice, here, effects its own 'judicial' ends without the consent of central authority. The situation was yet more complex: the Duke of York, who may have caused or at least welcomed this accusation and punishment of his rival Suffolk, was subject to, and further issued, accusations of treason himself. When York returned from his post as lieutenant of Ireland in September 1450 in order to defend his honour, his landing in Wales was opposed by the king's servants, who, York wrote to the king, 'afferm[ed] that I come ayenst your entent as your tratoure'. York complained in this bill that, when he was in Ireland on Henry's service, 'certeyn persones laboured instantly forto have endited me of treson, to thentent to have undo me, [and] myn issue'.[72] Soon afterwards in autumn 1450, York made his own accusations of treason in further bills both submitted to king and council, and published as widely as possible.[73] Here, York sought to convince the king of the need for justice against 'them that ben endited of tresone and other beyng openly noysed of the same', and volunteered to provide the required punishment, effectively threatening to arrogate royal authority as the king's replies to his bills did not offer him the assurances he sought.[74] In 1450, then, in response to government distrust, York widened the rifts in the political community by taking up the call for reform initiated by the parliamentary commons and Jack Cade

---

[70] *Paston Letters*, II, 450.1–3.   [71] *Paston Letters*, II, 450.16–31.

[72] R. A. Griffiths, 'Duke Richard of York's Intentions in 1450 and the Origins of the Wars of the Roses', *Journal of Medieval History*, 1 (1975), 187–209 (p. 203).

[73] Michael Hicks, 'From Megaphone to Microscope: The Correspondence of Richard Duke of York with Henry VI in 1450 Revisited', *Journal of Medieval History*, 25.3 (1999), 243–56 (p. 254).

[74] Griffiths, 'Duke Richard of York's Intentions', p. 204.

earlier in the year.[75] This bill was copied in John Vale's book,[76] and both copied and discussed between Paston correspondents, showing wider gentry and civic circulation of, and interest in, this textual sparring. By reproducing a full copy of this bill and enclosing it in a letter to John Paston I on 6 October 1450, William Wayte evidently viewed it as an important component of current affairs, a matter of which Paston should not remain ignorant. Wayte's explanation of the origins of the document suggests that it had widespread currency: York's bill 'is meche after þe Comouns desyre, and all is vp-on justice'.[77] Since such copying was widespread, knowledge of major political events and stances was by no means confined to (or only relevant to) the main contenders.[78]

During the Wars of the Roses, then, a plethora of conflicting agendas and the absence of one stable source of authority produced an environment seething with betrayals and with a multiplicity of actors attempting to exert control over how accusations of treason were issued and enforced; a discursive environment in which bills and letters constituted performative political actions, or events.[79] While bills discuss treason with an expectation of a wide audience, letters are usually intended for a specific audience, but are no less intent upon persuasion.[80] Letters are inherently about reception: they both respond to treason, and seek to produce responses to the treasons they discuss. These affective and persuasive functions often also apply to chronicles and political verses similarly concerned with current worldly affairs (as discussed below), but letters demonstrate particularly clearly the connection between the nature of treason accusations and the nature of the textual culture of this period. In this political environment, that is, where making people believe an accusation of treason and act as though it is true matters more than strict legality, letters—containing a

---

[75] We cannot simply assume, however, that York's intentions in 1450 were the same as when he claimed the throne in 1460: Griffiths, 'York's Intentions'; updated by Hicks, 'Megaphone to Microscope'.

[76] *Vale's Book*, pp. 185–90.

[77] *Paston Letters*, II, 460.1–8 and (Wayte's copy of the bill) 460A.1–23.

[78] Jack Cade's bills, for instance, were also transmitted among both Londoners and landed gentry: Scase, *Literature and Complaint*, pp. 114 and 135.

[79] As Nuttall writes, 'a text can be seen as a historical event', occurring 'at a particular moment using a particular set of linguistic and conceptual circumstances' (*Creation of Lancastrian Kingship*, pp. 1–3); see also J. G. A. Pocock, who writes of language as both influenced by and influencing its 'context of social relations': 'Texts as Events: Reflections on the History of Political Thought', in *The Politics of Discourse: The Literature and History of Seventeenth-Century England*, ed. by Kevin Sharpe and Steven N. Zwicker (Berkeley: University of California Press, 1987), pp. 21–34 (p. 25).

[80] Richard Beadle, 'Private Letters', in *A Companion to Middle English Prose*, ed. by A. S. G. Edwards (Cambridge: Brewer, 2004), pp. 289–306 (pp. 295–7).

layered latticework of purposeful language concerning treason—are significant interventions.

We see this sense of letters as persuasion about matters of treason, as making claims to legitimize the writers and delegitimize their opponents, in the way that the principal dynastic contenders heatedly and repeatedly deployed the same lexicon of treason in correspondence. For instance, a letter written on behalf of the seven-year-old Lancastrian Prince Edward complains to the City of London in late 1460 of 'that horrible and falsly forsworne traitor [Richard] calling hym selfe duc of [York]', condemning York for 'his subtilly contrived treasons'.[81] In this letter, the desire for Richard of York to be recognized as a traitor is continually reiterated in phrases such as 'the malicious coniecture of the said traytor' and 'the same fals traitour'.[82] Reciprocal (and therefore contradictory) accusations were made in the Yorkists' letters in similar attempts to ensure that public perception would sanction them and decry their opponents. Edward IV wrote to James III of Scotland in 1462 of his English 'traitours and rebellis', repeating the phrase half a dozen times in one letter seeking to prevent James from aiding the Lancastrians.[83] Edward used the same terms in a series of letters to the mayor and aldermen of London soon afterwards, informing the civic leaders that 'oure enemyes of Scotlande purpose tentre oure lande...at thinstaunce and provocacion of our great traitours and rebelles Henry, late usurpaunt king...and Margarete, his wife'.[84] Edward justified his request for funds to fight against the Lancastrian advance by explaining, 'we applie us to the diffence of our said reaulme and of our subgiettes therof to the rebuke of oure traitours, rebelles and enemies'.[85] Like the citizens importuned and implicated by means of these letters, the gentry's loyalty and material support were also solicited through the rhetoric of treason, as in two letters collected by the Yorkshire Plumpton family and Oxfordshire Stonor family. Both of these letters were issued by the privy seal office, sought military support, and employed the same language to indict the enemy, but they emerge from opposite camps. In one, Henry VI writes to Sir William Plumpton on 13 March 1461 concerning the movements of 'our great trator, the late earle of Mearch [i.e. Edward]', requesting military aid 'to resist the malitious entent and *purpose* of our said

---

[81] *Vale's Book*, p. 143; this and the only other extant copy (by John Stow, in British Library, MS Harley 543, ff.147v–148r) both replace the proper nouns in this indictment with 'n.', as discussed below.

[82] *Vale's Book*, p. 143.

[83] *Vale's Book*, pp. 144–5; similar expressions occur in other documents copied in this late fifteenth-century manuscript (British Library, MS Additional 48031A).

[84] *Vale's Book*, p. 151.   [85] *Vale's Book*, p. 150.

trator'.[86] We know that Sir William answered this summons, for his eldest son died seeking to oppose Edward's triumph at the Battle of Towton two weeks later (29 March). On 3 April 1470 Edward IV issued a very similar letter to the Stonor family, writing of the worrying westward progress of 'our Traitours and Rebelles þe Duc of Clarence and Therl of Warrewik' and charging Thomas Stonor to join him with an armed fellowship to 'represse þeir fals and *traiteroux purpose*'.[87] These letters' shared formulaic (but not inconsequential) phrasing suggests that most such letters written during the Wars of the Roses would have made the same rhetorical moves, and shows that not only the more aggressive Pastons, but also more typical gentry families, were affected by the contemporary discourses (and deeds) of treason. For the gentry and burgesses as for the aristocracy, then, this was no mere matter of idle curiosity; they were often implicated by their ties of loyalty to one great lord or another, and their lives were affected by periods of upheaval and regime change.

The lexical web of treasonous actions and accusations not only affected gentry and citizens, but was also employed by them; most of the gentry and merchant letter collections which survive from the Wars of the Roses reveal implication in and anxiety about both treason and accusations of treason. John Paston II reported to his brother John III in 1473 that 'the worlde semyth qweysye', recording a widespread uneasiness about how the magnates in power, while maintaining a superficial attitude of solidarity, strove against each other for preeminence. Although Clarence and Gloucester outwardly professed support for their brother Edward IV, John II observes, 'som men thynke þat vndre thys ther sholde be som other thynge entendyd and *som treason* conspryed', a curiously agent-less formulation that seems to speak either to the uncertainty of motives or an unwillingness to court danger by specifying. The letter further dwells on the instability of the situation, concluding, 'what shall falle can I nott seye'.[88] That the gentry were affected not only by the treasons of others but also those within their own circles is clear in the letter Margaret Paston wrote to her husband John I on 3 March 1451:

> there is a gret noyse in þis town þat my lord of Oxforth and Yelverton and ye ben endytid…and Jon Damme is endytyd þere also of treson be-cawse þat he dede Heydon endytyn of treson…And the pepyll þat ben ayens Sere

[86] *The Plumpton Letters and Papers*, ed. by Joan Kirby (Cambridge: Cambridge University Press, 1996), p. 26.

[87] *Kingsford's Stonor Letters and Papers*, 1290–1483, ed. by Christine Carpenter (Cambridge: Cambridge University Press, 1996), pp. 203–4.

[88] *Paston Letters*, I, 281.2–8.

Thomas Todenham and Heydon ben sore aferd be-cawse of þis noyse and of oþer langage that is had boþe in þis town and in þe contré.[89]

Here, there is both a recognition that treason is a present possibility, and an anxious awareness that the fates of the members of this gentry circle depend on the outcome of the civil strife. The privy seal letters requesting aid from the Stonors and Plumptons against traitors (as quoted above) show one of the ways in which these gentry families were entangled in discourses of treason; in addition, their own letters manifest anxiety about instability, as they shared their worries over the uncertainty of 'tydynges' in moments of treason-related crisis. For instance, Simon Stallworth wrote two letters to Sir William Stonor from London in June 1483 regarding the political turmoil and uncertainty there; in the second, he concludes, 'for tydynges I hold you happy that ye ar oute of the prese, for with huse is myche trobull, and every manne dowtes other…what schall happyne hyr I knowe nott'.[90] Similarly, on 13 December 1485 Thomas Betanson informs Sir Robert Plumpton of the attainders of treason meted out to the deceased Richard III and many of his supporters, and testifies to the uncertainty of the times a few months after Bosworth: 'Sir, other tydings is none here as yett. Ther is much runyng amongst þe lords, but no man wett what it is. It is sayd yt is not wele amongst them.'[91] The Paston letter with which this chapter opens, describing the accusations of treason in the confrontation between rival lords in Calais in 1460, shares this concern to establish as much as can be known about political affairs, while displaying anxiety about the contingencies of such news.

While neither the remaining gentry collection (of the litigious Armburgh family), nor the Cely merchant family letters (largely preoccupied with the wool trade), discusses current political events, the latter contains suggestive gaps which imply similar anxiety about times of treason and political uncertainty as in the majority of the gentry letter collections. The Cely letters run from 1472 to 1488, but no letters survive from November 1482 to November 1483—a year encompassing Edward IV's death and Richard III's usurpation—except for a note that makes a guarded reference to the circumstances of June 1483 when Richard was in the process of deposing his nephew. Neither are there any letters extant for 1485–6, when Richard was threatened and deposed in his turn by Henry VII.[92] This suggests that the Cely correspondents may have deemed these moments of crisis too dangerous for sending letters, or, perhaps more

---

[89] *Paston Letters*, I, 137.2–8.   [90] *Stonor Letters*, p. 417.
[91] *Plumpton Letters*, p. 63.
[92] Alison Hanham, ed., *The Cely Letters 1472–1488*, *EETS OS 273* (London: Oxford University Press, 1975), p. ix.

likely, deemed the letters they had written then too dangerous to keep—showing the extent to which they also were profoundly affected by contemporary anxieties about treason. Merchants were, however, like the gentry and aristocracy, more than just observers in this culture of treason. The wealthy draper Thomas Cook, for instance (mayor of London 1462–3), was one of several prominent Londoners and many more townspeople and knights elsewhere accused of treason, after letters, addressed to them from the dispossessed Lancastrian Queen Margaret and soliciting financial aid, were intercepted. Although Cook did not send any such aid, this indication of his suspected Lancastrian connections was enough to earn him an accusation of treason, and an eventual conviction of misprision of treason, by the mistrustful Yorkist regime.[93] This episode of widespread denunciations, incarcerations, and executions for treason is addressed in both gentry letters and civic chronicles, which evince concern about the prevalence and unpredictability of denouncements for treason of people of similar standing to the writers and readers.[94]

In England during the Wars of the Roses, positive and negative identities were constructed through treason, and hence palpably unstable. When calling someone a traitor, the accuser often deliberately contrasted this label with the identity that the accused claimed for him or her self, that is, what the accused is 'called': for instance, Henry VI denounced 'oon John Cade…whiche *callith* hym selfe John Mortymer and in some writyng *callith* hym selfe capiteigne of Kente, the whiche is openly knowen for a fals traytour'; Edward IV wrote to the mayor of London of 'Henry, late *called* king, our greate traitour and rebell'; the Lancastrian Prince Edward's letter discredited 'that horrible and falsly forsworne traitor [Richard] *calling* hym selfe duc of [York]'; and Henry VII's attainder denounced his predecessor for '*callyng* and namyng hym self, by usurpacion, Kyng Richard the.iij.d'.[95] Such figures claimed identities for themselves through their 'calling', just as oppositional identities were articulated for them through their enemies' own 'calling' in accusations of treason. The way in which many among those who discussed treason located their assaults and fears explicitly in language itself testifies to the extent to which treason, as a concept and a charge, was both constituted by and dependent upon words; unlike murder, for instance, treason sometimes *was* words, as well as being proved or prosecuted by words. We might observe that if fifteenth-century England had known the term

---

[93] Sutton and Visser-Fuchs, 'Provenance of the Manuscript', p. 88.

[94] Godfrey Greene, letter to Sir William Plumpton, 9 December 1468 (*Plumpton Letters*, pp. 39–40); 'Gregory's Chronicle', pp. 236–7.

[95] *Vale's Book*, pp. 207, 148, and 143; *Parliamentary Rolls*, XV.107.

'spccch act', contemporaries would have applied it to the inherently sociolinguistic operations of discourses of treason. When Margaret Paston reported (in the 1451 letter to her husband quoted above) that some local members of the gentry, who had supported those recently indited for treason, 'ben sore aferd *be-cawse of þis noyse* [i.e. the indictments] *and of oþer langage* that is had boþe in þis town and in þe contré', we see Margaret's and her contemporaries' awareness of the forceful, active dimensions of utterances such as accusations of treason.[96] The illocutionary function of calling someone a traitor is an accusation or denouncement; if the speech act is successful, the perlocutionary effect is to bring about the accused's status (or perception) as a traitor.[97] Thus, these Paston acquaintances are right to fear 'þis noyse', this 'langage' of treason, because they recognize that such acts of speech interpellate traitors as such—that is, oral and/or textual utterances, provided they are successful, create or constitute the figures' socially relative identities as traitors.[98]

Yet this discursive function and preoccupation is not, of course, limited to the strictly political or epistolary; chronicles likewise discuss and dread treason as they record and seek to make meaning of recent events. In doing so, they both respond to and emulate textual interventions such as the parliamentary attainders, which not only record, but also publish, the status of traitors: for instance, in the 1450 proclamation that Cade 'be called within youre seid reame fals traitour for evermore' (XII.203), and the 1459 declaration that the Yorkist lords are to 'be reputed, taken, declared, adjugged, demed and atteynted of high treson, as fals traitours' (XII.460–1). This focus on proclaiming the condemnation of traitors is reported by contemporary chronicles, as in the comment that 'the sayde camptayne

---

[96] *Paston Letters*, I, 137.7–8.

[97] The foundational study examining the performative and active dimensions of utterances is J. L. Austin, *How to Do Things with Words*, ed. by J. O. Urmson and Marina Sbisà, 2nd edn (1962; Cambridge, MA: Harvard University Press, 1975).

[98] For an insightful discussion of Louis Althusser's term 'interpellation', see Judith Butler, *Excitable Speech: A Politics of the Performative* (New York: Routledge, 1997), where Butler remarks that 'it is by being interpellated within the terms of language that a certain social existence of the body first becomes possible' (p. 5). Louis Althusser points out that ultimately there is no temporal element to the process of interpellation, since 'individuals are already-always-interpellated by ideology as subjects'. However, Althusser's analogy of a policeman's 'hailing of suspects' to explain the operation of what he glosses as 'interpellation or hailing' is useful for conceptualizing the effect of an accusation of treason: when a policeman utters, '"Hey, you there!" ... in the street, the hailed individual will turn round. By this mere one-hundred-and-eighty-degree physical conversion, he becomes a *subject*. Why? Because he has recognized that the hail was "really" addressed to him, and that "it was *really him* who was hailed"': Louis Althusser, 'Ideology and Ideological State Apparatuses', in *Lenin and Philosophy and Other Essays*, trans. by Ben Brewster (London: NLB, 1971), pp. 121–73 (pp. 162–4).

was cryde and proclaymyd traytoure, by the name of John Cade, in dyvers placys of London, and also in Sowtheworke, whythe many moo'.[99] Here, condemnation and publication led to punishment, since, with this proclamation and a bounty of a thousand marks on his head, Cade was captured and killed; his head, set on London Bridge, offered a warning to potential traitors both as a grisly presence and as a unit of chronicle narrative. By reporting proclamations and outcomes such as these, the chronicles perform or participate in attempts to broadcast accusations of and admonitions about treason—yet they do so not without misgiving.

The *Chronicle* formerly attributed to John Warkworth, Master of St Peter's College, Cambridge, a retrospective account of the first thirteen years of Edward IV's reign (1461–74), treats treason with a concentration and concatenation that exemplifies a mode common to many fifteenth-century English chronicles. Although this chronicle may have been written during Edward IV's reign (and certainly before Henry VII's), it criticizes Edward's officials and policies; in this vein, a chronology of accusations of and punishments for treason in the mid- to late 1460s and early 1470s is given prominence:

> in the vth yer off Kyng Edwarde the erle off Oxenford, the Lord Abrey, his sonne, & Sir Thomas Todenam, knyght, wer taken and brought into the Tour off London; *& þer was leyd to them hye tresoun* and aftyrwarde thay wer brought byfor þe erle off Worsetre and iudged by law Padowe þat þei shulde be had to þe Tour Hyll, wher was made a scaffotte off viij foote hy3t; & þer wer ther hedes smyten off þat all men my3t se, where off þe moste peple wer sory.
>
> *And* in the sext yer off Kyng Edwardes regne þe Lord Hungerford was taken & beheded *for hight tresoun* at Salesbury.
>
> *And* in the vij yer of Kyng Edwarde Sir Thomas Cooke, Sir John Plummer, knyghtes & aldermen of London, and Humfray Haywarde & oþer aldermen wer *arested and tresoun surmysed vppon them*, wheroff they wer acquyte; but the loste gret goodes to þe kyng, to the valow off xl M marke or mor; *and diuerse tymes in diuerse places of Englond many men wer arested for treson*, and som wer put to deth and some scaped.[100]

[99] 'Gregory's Chronicle', p. 194.
[100] 'Warkworth's' Chronicle*, in *Death and Dissent: Two Fifteenth-Century Chronicles*, ed. by Lister Matheson (Woodbridge: Boydell, 1999), p. 97.4–18. The author may have been a fellow of Peterhouse, responsible for the earlier copy of the chronicle (University of Glasgow, Hunterian MS 83), from which Peterhouse, Cambridge, MS 190 was copied and presented to Warkworth (Matheson, p. 81). Because John Tiptoft (the Earl of Worcester) had studied law at Padua, this chronicler criticized him for conducting trials according to civil rather than common law, even though the former was in fact appropriate for Tiptoft as Constable of England: David Rundle, 'Was There a Renaissance Style of Politics in Fifteenth-Century England?', in *Authority and Consent in Tudor England*, ed. by G. W. Bernard and S. J. Gunn (Aldershot: Ashgate, 2002), pp. 15–32 (pp. 19–20).

In this episodic and lexical emphasis on treason, the chronicler presents the past decade as imbued with a constant threat of arrests and treason. The polysyndetic 'and, and' of each further action against treason speaks to the prevalence and sense of inevitability of these occurrences; the chronicle continues, '*And* the viij yere off the regne of Kyng Edward… Sir Thomas Hungerford, knyȝt, son to the Lord Hungerford, & Harry Courteney, þe erle of Devenschir of ryght, *wer taken for treson and beheded*.'[101] While coordinating conjunctions are of course a common feature of chronicle writing, they are put to a particular purpose here: Edward IV's reign is told as a parataxis of treasons and their confrontation. Other chronicles contain comparable strains—from varied political perspectives, but with shared uneasiness.

A number of *Brut* chronicles, which follow the history of England from its mythical origins to the present day through continuations added to the late thirteenth-century original,[102] contain continuations for the Wars of the Roses that report England's treasons and lament its social instability. Some of these continuations are general, and others have a civic focus; both types tended to be produced for private remembrance and reading. One London chronicle shows a sense of a departure in the mid- to late 1430s towards a darker, more treason-filled England by declaring (in its entry for 1436) that 'the lond whas at that tyme full of treson aftyr the deth of the Duke of bedford and regent of ffraunce': Bedford's death in 1435 was thought to contribute to the growing uncertainty in Henry VI's government thereafter.[103] Indeed, these *Brut* chronicles tend to break and/or change hands part way through the Lancastrian period before a continuous scribal stint to their chronological end (be it Edward IV's coronation, or the midpoint of his reign, or the first half of Henry VII's), suggesting that these decades were seen as a distinct period—and one for which many treasons and accusations of treason are reported. One such continuation, for 1440–61, survives in two manuscripts, appended to a more common 1377–1437 continuation. The 1440–61 continuation comments on matters of treason from a Yorkist angle throughout.[104] Caxton's *Brut*, printed

---

[101] '*Warkworth's' Chronicle*, pp. 97.19–98.4.

[102] For further details of the *Brut* tradition and its manuscripts, see Lister M. Matheson, *The Prose Brut: The Development of a Middle English Chronicle* (Tempe, AZ: Medieval & Renaissance Texts & Studies, 1998).

[103] 'Cotton Cleopatra C IV', in *Chronicles of London*, ed. by Charles Lethbridge Kingsford (Oxford: Clarendon Press, 1905), pp. 117–52 (p. 141); the chronicles in this edition are not discussed in detail because they end near the beginning of the decades studied here (1443, in this case).

[104] Such matters of treason run from Duchess Eleanor Cobham (Humphrey of Gloucester's wife), 'endited of treson' in 1441, and Humphrey's summons to parliament in 1447 to 'answare to suche articles of treson… as were falsely put on hym', to Jack Cade's rebellion in 1450 when 'all þe peple of þis lond and specialli þe comunez cride ayens þe said

in 1480 and 1482, employs a similar treason-filled final continuation (1419–61),[105] and another is appended to the *Polychronicon*, a 'universal' history he printed in 1482.[106] Later fifteenth-century London chronicles that likewise dwell on these narratives of treason include a 'Short English Chronicle', 'Robert Bale's Commonplace Book', and 'Gregory's Chronicle'.[107] These chronicles end in Edward IV's first reign, and, although from a Yorkist perspective, they, like 'Warkworth's' chronicle, focus on the accusation and punishment of Edward's enemies after he is established on the throne: 'This yere was imagened and wrought grete treyson a yenes the kynge by the menys of the Erle of Oxenford and his sone Aubry, with oþer... traytors... and anon they were taken and juged to dethe.'[108] A further London chronicle that contains the same treason commentaries up to the 1460s is then incomplete until its concluding account of the treason trials concerning Perkin Warbeck's attempted usurpation in 1494–5; recording those 'endyted of Treson' and executed, it was probably written soon after.[109] Such passages bear witness to the important role that treason played in the mentalities and memories of contemporaries of the Wars of the Roses.

Some chronicles that participate in this mode of recording matters of treason ensure that the resonant, incendiary treason keywords are broadcast as a way of legalistically stigmatizing motive and action, thereby producing utterances as intent upon persuasion as those in the letters addressed in the previous section. Written by an anonymous Yorkist, the *Chronicle of the Rebellion in Lincolnshire* offers a partisan condemnation of the rebellion in March 1470 under the leadership of the Welles family, and as such this

Duke of Suffolk, and saide he was a traitour', and the 1459 parliament at Coventry, when the 'Duk of York and the iij erles... as traytours and rebelles to the kyng were atteynt of treson... and by the kyngis commyssion in euery cyte, burgh, and toune cryed opynly and proclamed as for rebelles and traytours': *An English Chronicle 1377–1461*, ed. by William Marx (Woodbridge: Boydell, 2003), pp. 63.4–5, 66.6–19, 70.29–31, and 81.8–13.

[105] See *The Brut, or, the Chronicles of England*, ed. by Friedrich Brie, EETS OS 131 and 136 (London: Paul, Trench, Trübner, 1906–8), pp. 491–533 (e.g. pp. 508, 513, 517.33, and 528.12–13).

[106] William Caxton, *Polychronicon Ranulphi Higden*, ed. by Joseph Rawson Lumby, 9 vols (London: Longman, 1865–6), VIII, 522–87.

[107] 'Short English Chronicle', in *Three Fifteenth-Century Chronicles*, pp. 63, 65, 66–7, and 78; 'Bale's Commonplace Book', pp. 115, 121, 128, 129, 142, 148–9; and 'Gregory's Chronicle', pp. 183–4, 188, 191–7, 218, 220–4, and 236–7. Though editorial titles are preserved here for ease of reference, the fifteenth-century London chronicles are anonymous and collaborative, based on a common tradition: Mary-Rose McLaren, *London Chronicles of the Fifteenth Century: A Revolution in English Writing* (Cambridge: Brewer, 2002), pp. 25–39 and 47–8.

[108] 'Short English Chronicle', p. 78; also in 'Gregory's Chronicle', p. 218, and 'MS Gough London 10', in *Six Town Chronicles of England*, p. 163.

[109] 'MS Gough London 10', pp. 154–7 and 164–6.

chronicle constitutes a political assault. The chronicler reports that Edward IV captured Lord Welles and ordered his son, Sir Robert, to submit, 'or elles thay for theire seide treasons shulde have dethe, as they had deserved'.[110] However, Sir Robert disobeyed, 'disposing him... *traytourly* to levie where [war] ayeinst his highnes, arredied hym and his felaship that day to have sett uppon the king...and so to have destrest hym and his oost, and so rescued his fadre lyf.'[111] Here, this chronicle articulates in no uncertain terms that Welles and his son have committed treason and shall be punished accordingly. It does not simply indicate that Sir Robert intended to levy war against the king, even though (as discussed in the first section of this chapter) such an act was definitively understood as treason in itself; rather, it specifies that his purpose was '*traytourly* to levie' war against the king, ensuring that even the most casual reader could not miss the condemnation, and employing the legal formulae of parliamentary attainders to do so.[112] The chronicle implicates Clarence and Warwick in even stronger critical language, stating that they:

> falsly and subtylly dissimiled with his highenes; for undre [their messages proclaiming loyalty to Edward] they sent theire messages daily to the kinges rebelles...they promised to have joined with theym and utterly to have taken theire parte, *wherby theire unnaturelle and fals double treason apperethe*.[113]

This chronicle's account of Warwick's and Clarence's conduct reads like a legal argument, with evidence, a 'wherby', and a concluding indictment for treason.[114] We also see this legalistic mode of treating treason in the other official Yorkist chronicle, the *Historie of the Arrivall of Edward IV*, written within a year of Edward's 1471 reacquisition of the throne, which it narrates as an expansion, with greater attention to political symbolism, upon earlier eyewitness accounts.[115] This text is peppered with keywords such as 'treason',

---

[110] 'Rebellion in Lincolnshire', p. 7.   [111] 'Rebellion in Lincolnshire', p. 9.

[112] See especially note 22 above.   [113] 'Rebellion in Lincolnshire', pp. 9–10.

[114] By terming the treason 'unnaturelle', the chronicler shows that the corollary of the widespread belief that the lords of the king's blood were his 'natural' advisors and allies was that Edward IV's brother (Clarence) and uncle (Warwick) were seen as especially reprehensible for betraying him.

[115] Wendy Scase, 'Writing and the "Poetics of Spectacle": Political Epiphanies in *The Arrivall of Edward IV* and Some Contemporary Lancastrian and Yorkist Texts', in *Images, Idolatry, and Iconoclasm in Late Medieval England*, ed. by Jeremy Dimmick, James Simpson, and Nicolette Zeeman (Oxford: Oxford University Press, 2002), pp. 172–84. Since this study addresses how the English represent themselves to themselves, the long version of the *Arrivall* is referred to here; the shorter ones were written (possibly first in French, and subsequently translated into English) for continental audiences as propagandist newsletters, as discussed in J. A. F. Thompson, ' "The Arrivall of Edward IV": The Development of the Text', *Speculum*, 46.1 (1971), 84–93, and updated in Richard Firth Green, 'The Short Version of The Arrival of Edward IV', *Speculum*, 56.2 (1981), 324–36, and Livia Visser-Fuchs, 'Edward IV's "Memoir on Paper" to Charles, Duke of Burgundy: The So-called "Short Version of the Arrivall"', *Nottingham Medieval Studies*, 36 (1992), 167–227.

'traitor', and 'evil will'. For instance, the chronicler calls the Earl of Warwick a 'traytor and rebell', writes of the 'malice, or evill will' of 'haynows traytouwrs and robbers', and 'the falcehode of all them that so falcely and so *traytorowsly* had conspired agaynst hym'.[116] To mount their political assault, these two chronicles wield the lexis and legal formulae of treason as some of the principal weapons in their arsenal.

In addition to recording matters of treason, these chronicles also register the fears such possibilities generate. For instance, reporting Humphrey of Gloucester's unjust accusation and death, Caxton's *Chronicles of England* comments, 'here may men mark what þis world is!' (513.6), and concludes: 'this began þe trouble in þe reame of Englond for þe deth of þis noble Duke of Gloucestre; & al þe communes of þe reame began forto murmure for it, & were nat contente' (513.25–8). When relating the same incidents, 'Gregory's Chronicle' similarly laments the state of 'thys wrecchyde and false trobely worlde'. Humphrey's unexpected arrest for treason and possible murder were alarming for English readers and writers, who could well fear that treasonous 'imaginings' would likewise be attributed to them if they were unlucky—as were the thirty-eight of Humphrey's squires arrested and put on trial for treason in connection with their deceased master's supposed treasonous intentions.[117] In a similar but broader reference to 1450, a London chronicler writes that 'the world was so strange that tyme that noo man might well ride nor goo in noo cooste of þis land wiþout a strength of ffelauship but þat he wer robbed'.[118]

Like letters, bills, and chronicles, mid- to late fifteenth-century verses were employed as polemic and propaganda;[119] written for a broad audience, they also paraded their fears and persuaded their readers through the language of treason. The majority of the political poems produced during the Wars of the Roses focus on civil strife,[120] often by dwelling on its general deleterious effects. One poem from the mid-1450s deplores the lack of loyalty and respect for social bonds in present-day England, commenting

---

[116] 'The Historie of the Arrivall of Edward IV', in *Three Chronicles of the Reign of Edward IV*, pp. 147, 153, 183, and 165–6. This language is also in the short (English) version: for example, 'Thomas bastard of Fauconbrege with other souldiers of Caleys *traytorously* conspyred againste' Edward (Green, ed., 'Short Version of *The Arrival*', lines 122–3).

[117] Five of these were sentenced to a full traitor's death, but, after hanging, they were pardoned and so spared death by drawing and quartering: 'Gregory's Chronicle', p. 188.

[118] 'Bale's Commonplace Book', p. 135.

[119] Charles Ross, 'Rumour, Propaganda and Popular Opinion during the Wars of the Roses', in *Patronage, the Crown and the Provinces in Later Medieval England*, ed. by Ralph A. Griffiths (Gloucester: Sutton, 1981), pp. 5–32 (p. 23).

[120] V. J. Scattergood, *Politics and Poetry in the Fifteenth Century* (London: Blandford, 1971), pp. 156–217.

(in a fashion reminiscent of the Rawlinson D82 poem with which this study opens) that 'No man may knowe hys frend fro foo' and 'Truthe ys turnyd to trechery'.[121] Another such poem, 'Nowe is Englond perisshed in fight', voices its concern that there is now

> fals couetyse with periurye;
> ...
> ffayned frenship & ypocrisye;
> Also gyle on euery syde.[122]

Such a preoccupation with the faithless conduct of the 'now' is also manifested in a 1450 poem of advice to the court, which complains that 'Trowth and pore men ben appressed, / And myscheff is nothyng redressed.'[123] A much longer advisory poem written *c*.1445–55 by and for gentry, Peter Idley's *Instructions to His Son*, contains similar commentary. Idley reproduces condemnations of treachery and deceit from his sources, Robert Mannyng's *Handlyng Synne* and Lydgate's *Fall of Princes*,[124] but also, more interestingly, includes deictic laments about treason and falseness that are *not* found in his sources. For instance, Idley writes that 'many oon' perform false witness and perjury

> at sessions and at assises—
> They recke not how falsely they forswere,
> So mony may be hadde fals witness to beere. (II.584–6)

These lines about contemporary England do not have a parallel in Idley's sources. Elsewhere, Idley creates five lines on how envy causes treason and how these two social ills have caused destruction in England; and, while he then concludes this rhyme royal stanza with a reference to Judas as a traitor sourced from *Handlyng Synne*, the connection between Judas' nature and actions on the one hand, and the 'oppressioun, murther, and false treasoun' 'in this lande' on the other, is unique to Idley, and highly resonant for contemporary England.[125]

---

[121] 'ffulfyllyd ys þe profesy for ay', in *Historical Poems of the XIVth and XVth Centuries*, ed. by Rossell Hope Robbins (New York: Columbia University Press, 1959), pp. 127–130 (lines 4 and 7). Poems in this edition are cited by first line for ease of reference.

[122] *Historical Poems*, pp. 149–50 (lines 20–3).

[123] 'Ye that haue the kyng to demene', in *Historical Poems*, pp. 203–5 (lines 13–14).

[124] For example, a stanza lamenting worldly instability and deceit (Peter Idley, *Instructions to his Son*, ed. by Charlotte D'Evelyn (London: Oxford University Press, 1935), II.2344–50) corresponds to Lydgate's *Fall of Princes*, ed. by Henry Bergen, EETS ES 121–4, 4 vols (Oxford: Oxford University Press, 1924), I, 2150–6.

[125] Idley, *Instructions*, lines 806–12; for lines 811–12 see *Handlyng Synne*, ed. by Frederick J. Furnivall, EETS OS 119 and 123 (London: Paul, Trench, Trübner, 1901–3), 4183–4. See also the allusions to Judas particular to the 1460 translation of Vegetius, *Knyghthode and Bataile* (lines 1170 and 1674–7; compare *Epitoma rei militaris*, pp. 130 and

In political verse as in other media, 'treason' and 'traitor' become more central keywords after *c*.1437;[126] moreover, political verses written in the mid- to late fifteenth century are more likely to dwell on contemporary troubles and treason possibilities without reference to providence than are earlier political verses. Wars of the Roses verses often engage with moments of particular crisis, such as the aftermath of the Yorkist lords' exile and attainder in 1459. In preparation for their return to England from Calais (in June 1460), Warwick, Salisbury, and March sent across the channel 'a stream of letters, proclamations, provocateurs, and spies, targeting the entire Southeast'; in March or April, one such poem was 'sette vppon the yates of the cyte of Caunterbury'.[127] Lauding the Yorkist lords, this poem calls for action in their favour (88.7). To demonstrate why a change is needed, it imagines the world observing and judging England for its shameful subjection to treason:

> *Grace ys withdrawe and Goddys mercyfulle hand*;
> Exalted ys falsehod, trowthe ys layde adoune;
> Euery reame cryethe owte on Engelondes treson.
> O falshod with thy colored presence! (87.3–6)

While attention has been drawn to the liturgical conventions of this poem,[128] it is worth dwelling on the secularity of the specification here that more concerted human action is needed in these times because God's grace is no longer ensuring that right will prevail. By contrast, when the poem 'God kepe oure kyng and saue the croune', written during the reign of Henry V (*c*.1415), refers to treason, it focuses on providential justice: 'Synne, morþere, derne tresoun / Not may be hyd fro goddis syʒt.'[129] Similarly, John Audelay's poem recollecting Henry V, written during the minority of Henry VI (*c*.1429), prays that God will act to save the king from traitors:

> Pray we þat lord is lord of all,
> To saue our kyng, his reme ryal;
> & let neuer myschip vppon him falle
> Ne false traytoure him to betray.[130]

---

158 respectively), and further discussion of Judas' role in treason rhetoric in Chapters 5 and 6; see also Nall, *Reading and War in Fifteenth-Century England*, p. 133.

[126] For example, while in the *c*.1415 poem 'Dede is Worchyng', 'treason' is discussed, 'falseness' receives more attention: *The Digby Poems*, pp. 204–14.

[127] Strohm, *Politique*, p. 173; *English Chronicle 1377–1461*, pp. 86.25–88.29.

[128] Strohm, *Politique*, pp. 180–1.

[129] *The Digby Poems*, pp. 192–201 (lines 94–5).

[130] 'A, perles pryns, to þe we pray', in *Historical Poems*, pp. 108–10 (lines 53–6).

These early-century poets match the faith in divine providence and corresponding moralizing about treason manifested in the narrative poems of their better-known contemporaries, John Lydgate and Thomas Hoccleve.[131] In contrast with such verses, mid- to late fifteenth-century ones usually do *not* place faith in or request aid from providence;[132] they focus instead on this-worldly regulation and/or lament. For example, concerning enemies of the commons including 'Suffolk, Moleyns, and Roos', a *c.*1450 poem hopes that: 'To suyche fals Traitours come foule endynge!'[133] This poem desires the punishment of traitors, but regulation of treason is here sought from human initiative—which is what Jack Cade's rebels, who produced poems such as this one, sought to embody.[134] A similar approach suffuses a poem that John Stow copied as 'a dyrge made by the comons of Kent... when Jake Cade was theyr cappitayn', which decries 'all this fals treson' and 'all the fals traytors that Engelond hath sold', desiring 'All fals traytors to come to evyll endynge'.[135] Another 1450 poem, or verse 'bill', again focuses on worldly initiative, warning the king: 'Let no lenger þy traitours go loos'.[136]

Vigilance against treason is likewise urged by three Yorkist poems written a decade or so later. 'Awake, lordes, awake & take goode hede' admonishes the Yorkist leaders to beware their enemies' promises of good faith:

> Trust not to moche in the fauour of youre foos,
> ffor þei be double in wirking, as þe worlde gos,
> Promysing feithfully obeissaunce to kepe,
> But perfite loue in þeire hertis is leyde for to slepe.[137]

Similarly, a 1461 Yorkist poem, although written at an optimistic time for the house of York, nonetheless articulates a need for continued policing against treason: the poet declares (or wishes) that the Yorkists' 'entent &

---

[131] On the containment of treason within a providential framework in Lydgate's *Siege of Thebes* and *Troy Book* and Hoccleve's *Regiment of Princes*, see Chapter 3.

[132] A similar argument concerning non-literary texts is made by Paul Strohm in *Politique: Languages of Statecraft between Chaucer and Shakespeare*, but in terms of princes' attitudes and political strategies: see Chapter 4, note 109.

[133] 'In the moneth of May when gresse groweþ grene', in *Historical Poems*, pp. 187–9 (lines 46 and 52).

[134] David Grummitt argues that the politics of Cade's rebellion were shaped by a contemporary discourse of complaint, within which 'contemporary poems and songs expressed popular sentiment, but they also provided a framework for men to interpret events': David Grummitt, 'Deconstructing Cade's Rebellion: Discourse and Politics in the Mid Fifteenth Century', in *Identity and Insurgency in the Late Middle Ages*, ed. by Linda Clark (Woodbridge: Boydell, 2006), pp. 107–22 (p. 110).

[135] *Three Fifteenth-Century Chronicles*, pp. 99–103 (lines 101–3).

[136] 'Ye that haue the kyng to demene', line 44.

[137] *Historical Poems*, pp. 206–7 (lines 13–16).

purpos' is 'to destroy treson, & make a tryall / Of hem þat be fauty'.[138]
Another, composed by a clerk in Holkham, Norfolk in the months following Edward IV's triumph at Towton in March 1461, specifies that treason
has been so prevalent in England that it cannot be hidden or avoided, and
that England was nearly destroyed by this treason: 'Henglond was al-most
lost, / Tretourys so fayre gon glose'.[139] The writer dwells on 'tresun' and
'tretourys' throughout the bulk of the poem, punctuating its lament of
what has befallen England recently and its hopes for Edward IV and his
lords with these words eleven times in 117 lines (usually mid-line, rather
than at the end of a line to enable a rhyme), as though its hopes for peace
are dependent upon a continued awareness of the possibility of treason
and contemporaries' responsibility for suppressing it. Another poem, written *c.*1456, seems to eschew partisanship, but is equally concerned with
the need for landowners and knights to work to secure social stability:

> *euery lord odur avauns,*
> And styfly stond yn ych a stoure;
> *Among ȝou make no dystaunce,*

---

[138] 'Yerly be þe morowe in a somer-tyde', in *Historical Poems*, pp. 218–20 (lines 64–6).
A 1460 poem which *does* place faith in providence, 'Of all mennys disposicion naturall', is
not an exception to this trend, but instead illuminates its parameters. This poem was written after the Yorkist lords, returned from exile in Calais, defeated the Lancastrian army and
captured Henry VI at the Battle of Northampton on 10 July 1460, with the intent of con-
trolling government thereafter. The struggle having reached an apparent (and favourable)
resolution, the poet writes that 'god of his speciall grace, / Heryng þe peple crying for mer-
cye' has redressed the 'falsehode in euery place', and thus the Yorkists have achieved victory
'Allonly þorough godes ovne prouysioun': *Historical Poems*, pp. 210–15 (lines 17–19 and
26). However, this moment was short-lived: Richard of York returned from Ireland, claimed
the throne, and was defeated and executed at the end of the year, before his son turned the
tables again at Towton in March 1461 and established himself as Edward IV—only to suffer
treasons throughout the first decade of his reign and further reversals thereafter. The way in
which this poet was able to write 'If god be with vs, who is vs agayne? / He is so nowe, blessid
mot he be' (149–50) perhaps represents apotropaic or wishful thinking, but also partially
distinguishes his poem's historical moment from the more bleak or uncertain periods of the
Wars of the Roses, offering a useful reminder that, as mentioned in the Introduction, these
decades were not universally infused with anxiety and strife. During such an optimistic
interlude, providence could be invoked *retrospectively* to explain successes and underpin
hopes that they will last; however, the quotation from 'Yerly be þe morowe in a somer-tyde'
above shows the more likely mode even at such moments, and, more broadly, Wars of the
Roses texts do not tend to seek recourse to providence *prospectively* for the sociopolitical ills
during difficult periods or reversals. This contrasts with previous generations: for instance,
a poem written *c.*1401, when Henry IV was not yet secure on the throne, nonetheless
expresses faith in providential outcomes: 'In that kyngdom ther trouþe is blamed, / God
sendes vengeaunce to make trouþe haue pes' ('ffor drede ofte my lippes y steke', in *Historical
Poems*, pp. 39–44 (lines 7–8)).
[139] Richard Beadle, ed., 'Fifteenth Century Political Verses from the Holkham Archives',
MÆ, 71.1 (2002), 101–21 (lines 19–21 and 56–7).

But, lordys, buskys ʒou out of boure,
ffor to hold up þis londus honour.[140]

This desire to inculcate social cohesion and the honouring of *troth* and relationships, and this pragmatic side-stepping of providence, link the non-literary with the literary texts addressed in Chapters 3, 4, and 5.

The moments at which treason and its destabilizing effect on community influenced contemporaries' lives and imaginations are emphasized by a concentrated and resonant vocabulary of treason that emerges most clearly where the pattern of authority is revealed as insufficient. When John Vale copied Prince Edward of Lancaster's letter denouncing Richard of York into his miscellany of documents related to contemporary strife, the text became 'that horrible and falsly forsworne traitor N calling hym selfe duc of N'. By omitting the names, Vale created a rhetorical template. This is no doubt partly due to the nature of Vale's book as a formulary and an archive of 'legal precedent and argument';[141] however, it also demonstrates that interest in the discourse of treason exceeded its subject. It illustrates the fluidity and pervasiveness of anxieties about treason or unexpected accusations at a time when anyone could be 'that traitor N', if his or her name were inserted into the ever-present discursive space. This chapter has elucidated the contours and contents of this discursive space with respect to non-literary texts. While, in the subsequent chapters, correspondence, chronicles, political documents, and verses will intermittently return to illustrate parallels, the more profound affinity between the material of this chapter and that of the following ones resides in the way that the literary texts engage, intently and didactically, with the concerns, keywords, debates, and reproaches detailed here. The following chapters concentrate on the implications of treason especially in order to suggest a better understanding of the neglected genre of prose romance. However, the prose romance genre participates in the same discourse about treason as the other genres addressed in this chapter and elsewhere. Thus, for another of the broader arguments of this book, considerations of genre or of divisions between literary and non-literary texts are less important than the convergences that unite these different groups of texts in their treatments of treason, and that thereby testify to a shared mentality about treason. The concept of *mentalité*, or mental attitude, is an especially appropriate critical category here because it pinpoints what any person has in common with other people of a given period and place; as attitudes 'governing

---

[140] 'ffulfyllyd ys þe profesy for ay', lines 73–7.
[141] Scase, *Literature and Complaint in England*, p. 147.

the immediate perceptions of social subjects', mentalities are necessarily collective.[142] As this chapter has shown through a close reading of types of texts that are not often accorded literary analysis, and as the following chapters show by examining often-understudied literary texts, a particular and pervasive set of collective fears and aspirations about treason informed the cultural imagination of the Wars of the Roses.

[142] Roger Chartier, 'Histoire des mentalités', in *The Columbia History of Twentieth-Century French Thought*, ed. by Lawrence D. Kritzman (New York: Columbia University Press, 2006), pp. 54–8 (p. 55).

3

'For treason walketh wonder wyde'

Treachery and Romance during the Wars of the Roses

In the late fifteenth-century *Squire of Low Degree*, the protagonist woos a Hungarian princess in a way that subjects the romance genre to derivative, almost parodic excess, and yet also conveys a fresh and serious commentary on treason. The Squire longs to be like 'Syr Lybius that gentell knyght' in order to win his lady's love, but seems an even less appropriate figure for chivalry than that ten-year-old boy hero of *Lybeaus Desconus*.[1] Surprised in a garden, the Squire bathetically and paradoxically tells the princess that he dare not speak of his love to her for fear of the consequences (116–28). While many romance heroines assume their suitors will display knightly prowess to win their love, this princess seems so aware of the Squire's shortcomings that she must explain to him precisely what he must do, focusing on the rather boy-scout-like logistics of riding 'Over hylles and dales, and hye mountaines, / In wethers wete, both hayle and raynes' (177–8), and lodging 'under a tre, / Among the beastes wyld and tame' (180–1). Reminiscent here of how a Sir Thopas might understand chivalry, the text continues its overzealous attempt to ape romance when the princess devotes twenty-eight lines to the accoutrements that she expects from a suitor (203–30); it is equally unable to find the right register when she offers to bankroll his required adventures (251–5). After their leave-taking goes hopelessly awry, the fetishization of courtly love is taken to an extreme: the princess embalms a dead body to kiss and keep her beloved, but she has mistakenly preserved the corpse of the envious steward. The Squire, meanwhile, languishes in her father's prison and in chivalric arenas abroad before they are eventually reunited—to the

---

[1] *Squire of Low Degree*, in *Sentimental and Humorous Romances*, ed. by Erik Kooper (Kalamazoo: Medieval Institute Publications, 2006), p. 78. Kooper's Introduction discusses the text's fifteenth-century composition. The *Squire* is extant in two early sixteenth-century fragments of a de Worde print based on a late fifteenth-century manuscript version; Copland's closely related 1560 print, the base text for the edition cited here, survives complete. There is also a condensed version in the mid-seventeenth-century Percy Folio manuscript.

sound of seventeen different musical instruments—and married. Yet the
Squire of Low Degree is more than a hackneyed rundown of earlier romance.
Mid- to late fifteenth-century English romances transform the genre by concentrating upon treason more intently and didactically than before, and this
text is no exception. The king instructs the steward that, if the Squire seeks to
enter his daughter's chamber to sleep with her, he should be imprisoned 'As
traytour, thefe, and false felon' (444). The text displays a repeated interest in
traitor appelations: the steward dies 'As a traitour untrewe' (650); the daughter calls him 'this traytour' (1040). Here, the *Squire of Low Degree* manifests
the distinguishing characteristics of the treatments of treason found in other
Wars of the Roses romances: treason or its possibility constitutes one of the
text's principal sites of instruction regarding proper conduct; both 'traitor'
and 'treason' are frequently reiterated; and horizontal as well as hierarchical
actions can be treasonous. This romance's ineptitude in presenting chivalry
turns to experienced precision and force concerning chivalry's antithesis,
treason. The characteristic of most contemporary romances which is lacking
in the *Squire* is an unhappy ending; however, in terms of treason, the text
exhibits a prevailing disillusionment: the narrator observes that the steward's actions, while reprehensible, are not surprising, 'For treason walketh
wonder wyde' (520). Such a disillusionment is particular to mid- to late
fifteenth-century English romances, which both worry about the ways in
which treason walks abroad—the ways in which it cannot be contained—
and seek to perform corrective responses to its errancy. This chapter assesses
the anonymous treason-laden romances of the Wars of the Roses, romances
produced in a culture for which 'treason walketh wonder wyde' could serve
as a proverb.

The first section of this chapter establishes synchronic and diachronic
contexts for an understanding of the Wars of the Roses romances. These
texts, with settings temporally and geographically distant from their readers, are ostensibly apart from contemporary life, yet they are insistently
connected to it; they are influenced by politics and society, and seek to
influence these realities in turn. John Scattergood has claimed that, unlike
other types of medieval literature, political verse was 'subject to pressures'
and characterized by 'practical intentions' and intended effect on 'the fabric of society'; however, as I argue here, these pressures and pragmatic
aims also inhere to other types of literature produced during the mid-
to late fifteenth century.[2] The way in which such literary texts use the
matter of treason to address contemporary problems is especially clear in

---

[2] Scattergood, *Politics and Poetry*, p. 14. Yet Scattergood's more recent definition of
'occasional' texts as 'responses to "external"' influences (sometimes 'precise' but sometimes
'broad social factors') suggests how a distant or 'fictional' setting does not prevent a text

contrast with their sources produced in different times and places. From Lydgate's late-career *Fall of Princes* in 1438/9, through the prose romances of Thebes, Troy, and Charlemagne produced mid-century, to the *Melusine* romances of the last quarter of the century, literary texts select and develop elements of narrative and rhetoric to respond to the understandings of treason circulating in contemporary England, and to treat the contagion of treachery in their own exemplary mode. To explore the ways in which these texts engage with treachery, the later sections of this chapter examine, first, the prose *Siege of Thebes* and *Siege of Troy*, reworkings of earlier English texts; and, second, the prose and verse *Melusine* romances, translations from French sources.

Prose becomes a viable medium for English romance only in the mid-fifteenth century, and, as discussed at the end of the chapter, it is significant that the majority of English romances produced in the following decades are in fact in prose. By decentring or questioning the role of providence, these texts both raise unsettling possibilities about the ineradicability of the possibility of treason, and create space for a performative response to treason through their speech acts. These romances, that is, bear witness to a cultural imaginary particularly invested in secular ethics and legal procedures. Their treasons and treacheries are horizontal as well as hierarchical, and they apply the language of the narrower institutional idea of treason to this wider set of transgressions to intensify their instructive condemnations. This chapter, then, elucidates an understanding of a mid- to late fifteenth-century literary culture distinguished by its texts' characteristically anxious mode of dwelling upon treason and betrayal: a mode that has a secular ethical framework and an admonitory and normative intent.

SYNCHRONIC AND DIACHRONIC CONTEXTS FOR FIFTEENTH-CENTURY ROMANCE

The Wars of the Roses romances' focus on treason is also characteristic of contemporary English texts from a variety of other genres. As addressed in Chapter 2, 'treason' and 'traitor', and concerns about them, suffuse the correspondence and chronicles of the Wars of the Roses. This is also the case in prose 'chronicles' of the legendary or distant past. For instance, the English *Pseudo-Turpin Chronicle*, translated *c.*1460, probably at the behest of Lancastrian gentry, repeatedly diverges from its

---

from having sociopolitical relevance: Scattergood, *Occasions for Writing: Essays on Medieval and Renaissance Literature, Politics and Society* (Dublin: Four Courts, 2010), pp. 11–12.

Latin source's neutral epithets in order to condemn oath-breakers and traitors.[3] The English version emphasizes 'the attractions of knighthood, nobility and Christian warfare ... at the expense of the kind of extended moralizing that characterizes other versions of the Pseudo-Turpin';[4] its commitment, instead, to a *secular* didacticism is demonstrated by two condemnations of Charlemagne's enemy Aigalonde's 'tresoune' and an indictment of 'þis false man Ganolion' that are not in its sources or analogues.[5] These types of source alterations are characteristic of contemporary English romances, as discussed below. Another English prose narrative, the *Life of Alexander*, similarly focuses on treason from within; while it is a fairly faithful translation of its Latin source, the *Historia de preliis Alexandri Magni*, in light of the contemporary English concentration on treason, it is not insignificant that it entered the vernacular in the mid-fifteenth century.[6]

Poetry exhibits a similar trend. As discussed in detail below, Lydgate's early-century *Siege of Thebes* and *Troy Book* have much less of a focus on treason than the prose versions produced a few decades later. However, Lydgate's later *Fall of Princes* (completed 1438/9) focuses on treachery more than his earlier work does.[7] Moreover, George Ashby's *Active Policy of a Prince*, written at the height of the Wars of the Roses (c. 1460–71) for Prince Edward of Lancaster, is as preoccupied with treason as contemporary prose romances. This mostly original poem addresses the troubles facing a prince in the present sociopolitical climate, and has a number of passages on treason, including:

> Be wele ware by discrete prouision
> For to suppresse youre false conspiratours,

---

[3] For instance, an oath-breaker is labelled 'untrew' and 'false' (lines 276, 277, and 290), uniquely to this version; as the only English translation, its closest parallels are in the *C* family of Pseudo-Turpin manuscripts, which include French, Welsh, and Irish as well as Latin exemplars: 'Introduction', in *Turpines Story: A Middle English Translation of the 'Pseudo-Turpin Chronicle'*, ed. by Stephen H. A. Shepherd, EETS OS 322 (Oxford: Oxford University Press, 2004), p. xxxviii.

[4] Stephen H. A. Shepherd, 'The Middle English *Pseudo-Turpin Chronicle*', *MÆ*, 65.1 (1996), 19–34 (p. 25); see also Introduction, *Turpines Story*, pp. xxxvii–xxxix.

[5] *Turpines Story*, lines 385, 409, and 1115.

[6] *The Prose Life of Alexander*, ed. by J. S. Westlake, EETS OS 143 (London: Oxford University Press, 1913); see, for instance, pp. 39.14, 44.11–14, 53.4–9, and 102.13–15. The *Prose Merlin*, similarly concerning treachery from within and faithful to its (French) source, was also translated mid-century; see, for example, the discussion of 'grete treson' in the *Prose Merlin*, ed. by John Conlee (Kalamazoo: Medieval Institute Publications, 1998), p. 61, and the comparable passage in *Merlin: Roman du XIIIe siècle*, ed. by Alexandre Micha (Genève: Droz, 1980), pp. 208–9.

[7] Lydgate's treatment of Mordred epitomizes the poem's discussions of betrayal: *Fall of Princes*, III, 3000–1, 3043–7, 3061, and 3126–8.

> Aftur the lawe & constitucion,
> Established ayenst opyn traiterous.[8]

Here, Ashby urges the deployment of legal procedures against traitors. This warning, as we shall see, would not be out of place in contemporary romances.

Drama offers another example of the pervasiveness of this admonitory mode. The *N-Town Play* and the *York Plays* have a much greater focus on treason in their representation of Judas' betrayal than do the other complete cycle plays or Nicholas Love's *Mirror of the Blessed Life of Jesus Christ* (a common source for cycle plays); significantly, *N-Town* and *York* are the only ones of these to have an association with the mid- to late fifteenth century. In representing the conspiracy and last supper, Nicholas Love's text calls Judas a traitor, and calls his actions treachery, malice, and betrayal—but *not* the more legal term treason. By contrast, in *N-Town*, rhetorical emphasis on treason conveys admonitory condemnations of Judas' actions. Jesus foretells that one of his disciples will commit 'treson' against him, and his disciples repeat this judgement in forcefully didactic lines such as those of Andreas:

> It is ryght dredfull such tresson to thynke,
> And wel more dredfful to werk þat bad dede!
> For þat fals treson to helle he xal synke,
> In endles peynes grett myscheff to lede.[9]

In this scene, most of the other disciples also condemn the as-yet-unknown traitor's actions *as treason*, providing a sequence of authoritative pronouncements that does not permit the audience to miss the point.[10] Furthermore, *N-Town*'s Judas accuses himself in these same terms before he hangs himself: 'I, Judas, haue synnyd, and treson haue don, / For I haue betrayd this rythful blood' (30.25–6). Thus the *N-Town Play* is determined to specify that Judas' actions are not only sinful, but also treasonous. Similarly, in the *York Play*, instruction about treason recurs, as when Pilate tells Judas:

> Hanged and drawen schulde þou be, knaue,
> And þou had right, by all goode reasoune.

---

[8] *George Ashby's Poems*, ed. by Mary Bateson, EETS ES 76 (London: Paul, Trench, Trübner, 1899), 380–3. On Ashby's sources and relative originality, see Margaret Kekewich, 'George Ashby's *The Active Policy of a Prince*: An Additional Source', *Review of English Studies*, NS, 41 (1990), 533–5, and John Scattergood, 'The Date and Composition of George Ashby's Poems', *Leeds Studies in English*, NS, 21 (1990), 167–76 (p. 173).

[9] *The N-Town Play*, ed. by Stephen Spector, 2 vols, EETS SS 11–12 (Oxford: Oxford University Press, 1991), I, 27.209 and 27.221–4.

[10] For instance, Thomas: 'For his fals treson þe fendys so blake / Xal bere his sowle depe down into helle pytt' (27.249–50).

Thi maistirs bloode þou biddist vs saue,
And þou was firste þat did hym treasoune.[11]

However, in the relevant parts of the *Towneley Plays* and the *Chester Cycle*, 'treason' is mentioned only in passing, and with much less admonition.[12] Nicholas Love wrote in the first decade of the fifteenth century, and the surviving copy of the *Towneley Plays* is *c.*1500, while the manuscripts of the *Chester Cycle* are primarily from the sixteenth and early seventeenth centuries. Given the *N-Town* manuscript's inscription of 1468, and the production of the principal manuscript of the *York Plays c.*1463–77, the extant form of these two cycles may be shaped by the same historical moment as Malory's *Morte Darthur* (completed in 1469).[13] While this admonitory mode of treating treason is particularly strongly and frequently a feature of romances such as the *Morte* and the anonymous ones addressed below, it is also widespread in the literary culture of the mid- to late fifteenth century.

While betrayal is not, of course, restricted to the fifteenth century within medieval English literature, the literature of the Wars of the Roses does treat this theme in a distinctive mode and to an unprecedented extent. Treason often figures more in Middle English literature than in French to begin with, as in the early fourteenth-century Middle English *Ywain and Gawain*'s emphasis on troth and treason rather than on the love that concerns its source, Chrétien de Troyes' *Yvain*.[14] However, in English romances before the mid-fifteenth century, treason words and recriminations tend

[11] *The York Plays*, ed. by Richard Beadle, EETS SS 23 (Oxford: Oxford University Press, 2009), 32.231–4. For other instances of 'treason' in this cycle, see 26.160, 28.129, 30.454, 30.460, 31.124, 32.289, 32.303, 32.363, 32.364, 33.333, 35.77, 36.54, 36.60, 38.450, and 45.32.

[12] The *Chester Cycle* only mentions 'treason' in the Resurrection Play, and without an admonitory gloss: *The Chester Mystery Cycle*, ed. by R. M. Lumiansky and David Mills, 2 vols, EETS SS 3 and 9 (London: Oxford University Press, 1974–86), I, 18.4 and 18.127. *Towneley* only mentions 'treason' thrice, for Lucifer's encounter with Eve, in the Harrowing of Hell, and in the Resurrection: *The Towneley Plays*, ed. by Martin Stevens and A. C. Cawley, 2 vols, EETS SS 13–14 (Oxford: Oxford University Press, 1994), I, 20.555, 25.365, and 26.224.

[13] As addressed in the Introduction, the dating of the *N-Town Play* is not certain, but is certainly suggestive. See Beadle's introduction to *York Plays*, esp. p. xii, on the date of their extant form. My focus on a Wars of the Roses context for these plays follows Pamela King's analysis of the York trial plays against late medieval English legal procedures, in which she argues for a reading of them as produced by and relevant to a mid-fifteenth-century context: Pamela M. King, 'Contemporary Cultural Models for the Trial Plays in the York Cycle', in *Drama and Community: People and Plays in Medieval Europe*, ed. by Alan Hindley (Turnhout, Belgium: Brepols, 1999), pp. 200–16 (esp. p. 212).

[14] J. A. Burrow, 'The Fourteenth-Century Arthur', in *The Cambridge Companion to the Arthurian Legend*, ed. by Elizabeth Archibald and Ad Putter (Cambridge: Cambridge University Press, 2009), pp. 69–83 (pp. 74–5).

to be vastly outweighed by *truth* words and praise of exemplary conduct, in a more positive primary mode of instruction. For instance, in the earliest extant English romance, *King Horn* (mid-thirteenth century), 'betray' words are employed *by* Horn and Fikenhild as they assert their honourable intentions, and *about* Fikenhild betraying Horn, but neither 'treason' nor 'traytour' occur.[15] Texts such as *Horn* and *Havelok the Dane* (late thirteenth century) focus more on laudatory conduct, as when *Horn*'s Athulf is called 'God knight mid the beste / And the treweste' (1007–8) and Horn is called 'Knight with the beste' (1340). Moreover, although the king's steward in *Amis and Amiloun* (early fourteenth century) wishes to destroy the two young knights 'With gile and trecherie',[16] it is important to keep in mind that 'treachery', 'treson', and 'traytour', in this text as in other thirteenth- and fourteenth-century romances, are vastly outnumbered by 'trewthe' words and by instruction through examples of praiseworthy (and praised) conduct; the latter form the didactic character of the popular romances of these centuries. By contrast, treason and treachery receive much lexical and ethical focus in the romances of the Wars of the Roses. For instance, in *King Ponthus and the Fair Sidone*, a mid-fifteenth-century prose romance that employs all the major plot elements and betrayals of the Horn narrative, 'treason' and '*un*truth' are emphasized more than in the earlier *King Horn*, often through departures from *Ponthus*' French source. The English version comments of Guenelete (Fikenhild's counterpart): 'neuer sith Crist was borne, was suche a tratour livyng, that thoght so fals a tresoune'. This emphasizes and condemns treason much more strongly than does the French text's 'oncques mais ne naquist plus faulx homme' ('a falser man was never born').[17] A similar trend will be observed in the English *Melusine* romances in the later sections of this chapter. Treason words also outweigh

[15] *King Horn*, in *Four Romances of England*, ed. by Ronald B. Herzman, Graham Drake, and Eve Salisbury (Kalamazoo: Medieval Institute Publications, 1999), lines 1263 and 1282. 'Biswike' (to deceive), at 294 and 671, is similar to 'betray'. Fikenhild, about to betray Horn, is called 'the wurste moder childe' (652): certainly a condemnation, but by no means a legalistic one. In a similarly limited fashion, treacherous actions in *Havelok the Dane* are described only a few times, with the stock phrase 'with trecherie / With tresoun, and with felounye': see *Havelok the Dane*, in *Four Romances of England*, 443–4, 1090–1, and 2988–9.

[16] *Amis and Amiloun*, in *Amis and Amiloun, Robert of Cisyle, and Sir Amadace*, ed. by Edward E. Foster (Kalamazoo: Medieval Institute Publications, 1997), 210 and 1076; the narrator further specifies that the steward acts 'with tresoun and gile' (407).

[17] *King Ponthus and the Fair Sidone*, ed. by Frank Jewett Mather (Baltimore: Modern Language Association of America, 1897), p. 135.16–17; *Le Roman de Ponthus et Sidoine*, ed. by Marie-Claude de Crécy (Genève: Droz, 1997), p. 168. The English version survives in two manuscripts, both from the middle of the fifteenth century. For further examples of the English version's greater focus on 'treason' and 'untruth' relative to its French source, see 68.15–17 (vs. 85); 123.4–6 (vs. 153); 128.11–12 (vs. 158); 129.3 (vs. 160); and 134.25–7 (vs. 167).

truth words in the *Morte Darthur*, and occur there more frequently than in Malory's French sources, as discussed in Chapter 4.

Moreover, betrayal in the earlier romances tends to be narrowly hierarchical; when it *is* horizontal, it is so only between members of a specific affinity group or individuals who have sworn a concrete oath to each other. The relationships to which the possibility of betrayal pertains in *King Horn* are all hierarchical and feudal, and similarly, in *Havelok*, Godrich and Godard betray their young royal charges and thus their oaths to, respectively, the dead kings Athelwold and Birkabein. Likewise in *Sir Launfal* (late fourteenth century), the eponymous hero, accused by Guinevere of attempting to seduce her, is taken before Arthur, who accuses him of being a 'traytour': here, in a feudal, hierarchical sense, since sleeping with the king's wife (or attempting to) constituted high treason.[18] Ricardian literature perhaps comes the closest to the fifteenth-century romances in terms of a broader conception of who can be a traitor to whom; yet treason, for the Ricardian poets, involves betraying an explicit affinity or contract, whereas for the fifteenth-century romances, treason is any deceitful or harmful action performed underhandedly. For instance, in Chaucer's 'Knight's Tale', it is because Palamon and Arcite have sworn an oath of brotherly loyalty to each other that, when they both pursue Emelye, Palamon is able to call Arcite 'false traytour wikke'.[19] This conception of treason is horizontal but limited to an explicitly made oath binding two people[20]—as is the conception of treason in *Sir Gawain and the Green Knight*.[21] Thus, while treachery and treason certainly figure in thirteenth- and fourteenth-century English romances, they are not as pointed there or

---

[18] Thomas Chestre, *Sir Launfal*, in *The Middle English Breton Lays*, ed. by Anne Laskaya and Eve Salisbury (Kalamazoo: Medieval Institute Publications, 1995), 761. For further discussion of the hierarchical nature of treason in thirteenth- and fourteenth-century romances, see Ojars Kratins, 'Treason in Middle English Metrical Romances', *Philological Quarterly*, 45.4 (1966), 668–87.

[19] Geoffrey Chaucer, *The Riverside Chaucer*, ed. by Larry D. Benson, 3rd edn (Boston: Houghton Mifflin, 1987), 'Knight's Tale', 1580.

[20] Chaucer treats high treason as well, as when Calchas betrays King Priam and Troy in *Troilus and Criseyde*. Chaucer's treatment of Calchas' defection is more legalistic than in his source: 'while Boccaccio vaguely implies that Calkas acted like a traitor (1, st. 10)', Chaucer calls him a traitor (I.87) and articulates his wrongdoing as specifically the crime of treason ('his falsnesse and tresoun', I.107, and again his 'treson', I.117): Joseph Allen Hornsby, *Chaucer and the Law* (Norman, OK: Pilgrim, 1988), p. 129. Chaucer's condemnation of Calchas is discussed later in this chapter in connection with the more strongly condemnatory prose *Siege of Troy*.

[21] For an overview of treason in Ricardian literature, see Chapter 6 (pp. 206–47) of Richard Firth Green's wide-ranging *A Crisis of Truth*; for studies of the individual poets' treatments of treason along reciprocal yet narrow lines, see: Hornsby, *Chaucer and the Law*; W. R. J. Barron, '*Trawthe' and Treason: The Sin of Gawain Reconsidered* (Manchester: Manchester University Press, 1980); Elliot Kendall, *Lordship and Literature: John Gower and the Politics of the Great Household* (Oxford: Clarendon Press, 2008), pp. 229–30.

addressed in the same manner as in the fifteenth-century ones, which are preoccupied with repetition and condemnation of treason, and also systematically define *as* treason all underhanded conduct committed even where there is no bond between perpetrator and victim. This mode dwindles at the end of the fifteenth century (as addressed in Chapter 6).

In thirteenth- and fourteenth-century romances, then, treachery is more part of the furniture than the architecture, especially since these texts focus on happy endings in which treachery is vanquished. These earlier works 'contain' their instances of treachery by restraining them within more positive narratives. The disastrous treachery of the fifteenth-century romances, on the other hand, refuses to be taken lightly; it is innovative both in emphasizing legal and social ways in which treason ought to be confronted if the dire results represented in the romances are to avoid repetition in contemporary England, and in how it confronts the possibility of unredressed disaster. The romance genre has been most productively understood through the theory of family resemblance, which recognizes that any given characteristic may be absent from a text without obscuring its nature as a romance[22]—even the happy ending commonly associated with romance but absent from texts such as the prose *Siege of Thebes* and *Siege of Troy* and Malory's *Morte Darthur*,[23] as addressed in the final section of Chapter 4. Medieval romance characteristically propounds cultural values and ideals,[24] but the romances of the fifteenth century are especially didactic. Fifteenth-century romance is, as Melissa Furrow points out, distinctive in 'the degree to which it insists it is instructive'; Furrow aptly suggests the word 'hortatory' for the self-presentation of fifteenth-century romances.[25] Of course readers read from very different perspectives and for different ends, but 'reading for the moral' was a pervasive habit for medieval people, who expected their reading material to have ethical import.[26]

---

[22] Ad Putter, 'A Historical Introduction', in *The Spirit of Medieval English Popular Romance*, ed. by Ad Putter and Jane Gilbert (Harlow: Longman, 2000), pp. 1–15 (p. 2); Helen Cooper, *The English Romance in Time: Transforming Motifs from Geoffrey of Monmouth to the Death of Shakespeare* (Oxford: Oxford University Press, 2004), pp. 8–9; Melissa Furrow, *Expectations of Romance: The Reception of a Genre in Medieval England*, Studies in Medieval Romance, XI (Cambridge: Brewer, 2009), p. 54. The concept is first articulated by Ludwig Wittgenstein, *Philosophical Investigations*, trans. by G. E. M. Anscombe (Oxford: Blackwell, 1953), pp. 31–2, and applied to literary genres more generally in Alastair Fowler, *Kinds of Literature: An Introduction to the Theory of Genres and Modes* (Oxford: Clarendon Press, 1982), p. 41.

[23] Cooper, *English Romance*, p. 9.   [24] Cooper, *English Romance*, p. 6.

[25] Furrow, *Expectations of Romance*, pp. 139–40 and 196; a similar argument is made in Arthur B. Ferguson's otherwise outdated *The Indian Summer of English Chivalry* (Durham, NC: Duke University Press, 1960), pp. 33–42.

[26] Furrow, *Expectations of Romance*, pp. 41–2; J. Allan Mitchell, *Ethics and Exemplary Narrative in Chaucer and Gower*, Chaucer Studies, XXXIII (Cambridge: Brewer, 2004), esp. pp. 13–15.

Thus the didactic dimension of Wars of the Roses romances is sustained by both textual intentions and readers' expectations, and it is from this perspective that we can approach the experience of reading them.

CONTRACTS AND CONDEMNATIONS: CIRCUMSCRIBING TREACHERY IN THE PROSE *SIEGE OF THEBES* AND *SIEGE OF TROY*

Modalities of Ethical Narrative

The ethical operations and rhetorical specificity of the prose *Siege of Thebes* and *Siege of Troy*—that is, the work they do, and how they do it—can best be illuminated in juxtaposition with their sources. The *Siege of Thebes* and *Siege of Troy* are extant only in one paper manuscript, Rawlinson D82; they appear to be by the same author, and are copied in the same hand (modelled on late fifteenth-century anglicana script with some secretary graphs), occupying the first ten folios and the following fourteen folios respectively. As much shorter reworkings of Lydgate's protracted verse versions of the early 1420s, his *Siege of Thebes* and *Troy Book*,[27] we might expect the prose *Thebes* and *Troy* to contain less of everything than Lydgate's works. The prose texts greatly reduce both Lydgate's positive examples of ideal chivalric behaviour and the 'consoling' rhetoric that, in Lydgate's works, circumscribes any successful treachery with an announcement of the divine retribution that will be meted out to all traitors, yet the prose versions also place greater emphasis elsewhere. Apart from Helen Cooper's identification of unresolved or disastrous treason from within kin and community as the core subject matter of the fifteenth-century prose romances, there has been no published assessment of the ways in which treason functions in the prose *Thebes* and

---

[27] Friedrich Brie demonstrates this derivation by comparing Lydgate's versions and the prose ones, and contrasting these to other Thebes and Troy texts: Introduction, 'Zwei mittelenglische Prosaromane: *The Sege of Thebes* und *The Sege of Troy*', *Archiv für das Studium der neueren Sprachen und Literaturen*, 130 (1913), 40–7. More recent articles on the prose versions (see notes 28 and 29 below) support Brie's assessment of their principal sources. Lydgate finished *Troy Book* in 1420 and wrote the *Siege of Thebes* shortly after, either just before or just after the death of Henry V on 31 August 1422. James Simpson has argued that Lydgate's *Siege of Thebes* demonstrates a pessimism appropriate to the months after Henry V's death because it is darker than Chaucer's Thebaid, 'The Knight's Tale' (James Simpson, ' "Dysemol daies and fatal houres": Lydgate's *Destruction of Thebes* and Chaucer's *Knight's Tale*', in *Long Fifteenth Century*, pp. 15–33 (pp. 15–16); Derek Pearsall, on the other hand, focusing on the prophecies for peace at the end of the *Siege of Thebes*, has argued that the poem reflects an optimistic ethos appropriate to the later stages of Henry V's reign (*John Lydgate*, p. 151). In either case, Lydgate's *Siege of Thebes* was completed *c*.1422, before Henry VI's minority had given grounds for further pessimism; moreover, the prose *Siege of Thebes* is, in its turn, much darker and less consoling than Lydgate's version.

Troy,[28] or of the ways in which its representation contributes to processes of community formation and identity construction in contemporary England. David Benson has noted an interesting debt that the prose *Troy* owes to Chaucer's *Troilus and Criseyde*, but this debt's relationship to the theme of treason has not been addressed.[29] Moreover, while, as Cooper points out, Lydgate's versions 'downplay...high chivalry and love, to emphasize treason and destruction',[30] the prose versions focus on treachery to a much greater extent than these sources, as well as in a significantly different spirit. These prose romances share a mode of narrating treachery that distinguishes them from the tenor of earlier literature; moreover, their engagements with treachery also differentiate them from each other.

Instead of ensuring that right order is restored in their narrative worlds, the prose romances often leave the disastrous treachery of their narratives unresolved—yet not in an unexemplary fashion. Because the prose *Thebes* and *Troy* break the conventions of romance by rejecting a happy ending or stable ordering principle, Cooper views them as working against 'the comforting ideologies of [earlier] verse romances'.[31] However, these texts' representations of instability also serve as rhetorical engagements with these situations; that is, they are commentaries that seek to mirror, maintain, or promote ideologies of their own, in addition to challenging those supported by conventional romances.[32] Thus, while the prose romances do '*express* a more realistic and bleaker view of the world' in which they were produced and received,[33] the expressions of such views of the world act not only as part of these texts' denials of narrative and ideological comforts, but also as exploration and instruction. The prose romances elide a providential framework, and in so doing both disclose disquieting ways in which the possibility of treason is ever-present, and offer a novel framework for ethical instruction: they use representations of speech acts and textual contracts as exhortations against treason.

The prose romances' shifted and intensified focus on treason emerges in their threefold manipulations of their sources, namely: what they retain, and what they do not retain, from Lydgate's versions; and what they portray that is not derived from Lydgate's versions.[34] Firstly, although as

---

[28] Cooper, 'Counter-Romance'.

[29] David C. Benson, 'Chaucer's Influence on the Prose "Sege of Troy"', *N&Q*, 18.4 (1971), 127–30.

[30] 'Counter-Romance', p. 145.   [31] 'Counter-Romance', p. 145.

[32] On ideology, see Chapter 2, note 40.

[33] Cooper, 'Counter-Romance', p. 144; emphasis mine.

[34] Other critics have observed that the prose *Siege of Thebes* includes some passages not found in its Lydgatean source, but only in terms of its realistic medieval siege details and the pragmatics of warfare: Malcolm Hebron, *The Medieval Siege: Theme and Image in Middle*

redacted versions of their sources the prose *Thebes* and *Troy* contain many fewer words and episodes overall, they selectively reproduce Lydgate's poetry to offer greater accentuation of treachery. Secondly, while Lydgate does include treason and destruction in his two poems, he also restrains them within a framework of divine justice that does not reappear in the prose versions. While James Simspon asserts that Lydgate's *Troy Book* presents 'a wholly secular vision of politics and war',[35] the examples below will show that Lydgate's *Troy Book* is by no means 'wholly secular' when compared to the anonymous prose version. Criticism of Lydgate's *Siege of Thebes* in particular has recognized that Lydgate 'strongly disapproves of human aggressiveness' and 'resorts quickly and frequently to Christian moralization' to mark his condemnation of such acts.[36] In both *Troy Book* and *Siege of Thebes*, Lydgate frequently adds moralizing exempla not found in his (prose) sources, Guido delle Colonne's *Historia destructionis Troiae* and a version of the *Roman de Thebes* respectively.[37] The exemplum, Larry Scanlon observes, illustrates a moral by recounting its enactment; in this performative model, the exemplum's ethical value is conveyed through a narrative that 'establishes a form of authority, enjoining its audience to heed its lesson, and to govern their actions accordingly'.[38] However, the prose author eschews Lydgate's moralizing exempla.[39] For instance, when Polynices' ally Tydeus defeats the assassins whom Eteocles underhandedly sends after him, an event that occurs in both versions of the siege of Thebes, only Lydgate's expresses a moral for this exemplum: 'By which ensample ye opynly may se / Ageynes trouth falshed hath no myght'.[40] The prose *Thebes*

English Romance (Oxford: Clarendon Press, 1997), pp. 9–33; updated in Nall, *Reading and War in Fifteenth-Century England*, pp. 101–3.

[35] Simspon, *Reform and Cultural Revolution*, p. 105.

[36] A. C. Spearing, 'Lydgate's Canterbury Tale: *The Siege of Thebes* and Fifteenth-Century Chaucerianism', in *Fifteenth-Century Studies: Recent Essays*, ed. by Robert F. Yeager (Hamden, CT: Archon, 1984), pp. 333–64 (p. 354); Simpson, 'Lydgate's *Destruction of Thebes*'.

[37] Robert R. Edwards, 'Introduction', in *John Lydgate: The Siege of Thebes* (Kalamazoo: Medieval Institute Publications, 2001), p. 4; Pearsall, *John Lydgate*, pp. 128–31, 138, 152, and 155.

[38] Larry Scanlon, *Narrative, Authority, and Power: The Medieval Exemplum and the Chaucerian Tradition* (Cambridge: Cambridge University Press, 1994), p. 33. While Scanlon applies this only to *Fall of Princes*, it is at least as applicable to *Siege of Thebes* and *Troy Book*.

[39] It is useful to view 'morality' as the sphere of Christian values or doctrine, and 'ethics' as the sphere of the practical pursuit of a virtuous life: Mitchell, *Ethics and Exemplary Narrative*, pp. 13–14. These spheres obviously overlap, and, as Alcuin Blamires points out, not in an equal fashion, since the 'Christian moral schema...systematically sought to subsume antique ethics', but the distinction remains a useful one: Alcuin Blamires, *Chaucer, Ethics, and Gender* (Oxford: Oxford University Press, 2006), p. 8.

[40] *Siege of Thebes*, 2236–7. Quotations from Lydgate's *Thebes* and *Troy* are cited by book and/or line number with reference to: *John Lydgate: The Siege of Thebes; Troy Book*, ed. by

does not include any such assurances. Exempla similarly concerning the divinely ordained punishment for the false and treacherous occur at many points in *Troy Book*, as in the figuration of the fate of Antenor:

> Lo! how þe riȝtful kynge,
> þat al may sene in his prouidence,
> Ful iustly can maken recompence
> Of doubilnes and simulacioun,
> And of al swiche contrived fals tresoun:
> For who avengeþ with falshed for his part,
> He shal ben hit wiþ þe same dart;
> …
> And who supplaunteþ shal supplaunted be,
> By good example, as ȝe shal after se. (IV.5486–500)

These reassertions of right order surface in Lydgate's moralizing exempla throughout both *Siege of Thebes* and *Troy Book*, which consistently highlight the dire and inescapable consequences of treachery. Neither these instances nor the vast majority of Lydgate's other moralizing exempla and rhetorical containments of treacherous behaviour are found in the prose versions.[41] Moreover, Lydgate was by no means the only early fifteenth-century writer to express such faith in providence (as the political verses discussed in the final section of Chapter 2 demonstrate), nor was the author of the prose *Siege*s the only mid- to late fifteenth-century writer to eschew such expressions (as the other romances discussed in the final section of Chapter 4 demonstrate).

The prose romances not only avoid reproducing Lydgate's expressions of faith in a divinely administered form of setting-to-rights, but also independently emphasize the prevalence and recurrence of treason without providential intervention. Two further examples will suffice here. Lydgate's *Thebes* ends on an optimistic note:

> But the venym and the violence
> Of strif, of werre, of contek, and debat
> That maketh londys bare and desolat
> Shal be proscript and voyded out of place,
> And Martys swerd shal no more manace,
> …

Henry Bergen, EETS ES 97, 103, 106, and 156 (London: Paul, Trench, Trübner, 1906–35). Citations of the prose *Siege*s refer to 'Zwei mittelenglische Prosaromane', ed. by Brie, pp. 47–52 and 269–85.

[41] For more such exempla that are elided from the prose versions, see Lydgate's *Thebes* 1742–1800, 2077–8, and 2544–52, and *Troy Book* I.244–9, II.73–112, II.1887–99, and V.1482–1662. The absence of such exempla in the prose versions is not absolute, as the final line of the prose *Troy* proclaims: 'And alwey the ende of euery tresoun and falsenes to sorowe

> But love and pees in hertys shal awake,
> …
> Thorgh grace only in dyvers naciouns,
> Forto reforme atwixe regyouns
> Pees and quyet, concord and unyte.
> And He that is both on and two and thre,
> Ek thre in on and sovereyn lord of pes,
> Which in this exil for our sake ches,
> For love only our troubles to termyne. (4690–707)

Here Lydgate's narrative world is underpinned by 'He that is both on and two and thre' (4704) ensuring peace and order. This is both elided from, and emphatically undermined in, the prose *Thebes*, which ends with what precedes this optimism in Lydgate's version: the placement of Thebes within a wider historical context (prose *Thebes* 272; Lydgate's *Thebes* 4608–25). Here Lydgate focuses on Theseus' rightful and exemplary revenge upon Creon (4520–64), but the prose version instead closes with Theseus finding 'Arcet and Palamon breþeren of Armes' after Theseus comes to seek revenge on Thebes (272). The prose author thereby pointedly connects his narrative to this third generation *not* mentioned in Lydgate's version, the chivalric subjects who break the oaths they have sworn to each other in Chaucer's 'Knight's Tale'.[42] Betrayal, in the prose *Thebes*, is not redressed, but rather regenerated. Likewise, in the prose *Troy* (in contrast to Lydate's version), treason begets more treason. In both versions, Hecuba plots Achilles' death in revenge for Hector's death. Lydgate construes Achilles' gruesome death as an illustration of the punishment destined to all traitors, and makes the role of providence in redressing treason explicit:

> Loo! here þe ende of falshed & vntrouþe,
> Loo! here þe fyn of swiche trecherie,
> …
> How *God quyt ay slauȝter by tresoun*!
> Loo! here þe guerdoun & þe final mede
> Of hem þat so deliten in falsehede:
> …
> As ȝe may se of þis Achilles. (IV.3210–19)

---

and myschef at the last. Amen' (285). However, this statement seems remarkably incongruous with the narrative proper; it draws attention to the failure of such a view to prevail, since (unlike the Lydgate texts) the trajectory of the prose text as a whole, particularly in its later sections, does not encourage such confidence. This will be further demonstrated below.

[42] 'Knight's Tale', 1139. The prose *Troy* uses Chaucerian material that is not contained in Lydgate's version (as noted by David Benson; discussed below); here, in its mention of Palamon and Arcite, we see that the prose *Thebes* does too.

In contrast to this 'narrative enactment of cultural authority',[43] the prose romance repeats its diagnosis of the act as treason, commenting, 'Ecuba thonking on this grete cruelte & fals tresoun of Achilles, purposed fully be some tresoun to bring him to his ende', and only moving on once the fact that Hecuba's actions constitute 'tresoun so don to Achilles' (284) has been reiterated. Thus both the prose *Thebes* and the prose *Troy* highlight the danger of recurring cycles of treason.

The prose *Thebes* and *Troy*, however, are neither simply nor unambiguously pessimistic; they also manifest their own didactic intentions by treating proper chivalric conduct and obligations in relation to their opposites, negation, or breach. That is, the prose romances' representations of treason operate as a form of paraenesis, as admonitions that are often specifically pointed towards the intended readers' conceptions of identity and community. This is a tendency shared, as discussed below, most strongly with Malory's *Morte Darthur* and other contemporary romances. In employing this rhetorical strategy, the texts present both an anxiety about the instabilities of *troth*, and instruction about the importance of honour and ethics. In other words, we can think of these texts' instances of treachery not only as events, but also, more interestingly, as narrative vehicles conducting characters, text, and reader through the conceptual geography of fifteenth-century English romance and its cultural concerns. Cooper views the prose romances as characterized by *family* strife: 'treachery and murder performed within the body politic or the kin-group, the slaying of father by son, the failure to pass on good rule in a strong and righteous order of succession, and sometimes also incest'.[44] However, the prose romances' rhetorical and thematic restructuring alters and exploits the narrative spaces offered by episodes of familial betrayal in order to emphasize a different dimension: that of the law. The prose romances' rewriting of the familial to place the greatest stress on legal processes and consequences of betrayal shifts the site of the moral reprehensibility of failing to honour commitments; it creates an ethic of social conduct that takes a secular and legal form.

The ethoi of these texts correlate with their historical moment, exemplifying a wider literary trend. Lydgate's *Siege of Thebes* and *Troy Book*, written either during or directly following the prosperity of Henry V's reign (1413–22), display much more moralizing and optimism than the prose *Siege of Thebes* and *Siege of Troy*, which, produced around the 1450s, emerge from a time of social and political instability similar to that of Malory's *Morte Darthur*. While it might be suggested that Lydgate's

43 Scanlon, *Narrative, Authority, and Power*, p. 34.
44 Cooper, 'Counter-Romance', pp. 141–2.

moralizing mode correlates with his profession as a monk, Lydgate's con-temporary Thomas Hoccleve—the other principal poet of the Lancastrian era and a secular clerk of the Privy Seal—circumscribes treason in the same ways that Lydgate does. In *The Regiment of Princes*, written for Henry V shortly before he became king in 1413, Hoccleve focuses on explicitly hierarchical treason (and how a prince ought to guard himself against it), and on 'Favel' or 'treccherie' as what can cause war 'twixt God and mannes soule'—as befits the text's didacticism as a mirror for princes.[45] More sig-nificantly, however, Hoccleve also declares the following about those who 'breke... bondes' or 'feith' (2201):

> for that synne, Goddes rightwisnesse,
> That punysshith falshode and treccherie,
> Nat mighte hem suffre endure in that woodnesse,
> But they destroyed were, it is no lye.
> Untrouthe, allas! The ordre of chivalrie
> Dampneth it; thogh that the persone it use,
> Knyghthode itself moot algate it refuse. (2234–40)

Here Hoccleve discusses secular treachery and breach of faith among chivalric subjects, but conveys both a semi-religious conception of such a transgression (as a 'synne'), and an assurance that God will provide suit-able punishment for 'falshode and treccherie'—which directly parallels Lydgate's *Troy Book* and *Siege of Thebes*. Such providential containments of treason also parallel those in contemporary political verses (written during the reign of Henry V and the minority of Henry VI, 1413–37);[46] and they contrast with the non-providential treatments of treason in the political verses of the 1450s and 1460s as well as those in romances such as the prose *Siege of Thebes* and *Siege of Troy*.

Lydgate's *Fall of Princes*, composed after Lydgate's siege poems and before the prose *Siege*s, is also intermediary in its treatment of treason: that is, while the *Fall of Princes* has a stronger emphasis on lamenting treason than Lydgate's earlier works, it still contains that treason within a providential framework. Translating from Laurent de Premierfait's second French prose version (*c*.1414), three times the length of Boccaccio's original *De casibus virorum illustrium* (*c*.1355–60), Lydgate made further omissions and addi-tions to produce the first English version of the text in 1438/9, around the

[45] Thomas Hoccleve, *The Regiment of Princes*, ed. by Charles R. Blyth (Kalamazoo: Medieval Institute Publications, 1999), 5258–64; see also lines 1941–6, 3053–9, and 4677–83.

[46] As discussed in the final section of the previous chapter; for instance, the poem 'God kepe oure kyng and saue the croune', written *c*.1415, specifies that 'Synne, morþere, derne tresoun / Not may be hyd fro goddis sy3t': *The Digby Poems*, pp. 192–201 (lines 94–5).

end of the increasingly unstable minority of Henry VI.[47] At the request of his patron Humphrey, duke of Gloucester, Lydgate appended explicitly didactic envoys to each narrative.[48] Of the sixty-nine envoys thus inserted into the *Fall of Princes*, fifty-eight 'consciously expound the significance' of the preceding narrative in an advisory idiom,[49] and it is here that we see Lydgate's attitude towards treason shifting late in his poetic career.

Unlike the later prose *Sieges* or Malory's *Morte*, the *Fall of Princes* neither questions the workings of providence, nor leaves room for potential criticisms, instead exhorting readers to understand the mutability of this world as the influence 'of Fate and Fortune' and to turn their thoughts to the life to come where all will be set right.[50] For instance, Lydgate uses the fall of Caesar as an opportunity for a homily:

> Princis considreth, in marcial policie
> Is nouther truste, feith nor assuraunce:
> ...
> Vp toward heuene set your attendaunce. (VI.2913–16)

This movement beyond the concerns of this world contrasts with the later texts. However, in the way that the *Fall of Princes* dwells upon treason more than its sources, and in a stronger fashion than Lydgate's Thebes and Troy texts, it prefigures the later romances. For instance, Lydgate's original 'Lenvoy' on Arthur (VIII.3129–64) concentrates more strongly on labelling Mordred's transgression as treason and on the dangers of treason than does the following 'exclamacioun' derived from his source (VIII.3165–206). Lydgate states that he has written his envoy to memorialize Mordred's treason as a universal warning:

> *to remembre* the gret vnkyndenesse,
> The conspiracioun, *þe tresoun*, the falsnesse
> Doon to kyng Arthour be his cosyn Modrede,
> Make a Lenvoye, *that al men may it reede*. (VIII.3126–9)

He further cautions fifteenth-century rulers to be on the alert for traitors:

> This tragedie of Arthour...
> Bit princis all bewar of fals tresoun;
> For in al erthe is non mor pereilous thing
> Than trust of feith, wher is decepcioun
> Hid vnder courtyn of fals collusioun. (VIII.3130–4)

[47] A. S. G. Edwards, 'The Influence of Lydgate's *Fall of Princes* c.1440–1559: A Survey', *Mediaeval Studies*, 39 (1977), 424–39 (pp. 424–5).
[48] Pearsall, *John Lydgate*, pp. 235–6; Edwards, 'Influence', p. 425; Mortimer, *Lydgate's 'Fall of Princes'*, p. 58.
[49] Mortimer, *Lydgate's 'Fall of Princes'*, pp. 58–9.
[50] Lydgate, *Fall of Princes*, VIII.3149.

Here, as elsewhere, Lydgate presents his text as explicitly admonitory,[51] and the fact that 'treason' and 'traitor' are used more frequently in these new sections than in the passages that he inherited likewise shows Lydgate's emphasis.[52]

Moreover, while the *Fall of Princes* as a whole remained popular in the generations after Lydgate wrote—surviving in more manuscripts than any other of his texts apart from the *Dietary* and *Life of Our Lady*, and owned and read by a 'broad social spectrum'—the frequency with which the poem's envoys were annotated or recopied as excerpts shows that these were the aspects of the work most valued in the mid- to late fifteenth century.[53] For instance, the following stanza, showing a concern with the prevalence of betrayal and threatening an appropriate fate to those who betray, appears on its own in eight copies:[54]

> Deceit deceyueth and shal be deceyued,
> For be deceite who is deceyuable,
> Thouh his deceitis be nat out parceyued,
> To a deceyuour deceit is retournable;
> Fraude quit with fraude is guerdon couenable:
> For who with fraude fraudulent is founde,
> To a diffraudere fraude will ay rebounde. (II.4432–8)

Thus, while others have emphasized the importance of the historical moment and princely commission that produced the *Fall of Princes*,[55] more interesting here is the extent to which the text's admonitory and regiminal material was seen as insistently relevant to the problems and sociopolitical climate of the next generation or two, when the prose *Thebes* and *Troy* themselves circulated with their parallel, though more daring, admonitory emphases.

The prose *Thebes* and *Troy* both bear witness to a culture particularly invested in legal procedures and prepared to question providence, and both deploy performative utterances to define treason; however, they are certainly not undifferentiated in their means of doing so. In the two

---

[51] Mortimer, *Lydgate's 'Fall of Princes'*, p. 59; see *Fall of Princes* I. ch. 9; III. ch. 19; IV. ch. II; VI. ch. 9; VIII. ch. 19.

[52] In contrast to Lydgate's envoy on Arthur, the source-derived 'exclamacioun' avoids using treason words, instead describing the betrayer as 'fals Modred' (VIII.3194) and specifying that Arthur 'Drouh to declyn be fals deuisioun' (VIII.3198) or 'be vsurping, conspiryng and falsheede / Of seide Modred' (VIII.3183–5).

[53] Mortimer, *Lydgate's 'Fall of Princes'*, p. 1; Edwards, 'Influence', p. 429; Pearsall, *John Lydgate*, p. 12.

[54] Edwards, 'Influence', p. 431. This stanza is also edited, from one of its independent appearances, as 'Deceit, I', in *Secular Lyrics*, p. 100.

[55] Mortimer, *Lydgate's 'Fall of Princes'*, p. 56.

Lydgate poems, treason words occur with comparable frequency, but are not specifically 'pointed' in either.[56] The prose *Troy* employs a more precise lexicon of treason; however, this lexicon is decidedly absent from the prose *Thebes*, where words such as 'traitour' and 'tresoun' do not appear at all (despite these words' reasonably regular occurrence in Lydgate's *Siege of Thebes*). This disparity between the prose romances in the use of 'treason' words is initially surprising, given the correspondences in their sources, themes, style, epoch, and joint survival. However, the divergences in fact imply a shared and coherent attitude towards treason, as well as an author sophisticated enough to apply this attitude to both texts. 'Treason' and 'traitor' do not stand out as much in Lydgate's poems as they do in the prose *Troy*, both because the percentage of the text formed by these words is greater in the prose version than in Lydgate's, and because Lydgate's treason words often occur as half of a balanced doublet or as part of a diffuse list including other words such as malice, felony, falsehood, fraud, cruelty, and deceit. Moreover, where the prose *Troy* insists upon an explicit accusation of 'treason' or 'traitor', Lydgate sometimes relies on other constructions, for instance when, in killing Hector, Achilles acts 'in meschef, of hate and of envie' (3.5387).[57] By contrast, 'treason' and 'traitor' have a particular emphasis in Wars of the Roses literature, as discussed below. Since each explores different aspects of treachery, it is no less significant that the prose *Thebes* does not use these words than that the prose *Troy* does use them.

The Prose *Siege of Thebes*

The legalistic implications and didactic intentions of the prose *Siege of Thebes* are visible in the divergences between the two unequal sections of its narrative of strife, and in the alterations made to its source in order to more effectively evoke documentary culture. In shifting from one generation of characters to the next, the prose *Thebes* also shifts its representations of discord in a fashion redolent of late medieval England's increasingly institutionalized procedures against treason. The text treats the actions of the later generation in a way that deepens its relation to the problems of contemporary society, enlarging upon a preoccupation with the operation and breach of oaths and contracts by its 'generation' of textual charters not found in Lydgate's version.

---

[56] For Lydgate's use of this lexicon, see, for instance, *Troy Book* I.188, I.733, I.4079, II.887, III.445, III.3635, IV.2597, IV.6441, V.400, and *Thebes* 863, 1156, 2150, 2639, 3096, and 3575.

[57] See also *Troy Book*, IV.2789, and Lydgate's *Thebes*, 2068–9.

The first portion of the text, concerning Oedipus, does emphasize familial strife and incest in the manner that Cooper has described. This familial interest is displayed near the beginning of the text in a resonant doubling of labels at the moment when Oedipus 'smote þe king his fader, and þere slowe him' (48). Lydgate's version, by contrast, indicates only that Oedipus 'mette / Kyng Layus and cruelly hym slogh' (580–1). The rhetorical 'pointing' of the horror of political patricide in the prose *Thebes* prefigures Malory's use of a nearly indistinguishable doublet in the climactic battle when Mordred 'smote his fadir, kynge Arthure' (1237.18–19). This moment of patricide is the only time Malory employs such a doubling or collocation;[58] to my knowledge, its occurrence in the prose *Thebes* has not been commented upon. The prose *Thebes* also contains a parallel damning collocation on the verso of the same folio: Oedipus, alone and partially disrobed in his bedchamber with Jocasta, is said to be 'sitting by *his moder and wife*' (48). Like the masculine collocation, this does not occur in Lydgate's version; although Lydgate does of course mention the closer kinship later (once Oedipus himself discovers it), at the proximal moment he instead writes only that Oedipus 'sat with the queen upon a certeyn nyght' (896). Moreover, whereas Lydgate's description of the generation of the incestuous children only mentions Jocasta by name (878), the prose text specifies that they were born because 'Edippes and Jocasta *his wife and moder* leueden togidre in lustes and likings by yeris' (48). The prose author, then, dwells upon the terrible truth in places where Lydgate does not. However, independent accentuations of incest occur only at the beginning of the prose *Thebes*, comprising not quite the first two folios out of its total ten.

The prose *Thebes* thereby makes Oedipus' story a brief prologue to that of his two sons; and, in its main story, it downplays the familial and focuses on the legal instead. Upon their father's death, Eteocles and Polynices start a quarrel over the throne that dominates the remainder of the text. The lords of Thebes seek to resolve, or at least regulate, the quarrel by proposing an accord to divide the rule of the city on an annual basis, with the non-ruling brother to leave Thebes until it is his turn to be king. This accord is 'in þe moost strengest wise *regestred* and *enrolled* with þe surest bondes and oþes vppon þeire goddis þat myght be done' (49). Here both verbs describe the action of entering a deed or contract into an official register, initiating the rest of the narrative's focus on the formation and breach of legal agreements, *not* on the expectations or violation of ideal familial behaviour.[59] Whereas Lydgate stresses that the Thebans have made

---

[58] Cooper, *English Romance*, p. 377.

[59] Compare Lydgate's *Thebes*, 1135–42. There is one narratorial comment later in the prose *Thebes* that evinces a focus on the familial: 'ffore hit preued well þere of þeym two, that

Eteocles and Polynices 'of on assent, / Of on hert *as brother unto brother*' (1114–15) and repeats that the principals of the accord are 'bretheren' (1136), the prose version merely terms the makers of the accord as 'bothe' (49). Thus, for the prose *Thebes*, the significance of the quarrel lies not in the fact that those fighting each other are brothers, but in the fact that these adversaries have sworn oaths not to do so—and that, moreover, these oaths are textual contracts.

While the first short part of the prose *Thebes* focuses on the familial and filial aspects of the strife, there are no oaths or contracts which *could* be emphasized there; however, the second part of the narrative would certainly have offered sufficient grounds for emphasis of matters of fraternal strife, if the prose author wished to place rhetorical stress there. Lydgate's version contains familial moralizations throughout, but the prose author does not follow suit. In Lydgate's *Thebes*, advice such as the advocation of proper filial respect and obedience that concludes Pars Prima (1019–43) delineates the obligations which ought to be fulfilled, and the standards by which conduct is to be judged. Lacking such advice, the prose *Thebes* shifts interpretation and emphasis away from the family towards the legal practices of the written contracts that its narrator insistently reiterates. The prose *Thebes* further removes attention from familial strife by making the latter latent after Oedipus' death. During Eteocles' first year of rule, the prose *Thebes* mentions Polynices' incestuous descent and his prior associations with familial strife only obliquely, when the narrator comments that 'of his ffather spak he [Polynices] no thing' (50). Here the text treats the cause of his friend Tydeus' exile—for fratricide—in a similarly masked way. These acts of biographical indirection seem concerted, not least in the way that both stories of familial betrayal are thereafter elided from the characters' histories when King Adrastus clears their slates by dwelling 'vppon þeire berth, and blode riall', and again on their 'noble and worthi blode' (50) in his process of deciding that Tydeus and Polynices are eligible husbands for his heiresses. Thus family strife becomes concealed or forgotten by both characters and text, whose focus shifts to an intensified concern with the legal operation and breach of contracts.

The prose *Thebes* generates a protean collection of charters not found in its source, thereby focusing on institutional and universal views of social bonds and codified ways of regulating disputes. When Eteocles' year of

---

weren so horribly goten ayenst all nature and ordenaunce, for as clerkes seyn, blode to touche blode, bringeth forthe the corrupt frute' (prose *Thebes*, 269). The prose text here addresses the reprehensible conduct of the *preceding* generation: that is, the incestuous relationship of Oedipus and Jocasta. However, in the narrative proper and in commentaries where Eteocles and Polynices are the agents, the text locates the reprehensibility of their strife in their breach of contract, indicating the *operative* system of moral or social culpability.

rule has ostensibly finished, Tydeus confronts him on Polynices' behalf to request the agreed-upon transfer of power. Lydgate's Tydeus speaks to Eteocles of 'the covenaunt and convencioun' for the division of rule (1929). The prose text's Tydeus goes further, expanding this reminder into an emphatic list: he tells Eteocles,

> ye shuld haue in remembraunce *þe grete and strong bondes, suerteis, oþes, and couenauntes*, made by a vice of al þe lordes of Thebes, with your consent, which is of so hie recorde, that hit may in no wise be repeled. (51)

These contracts, which receive so much of the prose *Thebes'* attention after Oedipus' brief appearance, not only symbolize the agreements made, but also constitute the functional manifestation of the text's more secular and legal ideas of proper conduct. The legal portion of the text constitutes the majority of the narrative, and also *supersedes* the prologue in a way that parallels the increasingly institutionally defined culture of fifteenth-century England. Conceptions of proper conduct and of treason that were oral, personal, and underpinned by communal justice were increasingly supplanted by written, legal, and institutional interpretations and enforcements from the mid-fourteenth century onwards.[60] While this transition was gradual rather than abrupt, the way in which the prose *Thebes* sites the change in the gap between its two generations of characters resonates with the shift in late medieval English practice.

The prose version of the struggle for the throne of Thebes acquires a further legal dimension not found in Lydgate's version when Eteocles refuses to honour his agreement to relinquish the city after his first year of rule and Polynices advances upon Thebes with an army of Greeks to attempt to compel his brother to adhere to the contract. Here, in both versions, unsuccessful parleys culminate in Eteocles' demand to be sole ruler of Thebes for life. Tydeus reminds Eteocles of the contract he is disregarding; again in both versions, these covenants have a written, material existence. Yet only the prose *Thebes* mentions that the Greeks possess *copies* of the textual covenants ready to show, as a form of legalistic clout with which they seek to enforce Polynices' claim:

> The Grekes sodenly maden answere þere, and namely Tedeus, seying playnly, þey wold in no wise entrete with him [Eteocles], but if he wold resigne crowne, septre, and all þe dignite aftre þe covenaunt and statutes made bifor tyme, *of which þey had þe copies redy to shewe.* (270)[61]

---

[60] Green, *A Crisis of Truth*.
[61] By contrast, in Lydgate's *Thebes*, Tydeus' reply to Eteocles' demands mentions 'the covenauntys and convencioun / Imad of olde, asuryd, and asselyd' (3774–5) in the city, but there is no suggestion that the Greeks possess any copies or legal textual evidence.

This relative clause serves as an authorial intervention in support of Polynices and the Greeks, since the material copies would strengthen their claims to Thebes. From the early fourteenth century onwards, the ability to produce the document concerning disputed land tenure was 'a formal requirement for those intending to bring an action of covenant in the king's courts'.[62] Increasing numbers of official documents were being produced in late medieval England, with claimants often assuming that 'their personal rights were encased in legal documents and must be proven by specific forms';[63] this practice may have influenced both the author's creation and the contemporary interpretation of the Greeks' copies. Yet are these 'copies' to be viewed as legitimate or forged? When describing the actual *making* of the accord, the prose *Thebes* only mentions the existence of the documents enrolled in the city. The Greeks' copies might be understood as one half of a chirograph, a reciprocal charter written in duplicate on the same piece of vellum and then cut in two so that each party could have a copy, 'usually authenticated by the seal of the other party', for proof of a legitimate claim.[64] This possibility speaks to the evidential truth that documentary culture sometimes held for contemporaries. On the other hand, however, forgeries—and anxieties about them—were on the rise in fifteenth-century England, particularly pragmatic forgeries produced 'to procure tax relief, a benefice, a licence to take collection or to sell indulgences', or for other money- or land-seeking purposes.[65] Either way, a fifteenth-century reader may well have viewed the diegetic origins of the copies, orthodox or otherwise, as secondary to the underlying 'trouthe' they represent. Because the reader already knows of the existence of a documentary accord between the two parties, even if the copies are forged, they meaningfully support a valid claim against the oath-breaker, Eteocles. The presence of the copies can therefore be seen as a fabrication on the part not most significantly of the Greeks but rather of the prose author: an embellishment of evidential truth that is not without its ambiguities, but that has a clear ethical instrumentality.

Thus, through innovations such as the clause in which 'the copies' are contained, the prose *Thebes* is infused with a more potent legal ethos and ethical imperative, which resonates with its sociopolitical climate. It generates contracts rhetorically, by expanding references to the accord into

[62] Green, *A Crisis of Truth*, p. 151.
[63] Emily Steiner, *Documentary Culture and the Making of Medieval English Literature* (Cambridge: Cambridge University Press, 2003), pp. 8–9.
[64] M. T. Clanchy, *From Memory to Written Record: England 1066–1307*, 2nd edn (1979; Oxford: Blackwell, 1993), p. 87.
[65] Alfred Hiatt, *The Making of Medieval Forgeries: False Documents in Fifteenth-Century England* (London: British Library, 2004), p. 29.

unmissable lists, and narratively, by deploying 'new' documents. In so doing, the prose *Thebes* intensifies the social judgement and didactic message it conveys in condemning breach of faith and underhanded conduct; it seeks to generate a contract with its readers as well—one that will bind them to its point of view.

The Prose *Siege of Troy*

In the prose *Siege of Troy*, the keyword 'treason' structures a parallel but distinct legal tone and ethical character. Like the focus on contractual processes and their breach in the prose *Thebes*, the rhetorical stress on treason in the prose *Troy* arises through the manipulation and embellishment of sources, and increases as the narrative progresses. 'Treason' is brought to the reader's attention at the beginning of this short text when it is employed to describe Pelleus' actions, and nine further instances of 'treason' or 'traitor' dominate the final few folios. The prose *Troy* is consistently interested in articulating the legal implications of its ethical framework by examining, and condemning, the ill-motivated intentions of its characters in instances of historically inflected treason. For instance, the phrasing of the comment that Pelleus '*compassed* tresoun ayenst' his nephew Jason, the rightful king, by seeking to send the latter to his death (273) seems directly informed by the 1352 Statute of Treason. As discussed in Chapter 2, according to the statute, 'compasser ou ymaginer' ('to compass or imagine') the death of the king constituted high treason, and intention was central to the crime.[66] The author of the prose *Troy* repeatedly connects characters' reprehensible motivations to judgements of their conduct, and seems to have made a concerted effort to construct this emphasis on treason by seeking out and incorporating relevant incidents and discourse.

The prose *Troy*'s representation of Calchas the traitor draws on Chaucer's *Troilus and Criseyde* in addition to Lydgate's *Troy Book*. David Benson points out that this choice is a remarkable one, since the prose author had to go 'against the entire medieval history of Troy tradition in order to agree with Chaucer's version of the treachery of Calchas'.[67] Noting that the prose text forgoes both 'stylistic distinction' and the parts of Lydgate's *Troy Book* that are not relevant to the war itself, Benson posits that a Chaucerian source was sought for part of the prose *Troy* out of respect for Chaucer's authority as a historian thanks to Lydgate's praise of Chaucer.[68] However, as Benson has observed, the prose author does

---

[66] *Statutes of the Realm*, I, p. 320.
[67] Benson, 'Chaucer's Influence on the Prose "Sege of Troy"', p. 128.
[68] Benson, 'Chaucer's Influence on the Prose "Sege of Troy"', pp. 129–30.

not borrow anything from *Troilus* beyond the material related to Calchas' engineering of the exchange of Criseyde and Antenor. It is therefore worth looking more closely at exactly what the prose author *does* integrate from his Chaucerian source. The rhetoric about treason in the correspondences between *Troilus* and the prose *Troy* offers another possible answer to the question of why the prose *Troy* supplements its main Lydgatean source with some Chaucerian material.

The section of the prose *Troy* that is dependent upon Chaucer rather than Lydgate contributes to the prose text's preoccupation with treason. This passage of the prose *Troy* not only mentions two instances of treason, but also consists of two accusations of traitors, Calchas and Antenor. Here the prose *Troy* explicitly calls Antenor a traitor: 'Antenor, he was after Traitour to him [Priam] and to þe Cite' (282). This appellation is reproduced from Chaucer's *Troilus*.[69] The prose *Troy* similarly labels Calchas as 'þe false traitour, Calcas' (282), but while Chaucer does refer to Calchas as a traitor elsewhere in his poem, the section of *Troilus* that the prose *Troy* reworks (IV.64–206) contains no such indictment. Both of these indictments are parenthetical comments in the prose *Troy*: doubly so, since the whole passage borrowed from Chaucer is extraneous to the main plot, and since, moreover, the hermeneutic labels of 'traitour' are themselves descriptive qualifications to 'Calcas' and 'Antenor'. This commentary is thus an extension that the prose author could have discarded (or refrained from creating) if the object had been solely brevity and/or historical accuracy. In other respects the author of the prose *Troy* seems to have been keen to produce a shortened war-focused account of Lydgate's verse, but here he instead expands his narrative by absorbing and embellishing an extract from a Chaucerian source that operates to replicate, and therefore intensify, emphasis on treason. This effect offers a more compelling rationale for the prose author's selective appropriation of parts of Chaucer's *Troilus and Criseyde* than does Benson's supposition of interest in historical accuracy. However, since Lydgate's construction of Chaucer's eminence would help to remind the prose author of Chaucer as literary authority and precedent, concerns with historical accuracy and explorations of treason could fuel each other.

The prose *Troy*'s new application of the parenthetical label of 'traitour' to Calchas provides insight into what its author foregrounds. The prose *Troy* does not indict the as yet innocent Calchas as a traitor the first time he is mentioned (282). However, between that mention of his name and the

---

[69] 'Antenor.../...was after traitour to the town / Of Troye': *Troilus and Criseyde*, IV.203–5.

one under discussion here (the next time Calchas' name occurs), Calchas has committed treason; and, in conjunction with this transition, the prose author weaves the label of traitor into the otherwise Chaucerian passage. The prose *Troy*, that is, inaugurates Calchas' status as traitor at the appropriate time. Moreover, the prose author's application of the label here to the borrowed passage (282) corresponds with his accusation of Calchas later as, again, 'þe false traitour Calcas' (284). Here and in the remainder of the prose *Troy*, the names of betrayers and discussions of them attract the signifiers 'traitor' and 'treason' to them as though magnetically. The prose *Troy* thereby exhibits both a narrow hermeneutic lexicon of treason and a certain insistence upon using it: other referential tags might generate identification of the subject or object in question equally effectively, but would not carry the same interpretation. This text's heightened emphasis on the indictment of traitors thus offers systematic accusations suggestive of the process of law after a treasonous act has been committed, producing a sharpened focus on responsibility for one's actions by policing intention, or 'purpos'—another word that insistently recurs in the narrative and that, like 'treason', has legal force. This focus on interpellating traitors—on creating or constituting the figures *as traitors* through speech acts—defines a category of otherness inhabited by transgressors in a way that resonates with the (oral) appeals by which one person could legally accuse another of treason in the late Middle Ages.[70]

Companion Narratives

In subverting the expected resolution of the otherwise exemplum-like components of their narratives, the prose *Thebes* and *Troy* replace the absent Christian cultural authority with another form of cultural authority, since their relocation of the links between members of an affinity group foregrounds a codified (and potentially enforceable) idea of social cohesion. These prose romances evince a shared determination not to let treacherous figures—Eteocles, Calchas, and Antenor—get away with their reprehensible behaviour without incurring a shameful reputation and communal ostracization. To define an exemplary text as one in which 'we recognize what we should be doing'[71] is to acknowledge the exemplum-like generic affiliations and praxis of the prose romances, but also to appreciate how they rely upon different rhetorical methods and ideological axioms to pursue exemplary ends. The prose *Thebes'* and *Troy's* denial of the 'comforting

---

[70] Bellamy, *Law of Treason*, p. 141. On speech acts and interpellation, see Chapter 2, notes 97 and 98.

[71] Mitchell, *Ethics and Exemplary Narrative*, p. 14.

ideologies' of the earlier verse romances suggests that in order for right to prevail, concerted action must be taken by society. If the divine cannot be relied upon, as the political and social upheavals of mid-fifteenth-century England seemed to indicate, then matters must be taken into human hands. The rhetorical specificity of the prose romances matches their focus on advocating action, since rather than editorially stating their exemplary aims or relying upon divinely enforced exempla, they *perform* their exemplary ethics by deploying documents or accusations of treason. The prose romances' layers of utterances concerning treachery—the characters' oaths or sociolinguistic commitments, and the texts' discussions of these bonds and their breach—are productive because they are informed by and animate a set of historically resonant conventions and cultural discourses. By employing language that evokes and enacts both communal judgements and the legal mechanisms that render these judgements intelligible and operational, the prose romances show treachery to be culpable and correspondingly transform the social position of guilty parties. Thus the pointed realism in the legal character of these texts' secular retributive framework contributes to their ethical effectiveness by inviting contemporaries to read such examples of unworthy behaviour in relation to their own experience, and thereby to learn to disdain and avoid them. By withholding one form of closure—in decentring a providential framework—the prose romances consider the possibilities of a different form of closure.

The prose *Thebes* and *Troy* exhibit neither a blind adherence to their sources nor a duplication of an undifferentiated idea; rather, they convey separate, coherent messages concerning what is significant about sociolinguistic bonds and their breach. The prose *Thebes* persistently passes over Lydgate's use of the lexicon of treason, instead foregrounding contracts as embodiments of interpersonal bonds to support processes of regulation. The prose *Troy*'s reliance on 'treason' and 'traitor' in accusatory labels and interpretative statements, on the other hand, creates a system in which people, rather than contractual processes, are the primary focus, thereby concentrating not on attempts to counteract uncommendable conduct but on 'after-the-fact' indictment of perpetrators. These texts thus express differing degrees of optimism in their desired cultural work, since *Thebes* seeks to encourage the keeping of promises, while *Troy* seeks to punish those who do not. Neither the apportioning of each of these priorities to its respective text nor the Rawlinson D82 manuscript's sequencing of the two narratives (in the order of the 'historical' sieges of Thebes and Troy) derive from Lydgate; these later choices produce companion narratives that foreground first an admonition to keep one's word prior to (complete) breach of faith, and then a diatribe regarding the judgement and punishment of those who dishonour their commitments. These complexities of composition show that there is more sophistication to these 'modest' works than has generally been attributed to them.[72] Their author seems to have been sensitive to the different potential contained in the two narratives and capable of refining sources to present texts more thematically and rhetorically coherent than Lydgate's.

Thus, in paying heed to the distinctive shape and facets of their treatments of treachery, we can retrieve the prose *Thebes* and *Troy* from the textual tailings heap to which they have hitherto been cast by critical approaches that have branded them simply 'redactions', and mine them afresh as moderately intricate and independent literary works. There is nothing to suggest that the two texts were *not* written by the same author unless we are determined to believe that their compositional differences must have been the result of different styles or circumstances rather than literary ability. Friedrich Brie, who in 1913 produced what is still the most recent published treatment of the relation of the two texts, assumed that they are by the same author on the basis of stylistic similarities.[73] However, while the two texts exhibit the same paratactic and trailing clause structure, their themes and rhetoric are not identical, but rather differ as the panels of a diptych.

The topical relationship between the two prose romances—the way they occupy different positions with a shared alignment—extends to the rest of the manuscript. The eight-line poem at the end of this manuscript, which offers a secular lament for deceit and breach of faith, has already been discussed (in the first paragraph of the Introduction); the remaining text in Rawlinson D82 is excerpted from Gower's poetry in a way that is also remarkably suited to the world view of the two prose romances. Following the three regular quaternions containing the prose *Thebes* and *Troy*, six hundred lines of the *Confessio Amantis* (VIII.2377–970), in a different yet similar hand, occupy the first eight folios of the concluding ten-folio quire. Entitled 'The Court of Venus', the Gower tale complements the prose romances in both pseudo-historical subject matter and themes: it deals with famous legendary figures who appear in the prose *Thebes* and *Troy*, such as Jason and Medea, Achilles, Hector, and Troilus and Criseyde (as well as Lancelot and Tristram); it mentions 'the grete sege of Troye' (f.28v) and Jason's earlier vengeance on Troy; and it is centrally concerned with 'vntrouthe' (f.28r)—albeit untruth or breach of faith in love rather than in chivalric bonds. Perhaps most intriguingly, this fragmentary copying of Gower's text ends immediately *before* a passage of the

---

[72] Benson, 'Chaucer's Influence on the Prose "Sege of Troy"', p. 130.
[73] Brie, 'Introduction', p. 40.

Confessio that treats 'eternal providence' (VIII.2973) in a direct appeal to God to arrange social stability:

> His grace and mercy forto fonde
> Uppon my bare knes y preie,
> That he this lond in siker weie
> Wol sette uppon good governance.[74]

Although there was space remaining at the bottom of the final verso that the Gower passage occupies, and on the following blank folio that later acquired the eight-line poem about deceit, the Gower copying concludes immediately *before* this tale-concluding address to divine providence. This is the only time these lines of Gower's *Confessio amantis* are excerpted as a stand-alone piece in the fifteenth century.[75] Given the parallels with the prose romances' elisions of providential statements in their reuse of Lydgate's verse, this is an intriguing place to conclude.

The selection and inclusion of this Gower tale thus seems the work of someone familiar with the two prose romances and seeking to add to them; indeed, the Gower quire is likely a slightly later addition to the manuscript. The fifteenth-century cursive hand in which it is copied is similar to that of the prose romances, the ruled area of the pages has exactly the same dimensions and placement, and the front page of the Gower quire (unlike the recto of the first folio of *Thebes*) is not weathered or dirty enough to suggest a prolonged independent circulation.[76] The Gower quire's associations with the prose romances are furthered by the presence of the eight-line poem, since while the poem, written in another fifteenth-century hand, follows the Gower tale, its concerns with friendship and homosocial betrayals (rather than betrayals in love) respond more

---

[74] John Gower, *The Complete Works of John Gower*, ed. by G. C. Macaulay, 4 vols (Oxford: Clarendon Press, 1899–1902), III, VIII.2984–7.

[75] Kate Harris, 'John Gower's *Confessio Amantis*: The Virtues of Bad Texts', in *Manuscripts and Readers in Fifteenth-Century England: The Literary Implications of Manuscript Study*, ed. by Derek Pearsall (Cambridge: Brewer, 1983), pp. 27–40 (pp. 29–33); see also A. S. G. Edwards, 'Gower in the Delamere Chaucer Manuscript', in *The Medieval Book and a Modern Collector: Essays in Honour of Toshyuki Takamiya*, ed. by Takami Matsuda, Richard A. Linenthal, and John Scahill (Cambridge: Brewer, 2004), pp. 81–6 (pp. 81–2).

[76] Indeed, Rawlinson D82 was once part of an even larger fifteenth-century vernacular miscellany composed by two scribes including the *Awntyrs off Arthur*, Hoccleve's *Regiment of Princes*, Lydgate's *Dietary*, and Dame Juliana Berners' *Book of Hunting*—texts with similar interests in chivalric and political self-fashioning. The evidence that Rawlinson D82 was once bound (or was intended to be bound) as part of this miscellany consists of correspondences of hands, watermarks, text layout, and quire and leaf signatures, as analysed in Kathleen L. Smith, 'A Fifteenth-Century Vernacular Manuscript Reconstructed', *Bodleian Library Record*, 7 (1966), 234–41. The prose *Thebes* and *Troy* were, as Smith claims, written by the 'Scribe A' who wrote most of the rest of the relevant manuscript booklets, but the Gower quire was (as Smith does *not* claim) written by 'Scribe B'.

insistently to the manuscript's prose romances than to the Gower lines; respond, that is, to the crisis of secular faith central to the literary culture of the Wars of the Roses.

MELUSINE TRANSLATED: THE FORM AND CONTENT OF TREACHERY

The admonitory mode of emphasizing treachery manifested by the prose *Siege of Thebes* and *Siege of Troy* is paralleled in other romances of the mid- to late fifteenth century that rework not earlier English sources, but rather French ones. Both Jean d'Arras' prose *Mélusine* (late fourteenth century) and Couldrette's abbreviated versification of it, *Le Roman de Parthenay* (produced a few years later, *c.*1403), were translated into English in the late fifteenth century. The English prose *Melusine* and the English verse *Romans of Partenay* survive in one manuscript apiece, both from near the end of the fifteenth century (though there is also a fragment of the prose version printed *c.*1510 by Wynkyn de Worde). The anonymous English versions, while faithful to their sources in narrative and most aspects of phrasing, adjust and increase emphasis on treason. While Cooper has focused on the extent to which the English and the French *verse* versions have less vio- lence and family murder than the corresponding *prose* versions,[77] of greater interest here are the characteristics that differentiate both *English* versions from their *French* sources. The English prose *Melusine* and the English verse *Romans of Partenay*, reiterating accusatory words such as 'treason', 'traitor', 'unlawful', 'untrue', and 'false', emphasize—and perform—the reprehensibility and legal dimensions of betrayal more than the French versions do. Moreover, that one of these English Melusine romances is in verse rather than prose allows a further nuancing of what is important about the 'prose' in the genre of treason-focused English (prose) romances with which Chapters 3, 4, and 5 of this study are concerned.

The English Melusine romances provide an origin narrative for the house of Lusignan, but they are also admonitory chivalric manuals. The narrative embraces three generations: Melusine's parents, the fairy Presine and her husband, King Elynas, who breaks the taboo his wife sets him and thereby loses her; Melusine and Raymond, who repeat her parents' tragic trajectory, but not before they found the Lusignan dynasty and Melusine has the formidable Castle of Lusignan built by mysterious workmen; and Raymond and Melusine's many sons, with their chivalric and bellicose deeds. However, both versions focus most of their energy

---

[77] Cooper, 'Counter-Romance', p. 157.

on Melusine and her husband Raymond themselves. Moreover, although the story of Raymond begins with his accidental betrayal of his lord, the Earl of Poitiers—a hierarchical betrayal, or petty treason—the principal focus of each narrative is Raymond's betrayal of his wife Melusine. This is perhaps the inverse of petty treason, since while the 1352 Statute of Treason defined a wife killing her husband as petty treason, it considered the opposite as merely felony. Although Raymond does not kill Melusine, his betrayal causes her to lose her mortal life and live forever apart from humanity, making her thereafter dead to society. The English prose and verse versions, despite their differences in medium, alter their sources in strikingly similar ways to construe Raymond's actions as treason, again testifying to the Wars of the Roses cultural imaginary with regard to treason.

The Prose *Melusine*

Raymond curtails his normative chivalric career when he accidentally kills his cousin and master, the Earl of Poitiers, and conceals his responsibility with the help of Melusine, a fairy whom he meets afterwards. When separated from the rest of their hunting party, the earl, a great astronomer, tells Raymond that the stars are so aligned that if a vassal were to slay his master, the vassal would become a great lord with renowned descendants. Raymond answers, as a proper vassal should, 'it were ayenst al right and reason / that a man shuld haue wele for to doo euyl, and for to doo suche a mortal treson'.[78] A boar attacks the pair, and Raymond breaks his sword striking the boar to defend his lord, but a fragment of the sword kills the earl. In this episode, the English prose *Melusine*'s choice of words to describe Raymond's transgression matches those in the French *Mélusine*. Distraught, the English Raymond laments, 'in certayn all they that shall here spek of this grett mysded shal juge me / & with good right, to dey of a shamfull deth, For a more false ne more euyl treson dide neuer no synner' (26.15–17), just as the French Raymond does: 'certes tous ceulx qui orront parler de ceste mesprison me jugeront, et à bon droit, de mourir de honteuse mort; car plus faulce ne plus mauvaise traison ne fist pecheur'.[79] That no one *does* hear of Raymond's accidental murder (except for Melusine, who knows of it without being told) is less important than that Raymond, his society, and the readerships of both the French and the English texts share an awareness that such a heinous misdeed deserves capital punishment. For this hierarchical betrayal, the labels 'treason' and 'traitor' are

---

[78] *Melusine*, ed. by A. K. Donald, EETS ES 68 (London: Paul, Trench, Trübner, 1895), p. 24.25–7.
[79] Jean d'Arras, *Mélusine*, ed. by M. Ch. Brunet (Paris: Jannet, 1854), p. 34.

applied in identical fashion by both the late fourteenth-century French and the late fifteenth-century English prose texts. However, when dealing with the contra-hierarchical or horizontal betrayals that constitute *Melusine*'s principal material, the English version   departs   from   its French source by turning lesser condemnations into accusations of treason and by further foregrounding the reprehensibility of treason.

When Melusine's mortal father Elynas breaks the oath he has made to her fairy mother Presine not to set eyes upon her during childbirth, a precedent is set for Raymond's betrayal of Melusine in condemnation as well as circumstance. The English text's labels for Elynas' transgression differ from the French text's in vocabulary, and in corresponding ethos. While Melusine and her sisters characterize Elynas' actions as 'desleaulté' (22) in the French version, they term his doings 'vnlawfulnes' (14.16) in the English. Again, shortly thereafter, the French version's sisters speak to Presine of 'la desleaulté que nostre père vous a fait' (23), whereas the English version eschews the word 'disloyalty' and replaces it with both 'vnlawfulness' and 'falshed' (14.22–3). Here the English text translates its source both linguistically and ideologically in line with the contemporary English emphasis on law in representations of betrayal, and stresses the reprehensibility by doubling the appellation to include two descriptors instead of one. These strategies of altered emphasis occur throughout the English *Melusine*. For instance, when Melusine asks Raymond to marry her, Raymond responds, 'I *lawfully* promytte you that so shal I doo' (32.5). Here, again, the word 'lawfully' replaces the French text's 'leaulment' ('loyally').[80]

The English version's most notable cultural translation involves a consistent and widespread transformation of its source's word 'triste' (sad or unhappy) into 'traitor'. Cursed by her mother to turn into a serpent from the waist down on Saturdays and to remain mortal only if her husband does not see her in that state, Melusine requires Raymond to promise her (in both the English and the French versions), 'vpon all the sacrements & othes', that 'neuer . . . ye shal not peyne ne force your self for to see me on the Satirday' (32.10–15). Raymond so swears, yet, as the narrator laments, Raymond 'aftirward faylled Couenaunt. wherfore Raymondyn lost his lady' (61.10–12). After some years of happy marriage, Raymond's brother visits Raymond on a Saturday and tells him (in both versions), 'wete it that the commyn talking of the peple is, that Melusyne your wyf euery satirday in the yere is with another man in auoultyre' (296.1–3). Raymond,

---

[80] The corresponding phrase in the French version is 'je vous prometz leaulment que ainsi le feray-je' (40).

provoked into jealous suspicion even more easily than Othello, punctures
his wife's door with his sword and, peering through, sees his wife bathing: with a serpent's tail, but entirely chaste. Realizing that he has broken
his oath, Raymond stops up the hole with wax and says (again in both
versions), 'My swete loue, now haue I betrayed you, & haue falsed my
couenaunt' (297.10–11). However, Raymond also lambasts his brother
for inciting his suspicion: 'Voyde this place, fals *traytour*, For thrugh your
fals reporte I haue *falsed* my feyth ayenst the moost feythfullest & *truest*
lady that euer was borne' (297.25–8). This differs significantly in wording
from the relevant section of the French text, which has Raymond tell his
brother, 'Fuiez d'icy, faulx *triste*, car vous m'avez fait, par votre *tresmauvais*
rapport, ma foy *parjurer* contre la plus loyalle et la *meilleure* des dames qui
oncques naquit' (332–3). Here, most importantly, 'triste' becomes 'traitor' in the English version. Moreover, words such as 'tresmauvais' (very
bad) and 'parjurer' (perjure) are transformed into more characteristically
English words of falseness and falsifying. Lastly, 'meilleure' becomes 'truest', reflecting the greater English concern with matters of truth or *troth*.
The English Raymond again calls his brother 'fals blynde *traytour* and
enuyous' (298.30–1), where the French Raymond instead says 'faulce bor-
gne [one-eyed], *triste* envieuse' (333).

Among the many other instances in the English prose *Melusine* where
'traitor' is employed instead of 'triste' (or its English equivalent) are those
that occur in the narration of Raymond's patrimony.[81] Raymond's father,
Henry of Leon, seneschal to the king of Brittany, is ambushed by the
king's jealous nephew (with an accomplice named Josselin), who 'sodaynly
cryed on hym, "now shalt thou dey, false traytour, that fro me woldest
haue and vsurpe myn herytage"' (67.11–13; the French version has 'Faulx
triste' (77)). Henry kills the nephew in self-defence, but is forced into
exile by Josselin's false accusations. Both texts term Josselin's conduct treason—Melusine tells Raymond to accuse Josselin of 'the treson' (66.8) or
'la traison' (78)—but the English version, which otherwise follows the
French version essentially word for word, focuses on 'traitor' labels instead
of the French version's 'triste' labels. For instance, Raymond tells the
Breton king, 'no kinge acompanyed of a traytour is not wel lodged ne
sure of his personne' (74.36–75.1; cf. 85 in the French version).[82] After
Raymond wins the trial by combat, the king hangs both Josselin and his
son as traitors. There is a counter-attack by Josselin's angered kin and their

---

[81] See also (among other examples) 332.4 (vs. 372) and 332.15–19 (vs. 372).
[82] The English Raymond further calls Josselin and/or his son 'fals traytour' (and the
French Raymond calls them 'faulx triste') at 76.6 (86), 77.19 (88), 78.4–5 and 78.15
(89), 83.11 (95), and 84.27 (95).

following, but Raymond, with his cousins' men, defeats them. Raymond's party captures some of the enemy, and the English text's narrator specifies that these reprobates are 'bounde bothe hand & feet *as traytours* and prysonners' (96.16–17), where the French text just has 'liez' (109) without the accusatory phrase afterwards. The English *Melusine* continues its heightened emphasis on treason when the king confronts the captives, asking them how they have been 'so hardy to doo suche *treson* and so shamefull dede' (96.29) instead of the French text's 'si hardi de faire tel *outerage* ne telle derrison' (109), before condemning them to the hangman as well. By such transformations, which occur throughout the text, the English *Melusine* creates an emphatically different register from its French source in treatments of transgressive behaviour, focusing on the legal sphere and on universalized and intensified condemnations of treacherous conduct in a way that correlates with other contemporary English romances.

In this text, otherworldly magic takes up the entirely this-worldly task of highlighting the importance of keeping faith in social bonds. Melusine's and Raymond's unhappy endings, and the monstrous deformities and conduct of their offspring, have nothing to do with divine justice; the principle in effect here is the retribution of faerie curses.[83] While Melusine knows Raymond has broken his promise, she initially forgives him because of his remorse; however, when Raymond blames Melusine for the sin of her progeny and calls her a serpent, she replies (in both versions), 'thou so falsly hast betrayed me / how wel thou art forsworn toward me' (315.28–30). She continues:

> *yf thou haddest not* falsed thy feythe & thyn othe, I...hadd lyued the cours natural as another woman; [but] thus I muste suffre & bere it, vnto the day of domme / & al through thy falsed. (316.6–17)

Here Melusine expresses the conditional past tense negatively rather than positively, in order to convey more effectively an admonition about the consequences of oath-breaking. Raymond never sees Melusine again; he goes on a pilgrimage to the pope, and then ekes out the remainder of his life as a hermit, doing penance for his sins and especially for his treasonous breach of faith.

The Verse *Melusine*

Couldrette's *Roman de Parthenay* redacts the prose *Mélusine* to one third of its length; the late fifteenth-century English translator rejects Couldrette's octosyllabic couplets in favour of rhyme royal, a shift with intriguing

---

[83] Cooper, *English Romance*, p. 384.

ethical implications. The English version's two extra syllables per line are more than 'filler' in the pejorative sense; the logistical, formal shift creates a space in which betrayal and oath-breaking are further highlighted by words such as 'treason', 'traitor', 'untruth', and 'falseness'. The English *Romans of Partenay* increases praise as well as condemnation, producing a heightened focus on, and contrast between, exemplary and transgressive conduct; but negatives are added more frequently than positives.

Whereas the French version describes Raymond entering the Earl of Poitiers' service as a youth who 'savoit bien avoir', the English version employs 'truth' instead of 'good'—'Off trouth he it knew ful wel verilye'— initiating its greater focus on issues of interpersonal bonds and honesty.[84] Similarly, where the French version says that Raymond is the earl's 'cousin' (261), the English version describes him as the earl's '*faythfull* cosyn' (113). Nonetheless, Raymond slays his lord, at least according to the narrator and to Raymond, who says 'By my grete mysded here hym slayn haue I' (298). However, the event does not seem to implicate Raymond in more than a failure to successfully protect his lord: rather than being pierced by a shard of Raymond's sword as in the prose version, the earl strikes the boar ineffectively, and falls to its tusks. This may explain why the verse version, unlike the prose, does not indict Raymond of treason for this failure. Having passed over this opportunity for a representation of hierarchical treason, the English *Romans of Partenay* proceeds to dwell upon horizontal treason more intently and reprovingly than its source.[85]

As in the prose version, Raymond breaks his oath to Melusine when his brother comes to tell Raymond that 'Men sain ouerall' that on Saturdays 'hir body Anothir man shall haue, / To you *trayteresse*, other so to craue' (2767–70). Here, instead of calling Melusine a 'trayteresse', the French earl tells Raymond merely that she 'vous fait *tricherie*' (3023), that is, that she *tricks* Raymond (by sleeping with another). To 'do trickery' (or to cheat) is a very different matter from being a traitor; where the former is a mode of acting deceitfully (without legal condemnation), the latter is an identity label and a much more serious accusation.[86] Raymond, finding

---

[84] *A Bilingual Edition of Couldrette's Mélusine or Le Roman De Parthenay*, ed. by Matthew W. Morris, Mediaeval Studies, XX (Lewiston, NY: Edwin Mellen Press, 2003), line 254; *The Romans of Partenay*, ed. by Walter W. Skeat, EETS ES 22 (London: Paul, Trench, Trübner, 1899), line 107.

[85] For example, compare the English lines 594 and 1049–51 with the French lines 769 and 1243–5 respectively.

[86] This switch from trickster to traitor also occurs when, after committing fratricide, Raymond and Melusine's son Geoffrey repents: in the French version he says, 'Bien suys mauvais et *tricherres*' (3647), but in the English he says, 'Wel shewith I am An ill fals traitour' (3336). According to Eugène Vinaver, in medieval French 'trecherie' means

Melusine (and her serpentine tail) chastely bathing, reviles his falsely accusing brother. Here the English text again heightens emphasis on matters of untruth and shameful conduct, as Raymond tells his brother:

> 'ye lye *vntrewly*,
> By your fals throte And youre teeth plain!
> In An ill houre here ye entred in surely;
> Fro my hous ye goo *with your felony*;
> Off my lady no more speke ye *for shame*,
> Sche is *pure* And clene Als without diffame.' (2830–5)

The italicized words and phrases are not in the French version.[87] Here the English text heightens behavioural contrasts, portraying the earl's attempts to sow dissension as all the more reprehensible by characterizing his actions as 'untrue' and as 'felony', by implying that he has done something of which he ought to be ashamed, and by juxtaposing him with Melusine's 'pure', or honest and loyal, character. Similar shifts in emphasis occur in the confrontation between Raymond and Melusine. Preparing to leave Raymond forever, Melusine indicts him: as 'Faulx *rigoreux* et faulx parjures' (3927) in the French, and, in the English, as '*Most* fals *traytour* And fals forsworn in-ded' (3602).[88] Whereas the French Melusine calls Raymond 'rigoreux' ('severe' or 'harsh'), the English Melusine instead calls him 'traytour', repeating the condemnation in this specific legal lexicon whenever the opportunity arises.

Cultural Translation

Thus the English verse Melusine romance, like its prose counterpart, exhibits a stronger focus upon words of treason than its French source. Like other Wars of the Roses romances (usually in prose), the *Melusine*s redact their sources and yet offer more discussion of treason. The author of the English *Romans of Partenay* observes that his version is shorter than his source:

> Als the frensh staffes [lines] silabled be
> More breueloker and shorter also
> Then is the english lines vnto see,
> That comperhended in on may lines to;
> And in such wise sondry times haue do. (6581–5)

---

deceit or trickery rather than paralleling the semi-legalism of the English word 'treachery' (*Commentary*, in *Works*, p. 1305).

[87] 'Vous y mentez par la / Faulce geule parmy les dens; / En mal heure entrastes dedens / Mon hostel; or vous en alez, / Et de la dame plus ne parlez, / Car elle est nette, sans diffamme' (3092–7).

[88] See also the English version's lines 3591–5, in contrast with the French (lines 3915–20).

While the English poet cannot be accused of false advertising here (his version is indeed four hundred lines shorter than his source's seven thousand
lines), the roughly ten-syllable rhyme royal lines, perhaps chosen with the
intention of creating a Chaucerian register, have also offered many oppor-
tunities for a decidedly non-Chaucerian type of thematic accretion and
alteration. In some ways, the type of translation that produced the *Romans
of Partenay* mirrors the act of writing in prose, of being a *dérimeur*, because
both prose and longer verse lines offer greater flexibility: they facilitate
expansion as well as elision, creating space for emphasizing and recast-
ing. Prose is conducive to the registers of this era's romances through its
associations with chronicle and bureaucratic writing; with authenticity,
verifiability, legalism, and a certain 'grittiness'.[89] Often a secular medium,
late medieval prose was associated with instruction in the form of courtesy
books and technical manuals as well as chronicles.[90] Yet in addition to these
ideological and generic connotations, one of the things that is important
about prose in the new fashion for such romances during the Wars of the
Roses has nothing to do with prose itself. Writers sought greater flexibility
and freedom of medium—a way of responding to the literary tradition in
a contemporarily relevant mode—and while the answer was most often
found in prose, the *Romans of Partenay* shows that reworked verse was also
a viable option. Together, the verse and prose *Melusine*s and the prose *Siege
of Thebes* and *Siege of Troy* demonstrate the cultural specificity of mid- to
late fifteenth-century English literature's preoccupation with treason as a
social problem and a mode of ethical didacticism. This focus was shaped
by geographical, political, and temporal translation as well as linguistic,
by shifting the significance of representations of reprehensible conduct
for new audiences while otherwise remaining faithful to their sources. The
following chapter examines how Malory, using sources both English and
French, verse and prose, likewise reshaped his material in order to dwell on
treason; and explores what this parallel suggests about the genre of prose
romance in relation to both its own literary culture and earlier romance.

---

[89] See Cooper, *English Romance*, p. 363; a similar argument is made with respect to medieval French literature in H. J. Chaytor, *From Script to Print: An Introduction to Medieval
Vernacular Literature* (1945; London: Sidgwick & Jackson, 1966), and French chronicles in
specific in Gabrielle M. Spiegel, 'History, Historicism, and the Social Logic of the Text in
the Middle Ages', *Speculum*, 65.1 (1990), 59–86 (pp. 80–2).

[90] Ian A. Gordon, *The Movement of English Prose* (London: Longmans, 1966), pp. 53
and 59.

4

Speaking (of) Treason in Malory's *Morte Darthur*

Fifteenth-Century Insular Romance and Chronicle

'I reporte me to all knyghtes that ever have knowyn me, I fared never wyth no treson, nother I loved never the felyshyp of hym that fared with treson.' (*Morte Darthur*, 1134.16–19)

'Where arte thou now, thou false traytour, sir Launcelot? Why holdyst thou thyselff within holys and wallys lyke a cowarde? Loke oute, thou false traytoure knyght, and here I shall revenge upon thy body the dethe of my three brethirne!'
   And *all thys langayge* harde sir Launcelot every deale. Than hys kynne and hys knyghtes drew aboute hym, and all they seyde at onys unto sir Launcelot,
   'Sir, now muste you deffende you lyke a knyght, othir ellis ye be shamed for ever, for now ye be called upon treson, hit ys tyme for you to styrre!' (1215.11–20)

The lexicon surrounding the *Morte Darthur*'s numerous references to betrayal communicates a powerful concern with treason and its relationship to chivalric community. Criticism has attended to the *Morte*'s rhetoric of ideals and their role in discourses of community. For instance, Jill Mann has catalogued terms crucial to connections between knights: 'aventure, worship, body, departe, hole, togidir, felyship'.[1] Elizabeth Archibald has elucidated Malory's ideal of fellowship, and recent scholarship has deepened our understanding of how the *Morte*'s communities are shaped.[2] These

---

[1] Jill Mann, 'Malory: Knightly Combat in *Le Morte D'Arthur*', in *The New Pelican Guide to English Literature*, ed. by Boris Ford, 9 vols (Harmondsworth: Penguin, 1982–8), I, Part I, 331–9 (p. 332).
[2] Elizabeth Archibald, 'Malory's Ideal of Fellowship', *The Review of English Studies*, NS, 43 (1992), 311–28; Radulescu, *Gentry Context*; Kenneth Hodges, *Forging Chivalric Communities in Malory's 'Le Morte Darthur'* (New York: Palgrave Macmillan, 2005).

approaches, however, focus on the positive ideals without considering the explicit centrality of antitheses such as treason to the definition and development of these ideals. Moreover, analyses of Malory's attitudes towards treason have not appraised the words that express these attitudes,[3] leaving unaddressed the implications of 'all thys langayge' for the text's values, and how and to whom it promotes them. The *Morte*'s persistent, emphatic articulation of 'treson' and 'traytour', often in direct discourse, is a distinct departure from its sources that has, to my knowledge, gone unremarked.[4] This chapter assesses how treason, as a key word and concept in the *Morte*, contributes to the politics of community and identity both diegetically and in contemporary England.

Treason is often Malory's mode of establishing and interrogating ideals. In the *Morte*, treasonous ideas and actions are the ever-present opposites to fellowship; traitors are situated at, and are therefore used to test, the boundaries of community, of inclusion and exclusion. The first half of this chapter addresses how Malorian treason works, and the work it consequently performs with respect to Malory's Arthurian world and the world of his contemporary readers. The language of treason surrounds instances of treason and its absence in the *Morte*, probing both the valorized and the devalued or subversive terms of behavioural binaries. In the utterances of traitors, their fellow characters, and narratorial interventions, as well as the rhetoric surrounding paragons of proper conduct (who explicitly avoid treason), the text construes and seeks to control treason while remaining troubled by its ineradicability. The text's vocabulary of treason operates as a hermeneutic system, a heuristic modelling of interpretation and exclusion. This system reimagines social organization and standards of conduct contentiously, renegotiating the late medieval intersections between different conceptions of treason to resonate with, but also challenge, contemporary concerns and world views.[5]

---

[3] Deborah S. Ellis, 'Balin, Mordred, and Malory's Idea of Treachery', *English Studies*, 68.1 (1987), 66–74; E. Kay Harris, 'Evidence against Lancelot and Guinevere in Malory's *Morte Darthur*: Treason by Imagination', *Exemplaria*, 7.1 (1995), 179–208; Robert L. Kelly, 'Malory and the Common Law: *Hasty jougement* in the *Tale of the Death of King Arthur*', *Medievalia et Humanistica*, NS, 22 (1995), 111–40.

[4] Ryan Muckerheide, 'The English Law of Treason in Malory's *Le Morte Darthur*', *Arthuriana*, 20.4 (2010), 48–77, and Mischa Jayne Rose, 'Malory's *Morte Darthur* and the Idea of Treason' (unpublished doctoral thesis, University of Wales, Bangor, 1992), dissect the forms of treason available to Malory, privileging categorizations rather than connections. Neither addresses the source alterations, lexicon, and performativity of Malorian treason that both are and lead to this chapter's findings.

[5] Recent studies have addressed attitudes shared between the *Morte Darthur* and its gentry readership: Hyonjin Kim, *The Knight Without the Sword: A Social Landscape of Malorian Chivalry*, Arthurian Studies, XLV (Cambridge: Brewer, 2000); Radulescu, *Gentry*

In an era of social instability and political turmoil, the *Morte* (1469) contemplates the menace of unchecked treason, yet also seeks to counteract it. The problems and pragmatism of this enterprise are explored in the second half of this chapter by reading the *Morte* alongside contemporary insular representations of Mordred in Hardyng's *Chronicle* and Scottish chronicles, as well as alongside contemporary English romances. Like romances such as the prose *Siege of Thebes* and *Siege of Troy* discussed in Chapter 3, the *Morte* addresses social instability by consistently condemning treason and minimizing reliance on providence. This chapter ends with the implications of these shared characteristics for Malorian ideas of both truth and treason, and for the romance sub-genre to which Malory's text belongs.

THE *MORTE DARTHUR*

Performative Rhetoric

The words 'treson' and 'traytour' occur in the *Morte* with notable frequency and discursive force. Of the ninety-seven instances of 'traytour' and its variants and plurals, the vast majority—eighty-nine—appear in dialogue.[6] 'Traitor' is thus primarily a form of address and accusation in the *Morte*. 'Treson' also concerns identification and interpretation: of 124 instances, seventy-two are spoken by characters in direct discourse.[7] Eight of the nine occurrences of the adverb 'traytourely' appear in dialogue.[8] In comparison, there are one hundred instances of 'trew' words (eighty in dialogue).[9] 'Trew', then, occurs with comparable frequency to 'traytour'; however, while 'trew' does often modify 'knyght' to create the opposite of the ethical label 'traytour knyght', many instances of 'trew' are used for purposes of factuality or agreement, as when Launcelot tells a hermit, 'all

---

Context; Karen Cherewatuk, *Marriage, Adultery, and Inheritance in Malory's 'Morte Darthur'*, Arthurian Studies, LXVII (Cambridge: Brewer, 2006). Although a Cambridgeshire or, more rarely, Yorkshire alternative is still occasionally upheld, most scholars accept P. J. C. Field's identification of the Warwickshire, Newbold-Revel candidate as the authoritative Sir Thomas Malory: *The Life and Times of Sir Thomas Malory*, Arthurian Studies, XXIX (Cambridge: Brewer, 1993). It is worth pointing out, as have others such as Kim and Cherewatuk (cited above), that the text's context of social class and historical moment remains the same regardless of which of these gentry candidates wrote it.

[6] *A Concordance to the Works of Sir Thomas Malory*, ed. by Tomomi Kato (Tokyo: University of Tokyo Press, 1974). Other orthographic forms are: 'tratoures', 'traytouras', 'traytourcs', 'traytours', 'traytowre', and 'traytur'.

[7] Also as 'treason', 'trechery', 'trechory', and 'tresoun', in *Concordance*.

[8] Variants are 'traytourly', 'traytourlyar', and 'traytyrly'.

[9] Also as 'trewe', 'tru', 'true', 'trwe', 'trewer', 'trewest', 'treweste', 'trewyst', and 'truest', in *Concordance*.

that ye have seyde ys trew' (898.36–899.1). 'Traytour', on the other hand, is always an ethical condemnation. Furthermore, instances of 'trouthe' and 'truly' (78 and 116 respectively),[10] while again primarily in dialogue, are predominantly declarative or corroboratory rather than ethical; the former is most commonly employed in statements such as 'that is trouthe', and the latter in the sense of 'indeed'. Significantly, then, 'treson' and 'traytour' not only occur in the *Morte* as frequently as 'trouthe' and 'trew', but, unlike the latter, always carry an ethical value.

While debates concerning the delineation of Malory's writings continue, most critics concur that his work can be productively analysed as a 'hoole book' (1260.16) due to its stylistic and thematic continuities.[11] The impact of Malory's work as a whole is manifested in 'the sheer consistency of its discursive habits', in the 'deliberate ... narrowness and simplicity of his vocabulary' that 'directs our attention, by insistent repetition, to the key words and concepts of his narrative'.[12] Accordingly, the *Morte*'s articulations of 'treson' and 'traytour' inform constructions of community accretively. Treason discourse is not substantially found in Tales II and VI (the Roman War and the Grail Quest); however, its presence is marked in the remainder. The *Morte* thus displays a preoccupation with treason when narrating the internal politics of the Arthurian realm, and at the points most central to the narrative's arc: in the establishment of Arthur's kingdom (Tale I); in the long middle section when the court is at its zenith but the seeds of the fall are also sown (Tale V); and during the disintegration of the community (Tales VII–VIII).

The Tristram section (Tale V) illustrates the *Morte*'s wider performative emphasis on treason. Malory uses 'treson' to mediate between communal unity and fragmentation quite pointedly here, especially in comparison with his source, the French *Roman de Tristan en Prose* (which does use 'traïson', but employs 'desloiauté' with much greater frequency).[13] For instance, when the *Roman de Tristan*'s Berluse, accusing Mark of a heinous

---

[10] Also as 'trouth', 'trowthe', and 'trewly', in *Concordance*.

[11] Carol M. Meale, '"The Hoole Book": Editing and the Creation of Meaning in Malory's Text', in *A Companion to Malory*, ed. by Elizabeth Archibald and A. S. G. Edwards, Arthurian Studies, XXXVII (Cambridge: Brewer, 1996), pp. 3–17.

[12] Andrew Lynch, *Malory's Book of Arms: The Narrative of Combat in 'Le Morte Darthur'*, Arthurian Studies, XXXIX (Cambridge: Brewer, 1997), p. xviii; Mann, 'Knightly Combat', p. 332. See also Joyce Coleman, 'The Making and Breaking of Language in Sir Thomas Malory's *Morte Darthur*', in *To Make his Englissh Sweete upon his Tonge*, ed. by Marcin Krygier and Liliana Sikorska (Frankfurt: Lang, 2007), pp. 93–110.

[13] French 'desloiauté' has diffuse implications, including 'disloyalty', 'faithlessness', 'falseness', and 'marital infidelity'; 'traïson', on the other hand, is a more specific legal term (*Old French–English Dictionary*, ed. by Alan Hindley, Frederick W. Langley, and Brian J. Levy (Cambridge: Cambridge University Press, 2000)).

crime, says 'Vous ocheïstes en Cornuaille mon pere, assés vilainnement et desloiaument' (IV.102; 'You slew my father in Cornwall, very cowardly and disloyally'), the corresponding accusation in Malory is 'ye slew my fader *traytourly* and cowardly' (582.27). Here Malory alters his French sources' representations of betrayal in similar ways to the English *Melusine*s. Moreover, Malory's Berluse concludes his address to Mark with 'all that ye do is but by treson' (582.33), a criticism not paralleled in the *Roman de Tristan*. When working from passages in the *Roman de Tristan* and in his other sources (such as the *Suite du Merlin*), Malory frequently selects and strengthens emphasis on treason in these ways.[14] Thus, despite the capaciousness of the French romances, the *Morte* concentrates on 'treson' and 'traytour' much more strongly.[15] Malory creates a narrower lexicon of betrayal while widening its application and forceful articulation.

Malorian treason rhetoric emphasizes that certain actions and actors are analogously destructive, immoral, and detestable by associating them with each other. While Malory habitually includes more direct speech than his sources,[16] this transformation is particularly powerful when it produces articulations as inherently performative as accusations of treason. Since Malory frequently presents interpretations of treasonous conduct in his characters' accusations (to a degree unparalleled in his sources), his text models the act of condemning deviant behaviour. In the *Roman de Tristan*, Berlés continues his confrontation with Mark: 'Rois March, rois March! Nous sommes hors de Cornuaille. Hui mais vous gardés bien de moi!' (IV.103; 'King Mark, King Mark! We are outside of Cornwall. Now defend yourself against me!'). Malory's Berluse, by contrast, says: 'Traytoure, kepe the from me, for wete thou well that I am sir Berluse!' (583.9–10). Here Malory foregoes the French text's double articulation of the accosted character's name (and title) in favour of the label of traitor. While combat in the majority of the *Morte* entails the confrontation of 'named knight against

---

[14] For example, compare 'Arthur and Accolon' in Tale I to the corresponding episode in *La Suite du roman de Merlin*, ed. by Gilles Roussineau, 2 vols (Genève: Droz, 1996). Malory condenses his source, but also expands such descriptions as 'uns chevaliers que on apiele Domas, le plus cruel et le plus felon qui soit en tout cest païs' (I.321; 'a knight called Domas, the most cruel and the most felonious in all this land') to 'his name is sir Damas, and he is the falsyst knyght that lyvyth, *and full of treson*, and a very cowarde as ony lyvyth' (138.23–5). Malory also independently reiterates 'this Damas ys so false and so full of treson' (139.12), and focuses more on Arthur telling Accolon 'thou art a traytoure' (146.18) and on other characters terming Accolon's actions 'false treson' (144.20) than his source.

[15] While Malory's copies of his sources may not have been identical to those extant, and Malory 'was not always translating line for line', these contingencies do not obscure how Malory emphasizes 'fellowship' more than his French sources (Archibald, 'Fellowship', p. 317), a similar trend in source alterations to this chapter's argument about treason.

[16] Catherine La Farge, 'Conversation in Malory's *Morte Darthur*', *MÆ*, 56 (1987), 225–38 (p. 227).

named knight, in a process of conferring honour' on the participants,[17] Malory sometimes decreases the *articulation* of names in challenges to combat, substituting 'traytoure' where appropriate. Yet also, where his source employs a character's name or another descriptor, Malory sometimes has his characters connect name and judgement, as in Bleoberis' challenge: 'Make redy, thou false traytoure knyght, sir Brewnys Saunze Pité!' (684.27–8). For the *Morte*, naming is secondary to publishing the characters' status as traitors, thereby decreasing the honour of those who do not perform proper knightly conduct.[18]

More broadly, Malory labels actions and agents as treason and traitors to foreground judgement and accusation of perfidy by capitalizing upon but also going beyond his sources. When Brewnys seeks to escape detection, the *Roman de Tristan* has him misidentify another knight straightforwardly: 'Sire, fait Breüs, ce est Breüs sans Pitié' (V.87; ' "Sir," said Breus, "that is Breus sans Pitié" '). In the *Morte*, however, Brewnys' abject status is determinedly repeated—even, in this case, by Brewnys himself: ' "A, fayre knyghtes!" seyde sir Brewnys, "here folowyth me the moste traytour knyght and the moste coward and moste of vylany, and his name is sir Brewnys Saunze Pité" ' (685.13–15). Similarly, the regicidal brothers Helyus and Helake are persistently referred to as 'thos traytoures', 'thes two traytoures', seven times within three pages of Vinaver's edition (712–14); although their actions are similarly understood as 'traïson' (V.188) in the *Roman de Tristan*, they are referred to only once as 'les deus traitours' (V.190; 'the two traitors') and elsewhere repeatedly as 'li doi serf' ('the two knaves'), 'li doi frere' ('the two brothers'), and 'dans cevaliers' ('sir knights') (V.186–202). Malory also strategically reminds his readers of traitors' shameful status in ritualistically comprehensive dialogue. For instance, when Palomides confronts Helyus and Helake, he asks, or recaps: 'Be ye the two brethirne, Helyus and Helake, that slew youre kynge and lorde sir Harmaunce by felony and treson, for whom that I am comyn hydir to revenge his dethe?' (717.31–3). Thus the *Morte*'s hermeneutic articulations regarding treason—in narrative recounting, discussion, and direct address—systematically denigrate and ostracize traitors.

---

[17] Cooper, *English Romance*, p. 401.

[18] Malory's female traitors often conform to the anti-chivalric function of male traitors: that is, apart from matters of love, they betray knights (or chivalric communities) with intent to harm their worship and well-being. Thus, in broad outline, the *Morte*'s women are called 'traytouras' when they behave in an 'unknightly' fashion, though sometimes through different means: notably, magic, on which see Carolyne Larrington, *King Arthur's Enchantresses: Morgan and Her Sisters in Arthurian Tradition* (London: Tauris, 2006), esp. pp. 33–8.

Circumscribing Community

Treason, then, often provides the language through which Malory defines community. Despite the fact that the *Morte* manifests 'a more realistic and bleaker view of the world' than is common in earlier romances, especially in connection with treason,[19] Malory's treason discourse is not unambiguously pessimistic, but instead contributes to a complex ideological commentary combining condemnation and instruction.[20] The following two sections assess, respectively, parts of Tales V and VIII to elucidate the cultural implications of Malory's treason rhetoric; and the complications of the *Morte*'s most treason-intensive sequences in Tales VII and VIII (concerning Launcelot and Guenevere, and Mordred). First, however, focusing on Balyn and on Tales III and IV (Launcelot and Gareth), this section shows how Malory's text uses treason to shape knightly communities by circumscribing them with admonitory limits, while also acknowledging and agonizing over the ineradicability of the possibility of treason.

Balyn is a controversial figure not only to Malory's characters but also to his critics, as some claim that Balyn is tainted with treason despite his ostensible status as a model knight. Deborah Ellis contends that Balyn's initial exemplar status is dismantled because his good intentions are 'continuously violated by death and unwitting betrayal'.[21] Kevin Whetter, however, reconciles the *Morte*'s 'insistence on Balyn's heroic qualities' with the events of Balyn's tale by suggesting that his actions be judged by the standards of epic-heroic honour rather than romance courtesy.[22] While it is indeed wise to accept Balyn as the exemplary figure the *Morte* proclaims him to be on its own terms, it is important that even—or especially— when Balyn is viewed as a paragon rather than a traitor, treason remains a central theme of his tale. The text's characterization of Balyn as without treason undermines the notion that Arthur, or the legal system he embodies, has espoused an acceptable definition of treason by imprisoning Balyn 'for sleyng of a knyght which was cosyne unto kynge Arthure' (62.35–6). This initial exclusion from community and Balyn's subsequent exile for killing the Lady of the Lake at Arthur's court seem, in light of Malory's

---

[19] Cooper, 'Counter-Romance', p. 144, as discussed in Chapter 3.
[20] On ideology, see Chapter 2, note 40.   [21] Ellis, 'Balin', p. 67.
[22] K. S. Whetter, 'On Misunderstanding Malory's Balyn', in *Re-viewing 'Le Morte Darthur': Texts and Contexts, Characters and Themes*, ed. by K. S. Whetter and Raluca L. Radulescu, Arthurian Studies, LX (Cambridge: Brewer, 2005), pp. 149–62 (pp. 152 and 156); see also Beverly Kennedy, *Knighthood in the Morte Darthur*, Arthurian Studies, XI (Cambridge: Brewer, 1985), pp. 218–30. However, later sections of this chapter disagree with the conclusions Whetter and Kennedy draw from Malory's representation of Balyn, which are, respectively, that the Tale of Balyn and the *Morte* are not romances, and that the *Morte* is unproblematically suffused by a providentialist view.

portrayal of Balyn as an exemplary non-traitor knight, to indicate a failure of institutional definitions to identify what truly constitutes treasonous behaviour. Arthur's apology to Balyn for having imprisoned him—'I was mysseinfourmed ayenste you' (64.27)—shows that idiosyncratic justice may also fail. Malory explores these possibilities in greater detail in connection with Launcelot and Guenevere (as discussed below).

In addition to raising these concerns about misapplication of the law and justice with respect to treason, Balyn also serves as a focal point for less tractable problems inherent to the definition of treason. The language defining Balyn's exemplarity testifies both to an abiding uneasiness about the potential for treason, and to a pervasive, admonitory mode of constructing chivalric identity. When the sword-damsel comes to Arthur's court seeking a knight *without treachery*, the negative expression of her aim is significant.[23] Balyn is repeatedly characterized by the phrase 'moste of worship *withoute treson, trechory or felony*' (64.2–3): treason provides the tools to define even this ideal knight. The fine line between good and bad knights in the *Morte*, where even non-traitors (or least-traitors) are surrounded by the lexicon of treason, shows that betrayal is a present absence at best, and a tragic menace at worst. Treason is fundamental to Malory's chivalric communities through its role in the processes of othering that intersubjective identity-fashioning entails. That is, the text's traitors, defining what chivalric identity is *not*, are created by the society they threaten, and are dialectically both within and beyond that society. Lacan's concept of *extimité*, or intimate alterity, is useful here as a way of conceptualizing the effect of the text's desire to reject the possibility of treason without ever being able to do so fully. In Lacanian psychoanalysis, the 'extimate' is what an interiority expels in order to create an illusion of integrity; at both the individual and the collective levels, treason is the possibility that Malorian chivalric subjectivity can neither accept nor eradicate. As the 'restless presence' at the centre of everything that a constructed identity 'abjects in order to materialize and maintain its borders', the *Morte*'s traitors and treasons can, I suggest, be understood as the *extimité* of individual chivalric subjectivity and also of a community such as the Round Table.[24]

Malory's emphasis on the intimate alterity of traitors is especially visible in how his descriptions of Balyn diverge from his source. In the *Suite du Merlin*, the sword-damsel seeks 'li mieudres chevaliers de cest païs et

---

[23] Ellis notes this expression without suggesting *why* it is important; 'Balin', p. 68.

[24] Jacques Lacan's term *extimité* ('external intimacy', or 'intimate alterity') is 'a phenomenon that conjoins the intimacy of self-knowledge to a foundational alterity, an exorbitance as frightening as it is familiar': J. J. Cohen, *Of Giants: Sex, Monsters, and the Middle Ages* (Minneapolis: University of Minnesota Press, 1999), pp. xiii and 4.

li plus loiaus sans trecherie et sans voisdie et sans traïson' (I.66; 'the best knight of this land and the most loyal without trickery and without guile and without treason'). However, the *Suite*'s damsel says this only once. The *Suite*'s Arthur calls for 'li mieudres chevaliers de son païs et...*si bien entechiés comme vous avés dit*' (I.67; 'the best knight of his country and...*so well endowed as you have said*'), offering a *positive* definition of an exemplary knight. Likewise, once Balyn has unsheathed the sword, the French version's damsel says: 'vous estes li mieudres chevaliers de chaiens' (I.69; 'you are the best knight here') and stops short of adding a 'without' clause as a negative reminder. Malory's sword-toting damsel, however, speaks of treachery and/or treason five times in her explanation of her search for a knight who lacks it (62–4). This repetition of the negative definition, both before and after Balyn becomes the successful candidate, accentuates the *Morte*'s admonitory conception of chivalry by continually reminding the reader that those who would earn 'worship' must do so 'withoute treson, trechory or felony' (64.2–3). However, the sheer repetition also suggests an element of desperation in this endeavour, as treason is shown to be a possibility that can never entirely be excluded from knightly identity, even in the latter's articulation.

An awareness of treason as the extimate of chivalric identity in the *Morte* inheres not only to the individual, but also, similarly, to the social body. In the Round Table oath, good characters and conduct are distinguished in part by their explicit relation to treason: 'than the kynge stablysshed all the knyghtes...and charged them never to do outerage nothir mourthir, and *allwayes to fle treson*, and to gyff mercy unto hym that askith mercy' (120.15–19). This code of conduct for the fellowship of the Round Table is unique to the *Morte*, and has been understood to encapsulate Malory's conception of chivalry.[25] Because the Round Table oath is reminiscent of the teachings of fifteenth-century courtesy books, it reminds contemporary readers that, in both the Arthurian world and their own, personal worship depends upon fulfilling social obligations, while contravening them leads to loss of community.[26] Indeed, in the Round Table oath, the punishment prescribed for treason is to be expelled from Arthur's community, in a geographic parallel of the creation of a mental

---

[25] Elizabeth Archibald, 'Beginnings: *The Tale of King Arthur* and *King Arthur and Emperor Lucius*', in *Companion to Malory*, pp. 133–51 (p. 141); Ellis, 'Balin', p. 69.
[26] Radulescu, *Gentry Context*, pp. 84–7. Malory's Round Table oath also has strong parallels with the injunctions given to initiate Knights of the Bath: Richard Barber, 'Malory's *Le Morte Darthur* and Court Culture under Edward IV', in *Arthurian Literature XII*, ed. by James P. Carley and Felicity Riddy (Cambridge: Brewer, 1993), pp. 133–55 (pp. 148–9); Ralph Norris, *Malory's Library: The Sources of the 'Morte Darthur'*, Arthurian Studies, LXXI (Cambridge: Brewer, 2008), p. 20.

extimate: the knights are to follow the code of conduct expressed in the Round Table oath 'uppon payne of forfiture of their worship and lordship of kynge Arthure for evirmore' (120.19–20). Since exile, and thus loss of community, increasingly took the place of execution as punishment for traitors in late medieval England (particularly aristocrats, who were required to abjure the realm),[27] Malory's articulation of the punishment for treason would likely have been highly evocative for, and therefore more effectively admonitory to, his contemporaries. Moreover, while the Round Table oath binds a community 'on shared ethical principles',[28] the contingency of these principles is inescapable. In accepting the oath's terms when they swear it 'every yere...at the hyghe feste of Pentecoste' (120.26–7), all the knights are vulnerable to, and aware of, potential exclusion. The repetition of the oath speaks to the permanence and order of Arthurian society,[29] but it also indicates darker aspects of this community, revealing that this community's bonds continually require renewal or reification. The knights' annual articulation of the abjectness of treason shows that treason is ever-present in their understanding of themselves, and this continual danger of slipping, of breaking, uneasily invokes the limitations of the Arthurian realm.

Thus, in his tragic representation of a moribund chivalric world, Malory foregrounds the fact that treason, as a breach of social contract, is never fully separable from idealized relationships. Fellowship, in the *Morte*, is the ideal of social cohesion; it encapsulates loyal relationships, both horizontal and hierarchical.[30] Yet the *Morte* frequently explores fellowship through its opposite, treason, as in the passage that begins this chapter. When Mellyagaunce tells Launcelot he hopes they will eschew treason before their legal duel, Launcelot's reply provides a striking picture of the relation between treason and fellowship: 'I reporte me to all knyghtes that ever have knowyn me, I fared never wyth no treson, nother I loved never the felyshyp of hym that fared with treson' (1134.16–19). In this utterance (not in Malory's source, the Prose *Lancelot*),[31] treason is figured as a travelling companion or fellow. The *Morte* represents treason as the destructive force capable of demolishing fellowship, and also shows that treason is the

[27] William R. Jones, 'Sanctuary, Exile, and Law: The Fugitive and Public Authority in Medieval England and Modern America', in *Essays on English Law and the American Experience*, ed. by Elizabeth A. Cawthon and David E. Narrett (Texas: Texas A&M University Press, 1994), pp. 19–41 (p. 30); J. J. Jusscrand, *English Wayfaring Life in the Middle Ages*, trans. by Lucy Toulmin Smith, 4th edn (1889; London: Benn, 1950).

[28] Hodges, *Forging Chivalric Communities*, p. 35.

[29] Archibald, 'Fellowship', pp. 317–18.

[30] Archibald, 'Fellowship', pp. 311 and 327.

[31] Compare *Lancelot: Roman en prose du XIIIe siècle*, ed. by Alexandre Micha, 9 vols (Genève: Droz, 1978–83), II, 77–9.

dark mirror or inverted reflection of communal and honourable identity, fundamental to the latter's existence.

Launcelot, as the mouthpiece for this definition of treason as the anathema of society, demonstrates the influential ways in which exemplary knights deploy 'treson' and 'traytour'. The narrator's statement that 'at no tyme' was Launcelot 'ovircom but yf hit were by treson other inchauntement' (253.10–12) invites particular attention because narratorial interventions are rare in the *Morte*;[32] to state that any setback Launcelot suffers is treason is to reinforce his judgement when he calls an enemy 'traytour'. For example, in Tale III, when informed of 'a knyght that dystressis all ladyes and jantylwomen' (269.19–20), Launcelot declares that this knight, Perys de Foreste Savage, 'doth shame unto the Order of Knyghthode, and contrary unto his oth' (269.23–4). Launcelot accuses Perys as 'false knyght and *traytoure unto knyghthode*' (269.35). Neither of these accusations is found in the corresponding episode in the Prose *Lancelot* (V.39–40);[33] this concern about treason *to knighthood* is Malory's. In episodes such as this, Launcelot demarcates the boundaries of knightly community from within.[34]

In Tale IV, Gareth, another exemplary knight, accuses a 'traytour' in a case that seems comically trivial, but that illuminates the text's attitudes towards treason. Lyonesse's brother Gringamour seizes Gareth's dwarf without violence; confronting him afterward, Gareth

cryed alowde that all the castell myght hyre:
    'Thou traytour knyght, sir Gryngamoure! delyver me my dwarff agayne, or by the fayth that I owghe to God and to the hygh Ordir of Knyghthode I shall do the all the harme that may lye in my power!' (330.11–16)[35]

Viewing the dwarf as a vital chivalric accoutrement may help to explain part of Gareth's furious reaction to his loss.[36] Significantly, however, the

---

[32] La Farge, 'Conversation', p. 227.   [33] Vinaver, *Commentary*, p. 1420.

[34] See also the accusation of treason that Malory's Launcelot issues at 285.12–14, again not found in the Prose *Lancelot* (Vinaver, *Commentary*, p. 1425).

[35] Malory's Tale of Gareth has no extant source. Vinaver's supposition of a French source (*Commentary*, pp. 1427–34) has been superseded by arguments for an English source based on vocabulary and syntax: P. J. C. Field, 'The Source of Malory's *Tale of Gareth*', in *Aspects of Malory*, ed. by Toshiyuki Takamiya and Derek Brewer, Arthurian Studies, I (Cambridge: Brewer, 1981), pp. 57–70; Norris, *Malory's Library*. However, since there is no extant source but there are partial analogues in both insular and continental romances, Malory may have synthesized his own tale. Regardless of which theory is correct, the fact that the Tale of Gareth contains the kind of treason discourse typical of the bulk of the *Morte* suggests that Malory made the same decisions regarding how to represent betrayal here as elsewhere.

[36] Emily Rebekah Huber, '"Delyver Me My Dwarff!": Gareth's Dwarf and Chivalric Identity', *Arthuriana*, 16.2 (2006), 49–53.

thievery is conducted underhandedly: at night, knowing Gareth is asleep, Gringamour, accoutred entirely in black, 'com stylly stalkyng behynde the dwarff and plucked hym faste undir his arme and so rode his way with hym' (328.24–6). The *manner* in which the offence is conducted causes Gareth to apply the label of 'traytour' to the perpetrator, as addressed below; Gareth, like Launcelot, tells the reader when the expectations of behaviour between knights are not met.

These utterances, and many more like them, shape chivalry not only by giving the appropriate interpretations to actions, but also by modelling the processes of exclusion that such actions warrant. While instances of treason are often unresolved in the *Morte*, no one gets away with treason without at least being noticed and denounced—in fact, accusers often aim to have as many people as possible hear their accusations.[37] The unrelenting way in which Malory's characters publicize treason creates expectations of an accusation whenever a character chooses unknightly conduct. The attentive reader internalizes—or is at least invited to internalize—the text's stance concerning treason, becoming complicit in reproducing it. This influence would be especially available to a readership situated within the legal traditions and political turmoil with which the text's representations of treason engage.

Historicity and Malory's Idea of Treason

Gareth's discourse on the moral turpitude of abducting another knight's dwarf in the darkness provides a useful starting point from which to examine the types of actions to which Malory applies the label of treason, and why. Robert Kelly and Kay Harris have sought to historicize Malorian treason, but focus only on the case of Launcelot and Guenevere in the final Tale as *the* historically inflected episode of treason in the *Morte*.[38] Yet critical perception has, in my view, been somewhat shortsighted in passing over the bulk of Malory's treason rhetoric without glimpsing the historical and legal frames of reference with which it intersects. Treason against the king is of course crucial to the *Morte*—especially in the cases of Launcelot, Guenevere, and Mordred, as discussed below—yet not exclusively so. The view that the bulk of treason instances in the *Morte* are not part of a cohesive system is something of a critical commonplace.[39] However, 'treson' is

---

[37] This is especially apparent when Agravain, Mordred, and company assault Launcelot in Guenevere's bedchamber, as discussed below. Another group accusation occurs when the Five Kings sneak up on Arthur's camp in the night: as Arthur's soldiers awake, 'many cryed "Treson!"' (128.10–11).

[38] See note 3.

[39] In addition to Kelly's and Harris' studies (note 3 above), see also Mischa Jayne Rose (note 4); Christopher Cannon, 'Malory's Crime: Chivalric Identity and the Evil Will',

a more 'precise' term (in the sense of accurate and appropriate) in Malory's work than has been recognized, and moreover 'precision' (in the sense of restricted classification) is not as useful a way of assessing the *Morte*'s treasons as is the text's manifest intent to create pointed associations through its deployment of the relevant signifiers. Malory's classification of transgressions as treason, that is, focuses less on distinguishing between orders of magnitude or types of wicked or guileful acts than on their collective association.

Malory's idea of treason supports order but does so by interrogating and transcending the models available in his society. The statute definition of treason, as discussed in Chapter 2, applied only to formal bonds of subservience; yet, as Green observes, to the popular medieval English mind, 'traitor' meant 'someone who had betrayed a trust', especially the trust expected 'between members of the same family or household'.[40] This less institutional, more personal understanding of treason and social bonds was subject to a continuing process of erosion by centralized authority;[41] its practical force diminished through the late Middle Ages, but it could retain ideological influence as a nostalgic standard, as in the *Morte*. Malory's representations of unresolved treason comment on the failure of the institutionalized attitudes and relationships of his time; yet also promote older, more personal forms of relationships. The *Morte* defines treason as almost any underhanded action, to anyone; this becomes clear by reading the text's accusations of treason accretively, as well as by paying heed to moments such as that in which Sir Patryse is killed by a poisoned apple and Malory's narrator comments that 'the custom was such at that tyme that all maner of shamefull deth was called treson' (1050.2–3). Since 'shamefull' could readily mean 'disgraceful', 'despicable', or 'deserving of reproach or condemnation', this narratorial comment aptly articulates both what makes an action treasonous in the *Morte*, and what sort of response treason ought to receive.[42] Through such broad condemnations of treason, the *Morte* seeks to inculcate a more honourable mode of interaction.

in *Medieval Literature and Historical Inquiry: Essays in Honour of Derek Pearsall*, ed. by David Aers (Cambridge: Brewer, 2000), pp. 159–83 (p. 181, note 62); Ruth Lexton, 'The Political Imagination of Malory's *Morte Darthur*' (unpublished doctoral dissertation, Columbia University, New York, 2010), pp. 246–311; and Lydia Fletcher, ' "Traytoures" and "Treson": The Language of Treason in the Works of Sir Thomas Malory', in *Arthurian Literature XXVIII*, ed. by Elizabeth Archibald and David F. Johnson (Cambridge: Brewer, 2011), pp. 75–88. As indicated in note 4 above, I do not agree that this widely held bipartite view accurately reflects what Malory does with treason.

[40] Green, *Crisis of Truth*, p. 214.   [41] Green, *Crisis of Truth*, p. xiv.

[42] See MED, 'shameful', entry 'c'.

Malory writes about and valorizes an imagined period when oral oath underpinned society, yet he also traces fifteenth-century legality onto it, bringing it closer to contemporary experience. As in the prose *Troy*, the *Morte*'s indictments of traitors imitate the process of law after a treasonous act has been committed. After King Mark expresses his intention to murder Tristram and kills a protesting knight, another, Amant, says that he 'woll *appele* you of treson afore kynge Arthure' (578.29–30). The word 'appele' is central to such accusations, which occur repeatedly.[43] This focus on interpellating traitors—on constituting the figures as traitors through speech acts—defines a category of otherness inhabited by transgressors in a way that resonates with late medieval accusations of treason. Oral appeals were, however, somewhat antiquated by Malory's time, when the more usual procedure consisted of written bills of indictment.[44] Appeals are found in Malory's French sources, but when replicated in the *Morte*, they, like the more 'original' emphases of Malory's treason representations, take on a resonance particular to a late medieval English milieu, functioning as part of the *Morte*'s nostalgic yet thoroughly contemporary ideology.

In Malory's representations of treason, therefore, his contemporary readers would recognize especially the part of their own social organization that was being eroded, in another instance of the personal and honourable crumbling before the institutional. The notion of this present-but-vanishing world is directly addressed when Malory's narrator intrudes on the story to state that 'the custom was suche tho dayes that and ony man were appealed of ony treson othir of murthure he sholde fyght body for body, other ellys to fynde another knyght for hym' (405.2–4). As discussed in Chapter 2, trials by battle were less common by Malory's time. Thus, in representing legal procedures as well as a personal conception of treason, Malory returns to resonant older customs. As in the prose *Thebes* and *Troy*, though with different complexities, the realism of the *Morte*'s engagements with treason and its punishment contributes to its ethical effectiveness. Although, in the Tale of Balyn, Malory does include a faerie damsel divining treason or its lack, the majority of his treatments of treason are more earthly. For Malory, the 'custom' in 'tho dayes' is worthy of contemporary emulation; it is the (flawed) golden age from which the present is declining.

The performative mode through which Malory's contemporary 'readership' may well have received the text further emphasizes its admonitions about treason. In the fourteenth and fifteenth centuries, for sophisticated audiences as well as semi-literate ones, 'the reading aloud of written

---

[43] For instance, 658.12–14, 661.10–12, and 1049.28–9.
[44] Bellamy, *Law of Treason*, pp. 138–41.

literature to one or a group of listeners' was 'the modality of choice'.[45] Critics have recently reappraised the *Morte* as a text meant for aural reception,[46] suggesting the heightened effect that the text's direct discourse—such as accusations of treason—would have. Moreover, the significance of the *Morte*'s narrowed vocabulary of treason would likely have been further enhanced by aural performance, since the individual reading aloud to the group 'would have instinctively "pointed," or emphasized', key words that Malory 'broadcasted' across the narrative.[47] While discontinuous reception might somewhat reduce the power of repeated keywords (since, while one or two hours of reading might occupy an evening, it would take over thirty hours to read the entire *Morte* aloud),[48] the reader would likely have been asked to pre-read the text for familiarity, and therefore would emphasize keywords even during a selective performance.[49] The potency of Malory's treason discourse would be further intensified by the collective aspect of aural 'reading',[50] mirroring the communal addressees of admonitions such as the Oath of the Round Table.

The *Morte* was likely widely read among not only the aristocracy but also the gentry,[51] many of whom either were or aspired to be knights, and whose concerns with self-fashioning mirrored the goals and ideals of Malory's characters. The *Morte* is preoccupied with personal 'worship' (or publicly recognized worth), friendship, fellowship (in the sense of affiliation and alliance), and good lordship; and, as Radulescu argues, these four concerns were those most central to gentry circles. Because 'belonging to a particular fellowship seems to have been a constant concern', of particular significance here is the fact that the consequences of being excluded from community were equally severe, and recognized, in fifteenth-century gentry society and in the *Morte*.[52] Malory's gentry audience, accustomed to

---

[45] Joyce Coleman, *Public Reading and the Reading Public in Late Medieval England and France*, Cambridge Studies in Medieval Literature, XXVI (Cambridge: Cambridge University Press, 1996), pp. 1–2.

[46] See all of *Arthuriana*, 13.4 (2003), in which especially Joyce Coleman, 'Reading Malory in the Fifteenth Century: Aural Reception and Performance Dynamics', 48–70; also, Cherewatuk, *Marriage, Adultery, and Inheritance*, pp. xv–xvi.

[47] Coleman, 'Reading Malory', p. 55.   [48] Coleman, 'Reading Malory', p. 57.

[49] D. Thomas Hanks Jr., 'Epilogue: Malory's *Morte Darthur* and "the Place of the Voice"', *Arthuriana*, 13.4 (2003), 119–33 (p. 124).

[50] Coleman, 'Reading Malory', p. 50.

[51] Despite the lack of evidence regarding specific readers, as Coleman observes, 'collateral evidence suggest[s] that the *Morte* appealed to, and was probably meant to appeal to, the armigerous class from which Malory himself came, as well as the higher ranks of nobility and the aspiring City men of Caxton's own ilk', particularly since these groups read other Arthurian romances and chronicles: 'Reading Malory', pp. 48–9; see also Thomas H. Crofts, *Malory's Contemporary Audience: The Social Reading of Romance in Late Medieval England*, Arthurian Studies, LXVI (Cambridge: Brewer, 2006), p. 6.

[52] Radulescu, *Gentry Context*, pp. 34 and 93.

perceiving courtesy books and romances as conduct manuals that could further their social aspirations,[53] would presumably have been well conditioned to attune themselves to Malory's text. Indeed, as Caxton's preface to his edition of the *Morte* informs the reader, the text instructs the reader about the importance of honour and ethics not only through 'the noble actes of chyvalrye, the jentyl and vertuous dedes that somme knyghtes used in tho dayes', but also by recounting 'how they that were vycious were punysshed and ofte put to shame and rebuke'. Caxton, instructing readers to 'Doo after the good and leve the evyl, and it shal brynge you to good fame and renommee', recognizes the *Morte*'s complex forms of didacticism.[54]

The Personal and the Political

> hit ys an olde-seyde sawe, 'there ys harde batayle thereas kynne and frendys doth batayle ayther ayenst other', for there may be no mercy, but mortall warre. (1084.4–7)

While previous sections discussed Malory's valorization of a universal, horizontal chivalric bond, this section explores the treatment of hierarchical bonds in the final sequences of the *Morte*, which promote personal loyalty to king and realm. Tale VIII is concerned with two cases of 'high' treason: Launcelot and Guenevere's affair, and the rebellion of Mordred and the English people that ends Arthur's reign.[55] Malory intensifies contrasts between the transgressors and accusers in these two episodes and saturates both with accusations of treason not found in his sources, offering a nuanced definition of treason in cases where intentions and institutionalized law are opposed. As argued above, the majority of the *Morte* does not show or encourage sympathy towards traitors. This attitude persists in the final movement, and is in some senses intensified there; however, in the shift to Tale VIII, the accusations of 'treson' and 'traytour' that had been spoken *by* exemplary figures are instead spoken *to* exemplary figures. In the short space between the two passages quoted at the beginning of this chapter, Launcelot moves from being the righteous spokesperson against treason to being the recipient of the dire and shameful rhetorical labels he

[53] Radulescu, *Gentry Context*, p. 8.

[54] William Caxton, 'Preface', in *Works of Sir Thomas Malory*, pp. cxlv.32–5 and cxlvi.7–8. The treason rhetoric in Caxton's version, as discussed in Chapter 5, does not differ substantially from the Winchester Malory.

[55] While 'hyghe treson' occurs only once in the *Morte* (in reference to Melleagaunt's accusation of Guenevere, 1135.14), the term is used here to designate any treason against the king.

earlier allocated. This transition signals the impending division and down-fall of the Arthurian world, but also qualifies earlier messages regarding treason. In Tale VIII, Launcelot and Guenevere do incur condemnation from their sovereign and society for their adultery. However, in discussing this treason within a more rigid legal framework than in his sources, Malory adds a proviso clause regarding intent to an otherwise consistent strategy of directing sympathy away from those who are labelled traitors. The text's defence of Launcelot and Guenevere's intentions connects with contemporary fears about being accused of treason for conflicted loyalties, yet also colludes with traitors in a way that jeopardizes the resolution of the *Morte*'s attitudes towards treason.

Through the ways in which, and figures by whom, Launcelot and Guenevere are accused of treason and put on trial or punished for it, Malory questions institutional conceptions of what constitutes loyalty to king and realm, and critiques the ill-intentioned actions that can be sanctioned by a letter-of-the-law perspective. Since Launcelot and Guenevere's perfidious consummation of their affair and its consequences are major components of the Arthurian story, Malory does of course treat them; however, the *Morte* seeks to emphasize not their guilt but rather the ways in which they are *not* culpable.[56] The text conceals the adultery as much as possible without denying its existence. When forced to address the notion of Launcelot and Guenevere alone in a bedroom, with Agravain and Mordred about to apprehend them, Malory's narrator is defensively circuitous: 'whether they were abed other at other maner of disportis, me lyste nat thereof make no mencion, for love that tyme was nat as love ys nowadayes' (1165.11–13). Malory here focuses on the nobility of the love between Launcelot and Guenevere, and is more concerned to articulate the motives of both the accused and their accusers than is common elsewhere in the text. Malory writes that 'the floure of chyvalry of alle the worlde was destroyed and slayne' because of 'two unhappy knyghtis whych were named sir Aggravayne and sir Mordred, *that were brethirn unto sir Gawayne*' (1161.7–11). By emphasizing Agravain and Mordred's familial connections, Malory stresses that they belong to an affinity group that often privileges itself above the kingdom it claims to serve. Here the Orkney clan divides, as Gawain, Gareth, and Gaheris refuse to have anything to do with Agravain and Mordred's denouncement of Launcelot (1162.22–30); however, Gawain later harms the community for the sake of his kin.

---

[56] Field has observed that Malory often writes as if constrained to include material he found in his sources and as if 'his only freedom lay in proportioning his narrative': *Life and Times*, p. 172.

Fifteenth-century Scots thwarted English desires for insular domi-
nance as 'an intractable and unabsorbable people', and, in Middle English
romances, Scottish disruption of English insular unity is often depicted
as treachery and guile.[57] Thus, as discussed further below, by participating in a more widespread expression of the English cultural imaginary
that depicted Scottish characters as treacherous, the *Morte* preconditions
the interpretation of the figures who accuse and assault Launcelot and
Guenevere as acting against the interests of the realm. The malevolent
nature of the Orkney clan is well established within the *Morte* prior to
Tale VIII, since several of the brothers (including Gawain, Agravain, and
Mordred) murder Lamorak. While this occurs early in the narrative, it is
a recurring preoccupation. The Arthurian community's last moment of
unity in 'The Healing of Sir Urry' is fractured, rhetorically as well as figuratively, by the present absence of treason when the roll call of attendant
knights is interrupted by an ominous recapitulation: 'there was never none
so bewayled as was sir Tristram and sir Lamerok, for they were with treson
slayne: sir Trystram by kynge Marke, and sir Lamorake *by sir Gawayne
and hys brethirn*' (1149.32–5). This comment also links the Orkney clan
with King Mark, who is the *Morte*'s other egregious traitor—and who,
as a Cornish figure, is again a dangerous insular Other to the English.
The narrator mentions, moreover, that 'sir Aggravayne and sir Mordred
had ever *a prevy hate* unto' Guenevere and Launcelot (1161.11–12). Here
Malory emphasizes that while Agravain and Mordred may side with the
law against treason in publicly denouncing Launcelot and Guenevere,
they do so out of ill will. By contrast, Launcelot and Guenevere are portrayed as honourable characters caught in a tragic conflict of loyalties; the
audience is expected to support Launcelot and Guenevere even during the
accusations spoken against them, because of the rebarbative figures against
whom they are defined.[58]

By emphasizing the good intentions of the accused and the malevolent
intentions of the accusers, the *Morte* seeks to skate over the cracks that
Launcelot and Guenevere introduce into its stance concerning the ethics

---

[57] Cory Rushton, ' "Of an uncouthe stede": The Scottish Knight in Middle English
Arthurian Romances', in *The Scots and Medieval Arthurian Legend*, ed. by Rhiannon Purdie
and Nicola Royan, Arthurian Studies, LXI (Cambridge: Brewer, 2005), pp. 109–19 (pp.
110–12).

[58] Comparable transferrals of blame occur in Tale VII when Mellyagaunce accuses
Guenevere of treason for sleeping with an unidentified member of her entourage after she
has in fact slept with Launcelot (1131–40): Mellyagaunce is portrayed as the villain because
of his wicked intentions and because he subsequently commits the unambiguously treasonous act of trapping Launcelot in a pit. Here deflection likewise qualifies the culpability of
the protagonists by emphasizing issues of intent, but legal consequences are suppressed
because Guenevere and Launcelot's love is not yet public.

of treason. As mentioned earlier, Launcelot and Guenevere's betrayal of Arthur is of course a common feature of the Arthurian tradition, but it is one that is especially problematic for the *Morte*, given Malory's stronger focus on condemning treason throughout. Accordingly, the *Morte* encourages the reader to commend or criticize Launcelot, Guenevere, and the Orkney clan based on *why* they behave as they do, rather than on legal niceties. A similar juxtaposition between the allegedly traitorous but still honourable Launcelot and a less than commendable accuser occurs when Gawain turns against Launcelot after the latter inadvertently kills Gawain's brothers Gareth and Gaheris. Gawain furthers the division of the Round Table by inciting Arthur to declare war on Launcelot for the sake of his personal (yet legal) blood vengeance (1186.5–12). Moreover, after the ensuing confrontation with Launcelot, Arthur wishes to be reconciled with Launcelot and Guenevere, but Gawain prevents him: 'sir Gawayne made many men to blow uppon sir Launcelot, and so all at onys they called hym "false recrayed knyght"' (1190.20–2). Here Gawain exploits collective accusations of treason to generate the public legal situation that necessitates Arthur's continuation of the war against the ostensible traitor, despite Arthur's desire to preserve the unity of the realm and his awareness of Launcelot's good character. Launcelot remains devoted to Arthur, articulating the personal loyalty that he will honour even when Arthur declares war on him: 'I woll never se that moste noble kynge that made me knyght nother slayne nor shamed' (1192.17–19). With 'sir Gawayne evermore callyng hym "traytoure knyght"' (1221.9–10), Launcelot is forced to finally respond to his besiegers' attempts to induce him to fight; as Launcelot and his kin recognize, accusations of treason are the one assault on his reputation that cannot be endured passively. Yet Launcelot is again defamed only diegetically, while Gawain is defamed in the readers' world—because Launcelot acts for the right reasons (if with reprehensible results) and Gawain acts for the wrong reasons. Gawain's fracturing of the Arthurian kingdom for the sake of his dead brothers is aligned with Mordred and Agravain's earlier motivations by the mention of Gawain's 'evyll wyll' when he is fighting against Launcelot (1220.13). The Orkney clan, those who act out of hatred rather than loyalty even if they are ostensibly obeying king and law, are the real enemies of the community, although Arthurian legal institutions do not or cannot define them as traitors. Here, that is, the strident articulations of treason (those that, throughout most of the *Morte*, indict the accused), when uttered over and over by the ill-willed accusers, 'indict' the speakers instead—at least to the *Morte*'s readership.

Thus the treason discourse that Agravain and company voice so clamorously through the bedroom door articulates a tension between, on the one hand, institutional notions of treason that supposedly reward loyalty and punish disloyalty, and, on the other hand, an alternative evaluation of conduct based on intent. In the *Mort Artu*, no accusation of treason is vocalized here;[59] in the Stanzaic *Morte Arthur*, a source which Malory sometimes privileged over the former for the culminating narrative, Launcelot *is* accused of treason, but Agravain and Mordred do not attempt to convey their accusations to other ears than Launcelot's and Guenevere's.[60] The *Morte*, however, shows the accusers seeking to broadcast their accusations:

> sir Aggravayne and sir Mordred wyth twelve knyghtes... seyde
>   with grete cryyng and scaryng voyce,
> 'Thou traytoure, sir Launcelot, now ar thou takyn!'
> And thus they cryed wyth a lowde voyce, that all the courte
>   myght hyre hit. (1165.14–20)

Here Malory's Agravain and company effect a public appeal of treason that generates the need for a legal trial, and exhibit a focus on proclaiming the status of traitors that matches Wars of the Roses practice.[61] While Arthur feels compelled to punish Guenevere and declare Launcelot his enemy, he nonetheless perceives a different way of interpreting the situation: ' "alas, that ever sir Launcelot and I shulde be at debate! A, Aggravayne, Aggravayne!" seyde the kynge, " ... thyne evyll wyll that thou haddist and sir Mordred, thy brothir, unto sir Launcelot hath caused all this sorow" ' (1184.7–11). It is not that Arthur does not recognize Lancelot's actions as treasonous; on the contrary, he earlier declares them to be treason after Agravain and Mordred report the affair (1163.11–13). Rather, because the adultery has been publicized, Arthur seems constrained to act in accordance with the laws of his kingdom instead of what he would rather have done for the sake of unity.

Therefore, it is not only the Orkney clan, those who act out of ulterior and malevolent motives but cannot legally be termed 'traitors', but also institutionalized law itself that is revealed as the (potential) enemy of community. Both Kelly and Harris find it problematic that Malory transforms Guenevere's charge from that of 'adultery', as construed by his French sources, to 'treason', because English law does not support such a categorization of Guenevere's crime.[62] However, this alteration of terminology

---

[59] Harris, 'Treason by Imagination', p. 194; see *La Mort le Roi Artu*, ed. by Jean Frappier, 2nd edn (1936; Genève: Droz, 1954), pp. 115–16.

[60] Stanzaic *Morte Arthur*, lincs 1810–13.

[61] As when, for instance, Henry VI sought military support by sending privy seal letters in which the Yorkist lords are 'called opon traytours' (*English Chronicle 1377–1461*, p. 86.3); see Chapter 2 for further examples.

[62] According to the 1352 statute, to sleep *with* the queen was treason, but the queen's actions were not treasonous. Yet because Malory habitually transforms his sources' more diffuse signifiers for most disloyal and/or underhanded actions into 'treson', we cannot (as

constitutes Malory's method of bringing the case into the internal logic of the *Morte*'s discussions of treason. Both critics focus on Malory's '*creation* of a law' that sentences Guenevere to death, and emphasize Arthur's agency, and therefore his error, in applying this law to judge Guenevere.[63] However, the *Morte* in fact emphasizes the influence that the law exerts on Arthur, figuring him as compelled to act against the best interests of his realm by the dictates of institutionalized legal practices:

> So than there *was made* grete ordynaunce in thys ire, and the quene *muste nedis* be jouged to the deth. And the law *was such* in tho dayes that whatsomever they were, of what astate or degré, if they *were founden* gylty of treson there *shuld be* none other remedy but deth, and othir the menour other the takynge wyth the dede *shulde be causer* of their hasty jougement. And right so *was hit ordayned* for quene Gwenyver: bycause sir Mordred was ascaped sore wounded, and the dethe of thirtene knyghtes of the Rounde Table, thes previs and experyenses *caused* kynge Arthure to commaunde the quene to the fyre and there to be brente. (1174.19–29)

The italicized verbs express the actions of the law or of its evidence, or have no expressed agent. Thus this law constitutes a rhetorical bombardment of external, inhuman pressure that leaves Arthur no option but to condemn Guenevere. Malory accords much of the critical agency involved here to the law itself, rather than to Arthur, suggesting that the former is more problematic than the latter.

In Tale VIII, then, Malory continues to engage with legal frameworks for treason in order to critique and refashion them. Harris and Kelly observe that many elements of this case have fifteenth-century legal parameters: not only accusation, but also proof, procedure, legal arguments, the trial's 'appeals' (in the modern sense of the word), and the summary judgement that prevails despite Gawain's remonstrations.[64] By providing the audience with a particularly draconian version of the law of treason in this case where the accused arguably retains the most sympathy of any traitor in the *Morte*, Malory critiques the heartless and unhelpful institutionality of codified legal systems and the ill-motivated policing it fosters. Although the narrative requires the recognition of Launcelot and Guenevere's culpability, the narrator manifests a desire to blame Agravain, Mordred, and Gawain instead, and attempts to pass this desire on to the reader.[65] Here, however, the *Morte* also acknowledges

---

Kelly and Harris do) privilege the one source alteration that pertains to Guenevere as the sole site of connections between Malory's text and treason laws.

[63] Harris, 'Treason by Imagination', p. 180; emphasis mine.

[64] For instance, Harris, 'Treason by Imagination', pp. 186–9.

[65] C. David Benson, for instance, writes of the assault on Launcelot in Guenevere's bedchamber that 'Lancelot kills all except, *unfortunately*, Mordred' ('The Ending of the Morte Darthur', in *Companion to Malory*, pp. 221–38 (p. 230), emphasis mine): to direct

fears that resonate with contemporary anxieties concerning accusations of treason. As addressed in Chapter 2, Malory's contemporaries, such as Jack Cade's rebels (in 1450), expressed concern over the lack of protection against both traitors and (potentially unfounded) accusations of treason:

> they say that whom the kyng woll shall be traytur and whom he woll shall be non, and that apperyth hederto, for yf eny of the traytours about hym wolde malygne ageynst eny person, hyghe or low, they wolde fynd fals menys that he shuld dy a traytor.[66]

When even the great and admirable Launcelot and Guenevere can (like Richard of York) be denounced for treason, and by those who have the king's ear but may themselves be traitors, those of lesser standing have good cause to worry about their fates.

The *Morte* continues its attempts to avoid self-contradiction in sympathizing with Launcelot and Guenevere despite its stance against treason by contrasting the latter's regrettable but noble conduct not only with the evil will of the Orkney clan, but also with the crime committed when Mordred usurps the throne and levies war against King Arthur. In the case of Mordred's treason, 'ultimate' in both gravity and plot position, intentions and institutionalized law codes are aligned: he is culpable on both counts. Malory invents several passages of treason rhetoric to emphasize the wickedness of Mordred's actions and to denounce his contemporaries' complicity. When he is made regent while Arthur fights Launcelot in France, Mordred usurps the throne. He commits high treason by usurping Arthur's place and by raising troops and waging war on the king's person when Arthur returns. Levying war against the king had been high treason since Edward I's reign; when high-ranking rebels raised troops against the king, the abridged legal procedure of the monarch proclaiming that the offenders were guilty could serve 'as indictment, or appeal, and verdict all in one'.[67] Appropriately, then, Arthur voices the text's final pronouncement regarding Mordred before the latter's death, in a passage that seems both indictment and verdict concerning Mordred's conduct:

> 'Alas, that ever I shulde se thys doleful day! For now,' seyde kynge Arthur, 'I am com to myne ende. But wolde to God,' seyde he, 'that I wyste now where were *that traytoure sir Mordred that hath caused all thys myschyff*.'
>
> Than kynge Arthur loked aboute and was ware where stood sir Mordred leanyng uppon hys swerde amonge a grete hepe of dede men.

---

a death-wish at Mordred is to participate in the *Morte*'s desire to condemn the destroyers of community.

[66] 'A proclamation made by Jacke Cade, Capytayn of the Rebelles in Kent', in *Three Fifteenth-Century Chronicles*, pp. 94–9 (p. 96).

[67] Bellamy, *Law of Treason*, pp. 56–7.

'Now, gyff me my speare,' seyde kynge Arthure unto sir Lucan, 'for yonder
I have aspyed *the traytoure that all thys woo hath wrought.*' (1236.17–27)

This battlefield denunciation of Mordred has no parallel in Malory's
sources, but is reminiscent of parliamentary attainders such as the 1459
indictment of the Yorkist lords for having 'falsely and traiterously rered
werre ayenst' King Henry (XII.456) with 'the grettest falsenes and treason' (XII.460). Mordred's treason does not effect the downfall of Arthur's
kingdom alone, but it does constitute the worst betrayal of king and community in the narrative; it is consequently the most condemned, and the
most worrying, because it is so disastrously successful.

MALORY AND MORDRED IN CONTEXT

Fighting for Mordred: The Geopolitics of Literary Treason

In fifteenth-century insular Arthurian narratives, Mordred is both most
vilified and most validated: the former by Malory and the English chronicler John Hardyng, and the latter by a group of Scottish chroniclers. In part
because of the indistinct boundary between history and fiction, Mordred
occupies a position that is not only diegetic, but also fundamentally
extra-textual in didactic and political implications. This section addresses
the cultural work this literary traitor figure performs in explorations of
collective identities and codes of conduct for insular communities, focusing on the role of pragmatism in conditioning what it means to fight for
Mordred, or in what Mordred is seen to be fighting for. Mordred's actions
and their reprehensibility or commendability contribute to discourses
concerning which loyalties ought to be privileged and to whom and how
one can be treasonous, supporting the political affiliations and/or ethically didactic intentions of each text. Malory, Hardyng, and the Scottish
chroniclers manifest an instrumental idea of truth in their portrayals of
treason and Mordred's relationship to it. For Malory and Hardyng, this
idea of truth as contingent and useful is informed by a secularist attitude
towards how to ensure good government and a stable community.

Malory's Mordred

While in earlier Arthurian narratives Mordred is characteristically a villain, he becomes especially sinister in Malory's *Morte*. Malory deviates
from his sources to create a darker portrayal of Mordred. This blackening
of Mordred produces an unsettling view of the power of treason to destroy
stability, but also contributes to the *Morte*'s use of the rhetoric of treason

to endorse a more stable, loyal society than Malory witnessed during the Wars of the Roses.

Even in the cradle, Mordred is aligned with Judas. Malory's portrayal of Mordred's infancy follows the *Suite du Merlin*, but forgoes the *Suite's* narration of Mordred's upbringing and arrival at Arthur's court as a youth. Here part of Malory's independence from his sources lies—as it so often does—in a selective reshaping that emphasizes what Malory does not discard. To protect against the nemesis that Merlin prophesies will be among those born on May day, Arthur gathers together the infants,

> And all were putte in a shyppe to the se;…And so by fortune the shyppe drove unto a castelle, and was all to-ryven and destroyed the moste party, save that Mordred was cast up, and a good man founde hym, and fostird hym tylle he was fourtene yere of age, and than brought hym to the courte. (55.26–32)

In the *Suite*, Mordred is the sole survivor of a shipwreck (I.58) but the other infants, on a different ship, are all saved by 'Nostre Signour' (I.61). In the *Morte*, however, Mordred is the only infant to survive the collective shipwreck. Although Malory's reticence shrouds Arthur's motives, Arthur presumably sets the infants adrift. If he wilfully attempts to procure their deaths, Arthur's action echoes Herod's Massacre of the Innocents.[68] However, the shipwrecked Mordred also has a biblical parallel.[69] Caxton's *Golden Legend* contains a biography of Judas' early years that it labels as apocryphal, but nonetheless narrates.[70] Here Judas, much like Mordred, is set adrift because his parents fear he may destroy his people (III.55), is shipwrecked, and returns to slay his father (III.56–7). Through this or another text, or through diffused cultural knowledge, many of Malory's readers were likely aware of such a backstory for Judas.[71] Mordred's infancy,

---

[68] Archibald, 'Beginnings', p. 138; see also P. J. C. Field, 'Malory's Mordred and the *Morte Arthure*', in *Malory: Texts and Sources*, Arthurian Studies, XL (Cambridge: Brewer, 1998), pp. 89–102.

[69] Archibald, 'Arthur and Mordred: Variations on an Incest Theme', in *Arthurian Literature VIII*, ed. by Richard Barber (Cambridge: Brewer, 1989), pp. 1–27 (pp. 15–18); Cooper, *English Romance*, pp. 375–7.

[70] William Caxton, *The Golden Legend, or Lives of the Saints*, ed. by F. S. Ellis, 7 vols (London: J. M. Dent, 1900), III, 54. The *Legenda aurea* was compiled *c*.1275 by Jacobus de Voragine, Archbishop of Genoa; Caxton's translation, printed in 1483, was based on a French incunable.

[71] The *Legenda aurea* was frequently reprinted between 1470 and 1530, in both vernaculars and Latin; over 800 manuscripts survive of the Latin *Legenda aurea*, and there were well-known French translations as well as an anonymous English prose translation from *c*.1438: Sherry L. Reames, *The 'Legenda aurea': A Reexamination of its Paradoxical History* (Madison: University of Wisconsin Press, 1985), p. 4. In some of the other prose romances printed by Caxton, such as his Charlemagne romances, vile traitors are likened to Judas with some frequency, indicating a cultural shorthand of characterizing a figure's actions as thoroughly reprehensible by association with Judas (see Chapter 5).

and thus Mordred's association with Judas, is all that Malory selected from Mordred's early history, and it stands in greater relief as the only detail of Mordred's childhood mentioned.

As well as these elisions, Malory elsewhere makes additions that likewise heighten Mordred's iniquity. As is well known, Malory has Mordred participate in crimes such as the murder of Lamorak, which Gawain alone commits in other versions, inventing the cowardly blow from behind with which Mordred slays Lamorak (699.25–6).[72] Malory also makes Mordred Agravain's accomplice in the exposure of Launcelot and Guenevere at the beginning of Tale VIII, thereby making Mordred partly responsible for exposing and widening the fractures in Arthur's community. In both the *Mort Artu* and the Stanzaic *Morte*, by contrast, this agency is attributed solely to Agravain.[73]

Less attention has been paid to other changes that Malory makes to attribute immoral and destructive actions to Mordred's agency. In the Stanzaic *Morte*, when Arthur is preparing to wage war on Lancelot, he asks his knights who ought to be regent. They reply that 'Mordred the sekerest was / . . . To save the reme in trews and pees' (2518–20): here Mordred has the admiration and confidence of his peers.[74] In the *Mort Artu*, Arthur does not ask his councillors' advice, but when Mordred suggests himself, Arthur 'dist que il velt bien que il remaigne et que il la gart' (166; 'said that he wished well that he [Mordred] remain and that he guard the queen'). However, in Malory's description of Arthur making Mordred his deputy, no one expresses trust or respect for Mordred. Arthur's choice of Mordred is instead configured as an obligation induced by blood relationship: 'bycause Sir Mordred was kynge Arthurs son, he gaff hym the rule off hys londe and off hys wyff' (1211.10–11). This motivation is unique to the *Morte*.[75] By stressing that Mordred is Arthur's son, Malory does give Mordred a plausible claim to regency; however, his emphasis is then on how Mordred treacherously exploits this claim.

---

[72] Vinaver, *Commentary*, p. 1513. Mordred and Agravain also murder Dinadan (615.5–7); this is not unique to the *Morte*, but Malory's Dinadan is a more sympathetic character than in other versions.

[73] Vinaver, *Commentary*, p. 1629.

[74] In the Alliterative *Morte*, the idea of Mordred as a trustworthy figure is also stressed. While Malory did not follow the Alliterative *Morte* in Tale VIII, his use of the Alliterative *Morte*'s Roman War section would have made him familiar with its account of how Mordred is chosen as deputy—with Arthur's lords' tacit assent (644–6). Furthermore, Mordred does not want the power when it is offered to him: he says to Arthur, 'I beseek you, sir, as my sib lord, / That ye will for charitee chese you another' and 'To pass in your presence my purpose is taken': Alliterative *Morte Arthure*, in *King Arthur's Death*, lines 681–2 and 687. Malory chose not to espouse this model of an honorable Mordred.

[75] Vinaver, *Commentary*, p. 1643.

Malory's version of the usurpation again presents Mordred's actions as appreciably more reprehensible than in the Stanzaic *Morte* and the *Mort Artu*. In all three versions, Mordred forges letters from France proclaiming Arthur's death and then becomes king, but his methods of doing so differ. The *Mort Artu* states that Mordred reminds the barons that Arthur named him as successor (149), and the barons

> trouverent *en leur conseill* qu'*il feroient de Mordret roi* et li donroient la reïne a fame et deviendroient si home lige; si le devoient fere por deus choses: l'une, por ce que li rois Artus les en avoit proiés; l'autre, por ce qu'il ne veoient entr'ex home qui si bien fust digne de tele enneur comme il estoit. (173)
>
> (found *by their counsel* that *they would make Mordred king* and would give him the queen as his wife and would become his liege men. And [they said] they should do it for two reasons: the one, because king Arthur had requested it of them; and the other, because they did not see among them a man who was as worthy of such an honour as he [Mordred] was.)

Here the barons believe it is their duty to Arthur to make Mordred king; however, they also show respect for Mordred and his claim to the throne. The Stanzaic *Morte* likewise shows Mordred chosen as king by a group acting voluntarily:

> Mordred let cry a parlement;
> The peple gan thider to come,
> And *holly through their assent*
> *They made Mordred king* with crown. (2978–81)

However, Malory's corresponding passage reads: 'sir Mordred made a parlemente, and called the lordys togydir, and there *he made them* to chose hym kynge' (1227.4–6). Malory's choice of 'lordys' rather than 'peple' favours the French over the Stanzaic version; more importantly, however, Malory deviates from both sources in order to more effectively emphasize Mordred's sinister agency. In Malory's version, it is neither the people's nor the lords' choice, but rather Mordred's treasonous compulsion, that results in his kingship.[76] Malory removes ambiguity from Mordred's actions and

---

[76] This pointed difference between Malory and his sources is not addressed in Vinaver's notes (revised by Field), which discuss only parallels between the Stanzaic *Morte* and Malory's *Morte* (*Commentary*, p. 1646); parallels between Malory's representation of Mordred in Tale VIII and his sources are similarly the sole focus in Peter Korrel, *An Arthurian Triangle: A Study of the Origin, Development and Characterization of Arthur, Guinevere and Mordred* (Leiden: Brill, 1984), p. 278. Cherewatuk does discuss Malory's manipulation of his sources to depict a more villainous Mordred, but focuses on incest rather than treason (*Marriage, Adultery, and Inheritance*, pp. 110–11 and 117–26). Ellis, on the other hand, expresses the surprising opinion that Malory 'dilutes Mordred's *traditional* faults' ('Balin', p. 71, emphasis mine). While Ellis posits a '*traditionally* nefarious Mordred' from which, in her view, Malory's representation of the figure departs (p. 71, emphasis mine), the notion of a 'traditional' Mordred who is more despicable than Malory's is not

presents him as the dark background against which other characters are sympathetically defined, and in connection with whom Malory's contemporaries are castigated.

In the final battle, Mordred alone, as the incarnation of treason, momentarily embodies all culpability by assaulting and destroying King Arthur, the sacred transcendental signifier without which the realm cannot survive. That treason can effect such a disastrous outcome realizes the fears of a society caught in a civil war, as Malory's is. Mordred dies too, but treason certainly does not die with him; Malory represents treason as a deplorable phenomenon still present in his readers' world, where it ought to be censured and avoided. Malory's blackening of Mordred makes the *Morte*'s urgings against treason all the more instructive (and unsettling) when Malory associates his contemporaries with Mordred and his supporters, with the treacherous and inconstant. When discussing Mordred's recruiting of voluntary troops and thus English complicity in Mordred's perfidy, Malory directly addresses his contemporaries in a rare authorial intervention (not found in his sources), accusing them of committing the same offence:

> Lo ye all Englysshemen, se ye nat what a myschyff here was? For he that was the moste kynge and nobelyst knyght of the worlde, and moste loved the felyshyp of noble knyghtes, and by hym they all were upholdyn, and yet myght nat thes Englysshemen holde them contente with hym. Lo thus was the olde custom and usayges of thys londe, and men say that we of thys londe have nat yet loste that custom. Alas! thys ys a greate defaughte of us Englysshemen, for there may no thynge us please no terme. (1229.6–14)

Rebellions against the current king(s) were, of course, familiar for Wars of the Roses readers; in this passage, Malory explicitly links the shifting allegiances in Arthurian Britain to the contemporary civil war.[77] In observing that 'the moste party of all Inglonde hylde wyth sir Mordred, for the people were so new-fangill' (1229.21–3), Malory emphasizes that it is not enough to locate and punish the single most vile manifestation of the abhorrent tendencies of which many are guilty. Deploring the continuation of 'the olde custom and usayges of thys londe', Malory castigates his contemporaries for colluding with treason and laments its inescapable presence. The treason discourse earlier diegetically contained in utterances between or concerning characters is here directed outwards towards Malory's society. On a symbolic level, Mordred signifies the contagion within the English

---

tenable except by considering Arthurian narratives that *post*date Malory, often themselves drawing upon Malory's version.

[77] Field, 'Fifteenth-Century History in Malory's *Morte Darthur*', in *Malory: Texts and Sources*, pp. 47–71.

people to whom Malory addresses his corrective admonitory exhortation; as the extimate or intimate other, Mordred can neither be accepted nor effaced.

Scottish Mordreds

Some Scottish texts similary put Mordred to use, for an equally pragmatic purpose though from a very different perspective. Most of the Scottish chroniclers from the late fourteenth century until the early sixteenth present *Arthur* as having usurped *Mordred's* rightful place, rather than the other way around.[78] These chronicles state that Arthur is illegitimate and therefore an usurper; that Mordred, displacing Gawain as the eldest legitimate son of King Lot of Lothian and his wife Anna (Arthur's legitimate half-sister), is the rightful heir to the British crown. First extant in John of Fordun's Latin *Chronica gentis Scotorum* (1380s) and copied by later chronicles such as Walter Bower's popular *Scotichronicon* (1440s), this rewriting of the Arthur–Mordred narrative legitimizes not only Mordred, but also Scottish claims to independence from their southern neighbours.[79] Fordun and Bower stress that Arthur was conceived when Igraine's first husband was still alive, and therefore barred from the succession as a child of adultery;[80] moreover, these chroniclers are at pains to lay out the pedigree through which Mordred, patrilineally a Scot, ought to have been king instead of Arthur. This reads as a reaction against English deployments of Arthur for political purposes, since, from 1301 onwards, one of the English arguments for overlordship of Scotland was the precedent of Arthur's authority over the whole island.[81]

---

[78] An exception is Andrew of Wyntoun (*c.*1408–20), who supports Arthur against Mordred in line with the Galfridian tradition: *The Original Chronicle of Andrew of Wyntoun*, ed. by F. J. Amours, 6 vols (Edinburgh: Blackwood, 1903–14), IV, 24. See Flora Alexander, 'Late Medieval Scottish Attitudes to the Figure of King Arthur: A Reassessment', *Anglia*, 93 (1975), 17–34, revising Robert Huntington Fletcher, *The Arthurian Material in the Chronicles* (Boston: Ginn, 1906); Cooper, 'Counter-Romance', p. 151. In the sixteenth century, accounts of Arthur, such as in Hector Boece's *Scotorum historiae* (1527), become yet more antagonistic.

[79] *Johannis de Fordun chronica gentis Scotorum*, ed. by William F. Skene (Edinburgh: Edmonston and Douglas, 1871), pp. 109–12; Walter Bower, *Scotichronicon*, ed. by D. E. R. Watt, 9 vols (Aberdeen: Aberdeen University Press, 1993). Bower first writes that Anna is Arthur's aunt (II.64), but later states the more common view that she is Arthur's sister (II.66).

[80] Malory, by contrast, specifies (unlike his source) that Arthur was conceived three hours after Gorlois' death, and is therefore *not* illegitimate (18.1–7).

[81] Ralph Hanna, *London Literature, 1300–1380*, Cambridge Studies in Medieval Literature, LVII (Cambridge: Cambridge University Press, 2005), pp. 90–1; Alexander, 'Scottish Attitudes to King Arthur'; Nicola Royan, 'The Fine Art of Faint Praise in Older Scots Historiography', in *The Scots and Medieval Arthurian Legend*, pp. 43–54.

These Scottish chronicles, by explaining and defending Mordred's right to the British throne, fight for Mordred and for Scotland intertextually and geopolitically. The *Scottis Originale* (*c*.1460s), a vernacular rendition of the Fordun tradition, explicitly relates Arthurian politics to contemporary Anglo-Scottish relations. Declaring that 'arthur þat tyrand maid weir on *ws* aganis his faith and promyss', the anonymous chronicle speaks as though for all Scots.[82] This diachronic community is reiterated in another comment on Arthur's perfidy to the Scots and to Mordred alike: 'Falslie he brak his allia *till ws* and maid weire *on ws* a quhile and tuke to him fra þe richtuiss aire The crovne of brettane That Is to say fra mordred' (190). This collective first-person pronoun associates the writer and readers of the chronicle with those who fought against Arthur: 'þis arthour had falsly vsurpit þe crovne of brettane ... Than callit he in helpe of þe falss saxonis ... nochtwithstanding *we* put þaim furth scharply' (191). In its account of the final reckoning, the *Scottis Originale* reiterates Mordred's rights:

> mordred ... gadderit all þe estatis and scottis men to londoun & schew þaim his richt and þar awysitly *þe brettonnis chesit him king* and crovnit him Incontinent and *in his richtuiss querell & defence* he slewe þis arthoure and arthure him. (190)

The statement that 'þe brettonnis *chesit* him [Mordred] king' would not be out of place in, say, the Stanzaic *Morte*; however, the *Scottis Originale*'s construal of the event as the Britons' *choice* certainly clashes with Malory's version of Mordred's 'usurpation' in which Mordred *compels* the lords to make him king (as discussed above). According to Fordun and Bower, in Arthur's time, Stirling and the Firth of Forth constitute the boundaries between Britain and Scotland,[83] and Scotland has its own king, who is *not* subject to the British king; it is to the Scottish king that Mordred, rightful king of the Britons through his mother, owes his primary allegiance as the son of the Scottish sub-king Lot. Thus the Scottish chronicles are at pains to show that Mordred's half-Scottishness ought not to have hindered him from taking his rightful place as king of Britain.

A wrongful Arthur and a rightful Mordred were instrumental to defining the Scots as just and honourable and the English as traitorous. The *Scottis Originale* specifies that an Anglo-Scottish 'allia was lang tyme weile consseruit & kepit vnto þe tyme þis arthur brak It' (191), thereby blaming

[82] 'The Scottis Originale', in *The Asloan Manuscript*, ed. by W. A. Craigie, 2 vols (Edinburgh: Blackwood, 1923), I, 185–96 (p. 189).

[83] Steve Boardman, 'Late Medieval Scotland and the Matter of Britain', in *Scottish History: The Power of the Past*, ed. by Edward J. Cowan and Richard J. Finlay (Edinburgh: Edinburgh University Press, 2002), pp. 47–72 (pp. 54–6).

the English for any hostilities thereafter. Whether due to different recensions or to the difference between the Anglo-Scottish rapprochement of the 1460s–1470s and the aftermath of the battle of Flodden (1513), the version of the *Scottis Originale* thus far quoted, produced after 1513, emphasizes English perfidy more strongly than the *c*.1460s version.[84] However, both versions contain the following generalization about English perfidy:

> *This is the nature of Inglismen* quhar ever thai mak straytest oblissing of faith and pes, thai dissave thame ereft...with fenȝeit falsehede and false colouris. And *this did thai ever till us all tymes bygane*, bot that suld thai nocht have done and thai had been trew.[85]

The Scottish chronicles eschew the idea of Trojan ancestry for the Scots because the Trojans were associated with the English, and they use this association to portray the English as traitors in their origins as well as in their present cross-border relations. The *Scottis Originale*, for instance, states that it is 'nocht trew...þat we come of brute quhilk come of tratouris of troye' (185). An alternative ancestry, originating in the thirteenth century or earlier and redeployed in the Fordun tradition to counteract English claims that the Scots were descended from Arthur's subjects, posits Scottish descent from a Greek prince, Gathelos, and his wife Scota, the daughter of an Egyptian pharaoh, who founded Scotland before the fall of Troy.[86] The *Scottis Originale* is thus able to point out that the Greeks were 'þe mast worschipfull nacioun' while the English 'ar succedit of þam þat bure & beris þe foull surname of þe tresoun of troye' (186). Thus here, as when dealing specifically with Mordred, these Scottish chroniclers use the rhetoric of treason to respond to the Arthurian legend in ways that define the Scots as righteous and the English as traitors.

The English and Scottish treatments of Arthur and Mordred were, of course, produced in different sociopolitical circumstances. Sharing similar institutional understandings of the nature of treason, what the English and the Scottish *could* agree on was that traitors were to be abhorred, punished, and ideally forestalled.[87] Yet while Scotland did experience rebellions such as that which resulted in James I's death in 1437, fifteenth-century

---

[84]   Royan, 'Older Scots Historiography', pp. 49–50.
[85]   'The Cronycle of Scotland in a Part', in *The Bannatyne Miscellany*, 3 vols, ed. by W. Scott and others (Edinburgh: Ballantyne, 1855), III, 35–42 (p. 42)—Dalhousie version; cf. *Asloan*, p. 195.
[86]   See, for example, Bower, *Scotichronicon*, vol. 1, Book I, Chapters 9–17; and, for discussion, Boardman, 'Late Medieval Scotland and the Matter of Britain', p. 49; Juliette Wood, 'Where Does Britain End? The Reception of Geoffrey of Monmouth in Scotland and Wales', in *The Scots and Medieval Arthurian Legend*, pp. 9–23 (p. 14).
[87]   The English and the Scottish laws of treason agreed in principle and outline. For the definitions of high treason, see the English 1352 Statute of Treason (discussed in Chapter 2 above), and the Acts of Parliament of James I: 'Acta Parliamentorum Regis Jacobi Primi,

Scotland worried less about dynastic wars than about English aggression;[88] accordingly, the Scottish chronicles' use of Arthurian material shows an interest in condemning treason from the outside. Malory, by contrast, writing during the Wars of the Roses, focuses on combatting treason from within. The Scots (like the Cornish) are a semi-separate people in the *Morte*, but are within the proto-English polity in Malory's conception of the whole island as Arthur's kingdom; Malory's Scottish Mordred commits *hierarchical* treason in fighting against Arthur. Yet in the Scottish pro-Mordred chronicles, while Arthur does perhaps commit hierarchical treason in fighting against the rightful king, Mordred, more attention is devoted to how Arthur breaks his promises and alliances with 'us', with the Scots as a whole, as *horizontal* treason. The pro-Mordred Scottish chronicles, while not the only Scottish view on the Arthurian legend or on the possibility of Trojan ancestry for the Scots, were central enough to provide the standard history of Scotland throughout the fifteenth century and into the sixteenth.[89] In their deployments of Mordred, contradicting a portion of the Galfridian history that they otherwise espouse in order to pursue pragmatic community formation, these Scottish chronicles are the mirror images of Malory's *Morte* and Hardyng's *Chronicle*.

Truth, Treason, and Secular Pragmatism in the Fifteenth Century

Like the Scottish chronicles, John Hardyng's *Chronicle* and Malory's *Morte* configure Mordred and Arthur in a manner that supports commentaries on treason and on Anglo-Scottish relations. In their portrayals of Mordred, Malory and Hardyng (and Fordun and his followers) espouse an ideology of pragmatism: an understanding of truth and treason as instrumental, as contingent and malleable. Each text makes use of discourses of treason and renegotiates attitudes towards literary traitors to construct, and instruct about, contemporary insular identities.[90] In discussing Scottish

---

19 January 1449', in *The Acts of the Parliaments of Scotland*, 1124–1707, ed. by C. Innes, 12 vols (Edinburgh: 1814–75), II (1424–1567), p. 35; cf. the 1424 parliament, p. 3.

[88]   Roger Mason suggests that this is because Scotland had already suffered dynastic wars in the early fourteenth-century struggle between Bruce and Balliol: 'Kingship, Tyranny and the Right to Resist in Fifteenth Century Scotland', *Scottish Historical Review*, 66.2 (1987), 125–51 (p. 143). Moreover, fifteenth-century Scotland, unlike England, always had an heir apparent.

[89]   Boardman, 'Late Medieval Scotland and the Matter of Britain', pp. 47–8 and 53–5; Mason, 'Fifteenth Century Scotland', pp. 146–7.

[90]   Unsurprisingly, something closer to Geoffrey of Monmouth's version is deployed for the 'historical' purposes of the Scottish chronicles and Hardyng's *Chronicle*, while Malory shows that 'romance' traitors can, of course, have 'historical' or political resonance too. As Richard Firth Green writes, 'there is little doubt that the numerous "histories" of Troy, Thebes

traitorousness, Hardyng's *Chronicle* is more explicit, yet not necessarily more determined to show the evils of insular division, than is the *Morte*. The laments concerning treason in Hardyng's *Chronicle* and Malory's *Morte* exhibit a shared secular world view that oscillates between a failure to find a satisfactory response to treason and a suggestion of a more hopeful sort of response.

Hardyng presented the first version of his *Chronicle*, narrating events to 1437 with a Lancastrian bias, to Henry VI in 1457; however, failing to obtain sufficient remuneration, Hardyng reworked his *Chronicle* for Richard of York, and finally presented it to Edward IV *c.*1464.[91] This second version extends the chronicle to Henry VI's flight to Scotland in 1461. Hardyng expresses anti-Scottish views in both versions, for instance in the second version's epilogue. Here Hardyng advises Edward IV to recapture Henry VI from Scotland if at all possible, because Henry is more of a threat when among the Scots, who 'wyll ay do you the harme they may'.[92] Hardyng further cautions Edward to be aware that the Scots are inherently treacherous:

> Ye shall neuer fynde the Scottes vnto you trewe,
> Where they maye with youre enemies ay beleuen,
> They wyll to you then alwaye be vntrewe,
> …
> Truste neuer truth in them ne perfeccyon. (414)

In the light of Hardyng's aim of urging English overlordship of Scotland, it is not difficult to see his vilification of Mordred as a contribution to his view of the inherent treachery of the Scots. In order to remove the taint of incest from Arthur, Hardyng makes Mordred, with Gawain, the legitimate offspring of King Lot of Lothian and Uther's daughter Anna (120); however, since Gawain is the eldest son, Mordred has no claim to the throne of Lothian, let alone of Britain (137). Like Malory, Hardyng vilifies Mordred as an arch-traitor for his usurpation of the British throne.[93]

---

and Alexander, or even of Arthur…were read largely as sober, factual accounts' (*Poets and Princepleasers: Literature and the English Court in the Late Middle Ages* (Toronto: University of Toronto Press, 1980), pp. 136–7). Since fifteenth-century readers did not perceive a boundary between history and fiction, we need not do so either.

[91] C. L. Kingsford, 'The First Version of Hardyng's Chronicle', *English Historical Review*, 27 (1912), 462–82. Hardyng may never have finished revising the second version of his *Chronicle*; surviving manuscripts do not provide evidence of a stable form of the text: A. S. G. Edwards, 'The Manuscripts and Texts of the Second Version of John Hardyng's Chronicle', in *England in the Fifteenth Century: Proceedings of the 1986 Harlaxton Symposium*, ed. by Daniel Williams (Woodbridge: Boydell, 1987), pp. 75–84 (p. 83).

[92] *The Chronicle of Iohn Hardyng*, ed. by Henry Ellis (London: Rivington, 1812), p. 410.

[93] Hardyng's Mordred usurps when Arthur is warring against Rome (145), not, as in the *Morte*, against Lancelot; this again serves Hardyng's agenda of purifying the Arthurian story.

Malory calls Mordred 'unhappy' in the sense of 'doomed to misfortune';[94] what is less well appreciated is that Hardyng does so too:

> O Mordred,
> ...
> What *vnhappe* thy manly ghost hath moued,
> Vnto so foule and cruell hardynesse,
> So many to be slayn through thyn *vnhappynes*. (149)[95]

Arther hastens home to confront Mordred, 'that sire / That trayterously agayn hym did conspire' (145). Hardyng accuses Mordred further:

> That great falshode thy prowesse did appall,
> As soone as in the entred periurie,
> By consequens treason and traitourie,
> Thy lorde and eme and also thy kyng souerayn,
> So to betraye thy felowes eke certayne. (Ellis, p. 149;
> Lansdowne 204, f.87r)

Malory similarly highlights the Scottish role in undermining English/ Arthurian unity (as discussed in the first half of this chapter), especially by giving Mordred and Agravain's companions in the assault on Launcelot in Guenevere's bedchamber names that belonged, in earlier romances, to specifically Scottish knights.[96]

However, for both Hardyng and Malory, traitors such as Mordred serve as a means not only for condemning transgressive behaviour, but also for worrying about, and interrogating, a lack of providence. Hardyng's and Malory's texts both manifest an ideology of secular pragmatism in their treatments of treason, which is especially interesting because Hardyng's *Chronicle* is one of Malory's minor sources.[97] After Arthur and Mordred kill each other in the final battle (146), Hardyng laments:

> O good Lorde God, suche treason & vnrightes,
> Why suffred thy deuyne omnipotente,
> That of theim had precience and forsightes,

[94] Cooper, 'Counter-Romance', p. 154; Beverly Kennedy, *Knighthood in the Morte Darthur*, pp. 233–4 (though we need not follow Kennedy to her conclusion that Malory's 'hap' and 'unhap' imply a providential order).

[95] Also in the first version of Hardyng's *Chronicle*: British Library, MS Lansdowne 204, f.87r. This passage is mentioned, but with different emphases, in Beverly Kennedy, *Knighthood in the Morte Darthur*, p. 335.

[96] Rushton, 'Of an uncouthe stede'. However, the only people whom Malory specifically lists as fighting for Mordred in the final battle are English (1233.5–7), a detail not found in Malory's sources. Further, 'muche people' among 'all the baronny of thys londe' (1228.34) fight for Mordred, though where the boundaries of 'thys londe' lie—whether between or encompassing insular peoples—we are left to speculate.

[97] Malory drew upon a version of Hardyng's *Chronicle* early in the composition of the *Morte*, and towards the end: Edward Donald Kennedy, 'Malory's Use of Hardyng's

That myght haue lette that cursed violence
Of Mordredes pryde, and all his insolence,
That noble kyng forpassyng conqueroure,
So to destroye *by treason and* erroure. (148)[98]

This is a lament for the lack of providence, for the way in which there is no insurance that the righteous prosper and traitors fail, at least as much as it is a lament for Arthur himself. Here Hardyng acknowledges the failure of a providential world view to account for the success of treasons such as those that plagued contemporary England; yet he also expresses pragmatism through this secularism. In casting doubts on providence, Hardyng suggests that solutions must be sought in societal self-regulation—in positive, rather than natural, law.[99] Malory does the same. The *Morte* manifests a form of disillusionment about divine intervention when King Mark wins a trial by battle for treason 'by mysadventure' (592.25): Mark is the traitor and his opponent Sir Amant is his just accuser. After Mark's victory,

two maydyns cryed alowde, that all the courte myght hyre, and seyde,
'A, swete Jesu that knowyste all hydde thynges! Why sufferyst Thou so false
a traytoure to venqueyshe and sle a trewe knyght that faught in a ryghteuous
quarell!' (593.9–13)

Chronicle', *N&Q*, 16.5 (1969), 167–70, 'John Hardyng and the Holy Grail', in *Arthurian Literature VIII*, ed. by Richard Barber (Cambridge: Brewer, 1989), pp. 185–206, and 'Malory and his English Sources', in *Aspects of Malory*, pp. 27–55; Robert H. Wilson, 'More Borrowings by Malory from Hardyng's Chronicle', *N&Q*, 17.6 (1970), 208–10; P. J. C. Field, 'Malory's Minor Sources', *N&Q*, 26.2 (1979), 107–10; Norris, *Malory's Library*. These studies focus on similarities in Arthur's crowning as Roman emperor and the Grail quest, and on similarities of place names and phrasing; however, they do not address the affinities in representations of treason. Comparatively little attention has been devoted to the ways in which Hardyng's *Chronicle* and Malory's *Morte* share not just some material, but also certain ideological attitudes; see, however, Sarah L. Peverley, 'Political Consciousness and the Literary Mind in Late Medieval England: Men "Brought up of Nought" in Vale, Hardyng, *Mankind*, and Malory', *Studies in Philology*, 105.1 (2008), 1–29. Further attitudes shared by Malory's and Hardyng's texts, which will be addressed here, include those invested in calling Mordred 'unhappy' and dwelling upon the vileness of his treason, and in lamenting providence's failure to ensure that right prevails against treason.

[98] Treason is a focus of both versions of the *Chronicle*; however, following Edward IV's seizure of the throne, the second version (12,500 lines rather than the earlier version's 17,000) dwells upon treason slightly more: we see this when, in the last line of this stanza, the first version's '*and waste thrugh his* error' (Lansdowne 204, f.87r) is changed to '*by treason and* erroure'. For a complementary view of Hardyng's composition as influenced by the Wars of the Roses, see Felicity Riddy, 'John Hardyng's Chronicle and the Wars of the Roses', in *Arthurian Literature XII*, ed. by James P. Carley and Felicity Riddy (Cambridge: Brewer, 1993), pp. 91–108.

[99] Hardyng's focus is again this-worldly when detailing the punishment that English traitors should receive: those who had rebelled against Henry IV 'on them selfes the hurte and all the anoye / Ay fell at ende that honged were and heded / As traytours ought to bene in euery stede' (371). Elsewhere, Hardyng similarly exhorts his intended (Yorkist) reader,

This plaint goes unanswered and unaddressed in the narrative. While this episode and lament were inherited from Malory's source (the *Roman de Tristan*), such disturbing failures of providence acquire different implications within the context of the rest of the *Morte* and when directed towards a Wars of the Roses readership, especially in connection with Malorian passages *not* found in his sources.[100] For instance, when his kingdom is beginning to fall apart, Arthur does not want to let Launcelot defend Guenevere's honour in a trial by battle: Gawain tells Arthur,

> 'as for sir Launcelot, I dare say he woll make hit good uppon ony knyght lyvyng that woll put uppon hym vylany or shame, and in lyke wyse he woll make good for my lady the quene.'
>
> 'That I believe well,' seyde kynge Arthur, 'but I woll nat that way worke with sir Launcelot, for he trustyth so much uppon hys hondis and hys myght that he doutyth no man. And therefore for my quene he shall nevermore fyght, for she shall have the law.' (1175.15–23)

Arthur fears Launcelot would win a trial by combat solely through physical prowess regardless of guilt or innocence, and he is determined that Guenevere shall be subject to 'the law' instead. Significantly, this expression of Arthur's disillusionment with trial by combat is unique to Malory.[101] Here, a gap has opened up for Arthur between trial by combat and law, which had once been perceived to be the same. Trial by combat was supposed to produce a just result through divine intervention; Arthur here recognizes that not divine intervention, but rather Launcelot's military prowess, dictates the outcome of any trial by combat in which he participates, bespeaking a wider doubt about the system of trial by combat and divine intervention as a whole.[102]

This view of the ineffectiveness of providence in ensuring that right prevails is shared not only between Malory's *Morte* and Hardyng's *Chronicle*, but also with texts such as the prose *Thebes* and *Troy* (as discussed in

---

'Good lorde when ye be set well vnder crowne, / With treytours and misruled ryatours / Dispence right so with all suche absolucyon, / And lette hym seke no other correctours, / But maynteyne theim your lawes gouernours; / And ouer all thyng be ye the chefe Iustyce, / To kepe the peace, that no false you suppryse' (94).

[100] On other aspects of the *Morte*'s troubled relationship to providence, see Batt, *Malory's 'Morte Darthur': Remaking Arthurian Tradition*, pp. 53–63.

[101] Gawain opposes Arthur in the *Mort Artu* (p. 121) and the Stanzaic *Morte* (lines 1920–41), but neither expresses anything of this sort. Vinaver remarks upon Malory's additions only in terms of how they highlight 'Gawain's affection for Lancelot and his sense of loyalty' (*Commentary*, p. 1633).

[102] For a positive view of the role of trial by combat in the *Morte*, see Beverly Kennedy, *Knighthood in the Morte Darthur*, pp. 39–47; for a more sceptical, thorough overview, see Jacqueline Stuhmiller, 'Iudicium Dei, iudicium fortunae: Trial by Combat in Malory's *Le Morte Darthur*', *Speculum*, 81 (2006), 427–62.

Chapter 3), likely also produced in the 1450s or 1460s.[103] This attitude contrasts not only with the 1420s Lydgatean sources for the prose *Thebes* and *Troy*, but also with Lydgate's 1430s work, the *Fall of Princes*. While Lydgate's Arthur section in the *Fall of Princes*—which Hardyng knew and may have used[104]—does discuss and condemn treason (as addressed in Chapter 3), it certainly does not set a precedent for Hardyng's and Malory's lament for a lack of providence; in fact, quite the opposite. In Lydgate's version of the Round Table oath, the emphasis is not, as in Malory's, on (fleeing) treason, but on being wedded to truth:

> bi ther ordre thei bounde wer of trouthe,
> Be assuraunce & be oth Isworn. (VIII.2829–30)

Lydgate further stresses the stability and accessibility of (the Arthurian world's) truth through faith in the justice of trial by combat—and therefore in providence as guarantor for the justice of trial by combat:

> In that court what kniht was requerid,
> *In the diffence of trouthe and equite,*
> Falshod excludid and duplicite,
> Shal ay be reedi to susteene that partie,
> His lyff, his bodi to putte in iupartie.
> Thus in Breteyne shon the cleere liht
> Of cheualrye and of hih prowesse. (VIII.2844–51)

Here Lydgate's poem shows faith in truth (and troth) as stable, and faith in trial by combat as a way of accessing truth. A few decades later, however, Malory and his contemporaries knew and were increasingly beginning to write about the fact that it was not enough to place all of one's faith in the supposed role of the king in generating stability, let alone in divine providence.[105] Lancastrian and Yorkist chroniclers tended to attribute the fortunes of Richard II and subsequent superseded monarchs to

---

[103] For Hardyng's *Chronicle* as for the *Morte* and the prose *Thebes* and *Troy*, contemporary readers probably included gentry and merchants as well as the aristocracy: Edwards, 'The Second Version of John Hardyng's *Chronicle*', p. 78.

[104] Edwards, 'Influence', p. 436.

[105] This contrast between early and mid-fifteenth century is especially apparent in how Lydgate, even when querying God on the subject of divine providence, maintains his emphasis on 'the inevitability of retribution' (Pearsall, *John Lydgate*, p. 141). When, in *Troy Book*, Agamemnon is murdered, Lydgate asks: 'O myȝti God, . . . / Whi wiltow nat of equite and riȝt / Punishe & chastise so horrible a þing' (*Troy Book*, V.1046–9). Lydgate, however, uses this question as a means to request, and expect, that God will 'Suffre non swiche to live vp-on þe grounde' (V.1059), again placing the emphasis on providence while the later texts leave their lament bleakly unanswered and focus instead on this-worldly means of regulating treason.

providential punishment for their sin;[106] denigrating such predecessors meant that they could be figured as deserving of the treasons by which they had been overcome. This chronicle trend shows the importance of providence to the propagandist aims of some fifteenth-century writers, but also highlights contemporary romanciers' decisions *not* to write within a providential frame. When these romanciers wrote about Arthur, Troy, Thebes, and Melusine, and when Hardyng chronicled the reign of Arthur, the geographical and/or historical remove from current politics perhaps freed them from the need to speak of providence to show support for the current regime. Accordingly, the romanciers' ideological stance may be closer to wider contemporary mentalities in the way that they are more fully able to acknowledge anxieties about a lack of closure or fitting repercussions in response to acts of treason—anxieties that are also expressed in correspondence and other occasional texts, as addressed in Chapter 2.

Moreover, it is not only in relation to distant settings that mid- to late fifteenth-century writers interrogated providence. The polemical *Somnium vigilantis* (produced *c*.1460; discussed in Chapter 2) displays this same pragmatic focus, urging all loyal English subjects to act against the Yorkist rebels whenever they have the opportunity: 'chescung fust de bone valour et courage a exposer tant son corps comme sez biens pour lexpedicion...a cause de sormonter et mettre a nyant cez faulx et desleyaux hommnes dessusdis' ('everyone be of good valour and courage to expose both his body and his goods for the purpose; [...everyone should] loan or give his goods to the king for the cause of overcoming and destroying these above-mentioned false and disloyal men').[107] The *Somnium* articulates a disillusioned yet hopeful theory: 'Il ne fault point du tout esprere en Die. Il conuient mettre la main a leure et puis Dieu donra son ayde.' ('Hope must certainly not be placed entirely in God. It is appropriate to put one's hand to the work and then God will give his aid.')[108] The implication here is that God will help the just who help themselves first. In this idea of secular, this-worldly action superseding providence, we see an instance of the pragmatic ethics that characterizes much of the literature of this era. It is not that Wars of the Roses texts reject a divine framework, but rather that they focus their attention elsewhere. As Strohm puts it, 'divine factors are likely to be moved to the back burner so that a more purely practical

---

[106] Henry Ansgar Kelly, *Divine Providence in the England of Shakespeare's Histories* (Cambridge, MA: Harvard University Press, 1970), pp. 37–9. Arthur B. Ferguson also views fifteenth-century writing as lacking in interrogation of providence: *The Articulate Citizen and the English Renaissance* (Durham, NC: Duke University Press, 1965), pp. 200 and 408. Neither Kelly nor Ferguson considers romance.
[107] 'Proscription of the Yorkists', p. 524.
[108] 'Proscription of the Yorkists', p. 524.

discussion can ensue...providential determination is not so much actively denied as infinitely postponed'.[109] The *Somnium*'s appeal against treason is inclusive: everyone in the community of the realm is supposed to help punish the identified traitors, and to keep active watch for further traitors. The *Somnium* advocates actively responding to the rifeness of treason in its society, just as Malory's *Morte* and the Arthurian section of Hardyng's *Chronicle* urge the same response in a more universal fashion.

Here the Malorian idea (or 'ideal') of truth is not ontological, theological, or intellectual; it is, rather, instrumental and ethical.[110] The 'truth' that Malory and his Arthur attempt to valorize by ignoring Launcelot and Guenevere's affair for as long as possible is a truth that has a use-value, a truth of a societally constructed (rather than divinely provided) ethic that ignores absolutes in a pragmatic attempt to preserve social stability. Thus Malory's conception of truth appears rather Foucauldian; in recognizing that the 'truth' or correct outcome produced by a means such as trial by combat depends on who takes part in the combat, Malory views truth not as absolute but (like Foucault) as 'an effect of particular relations of power', as a result of which there can be no truth that is not contingent.[111] In the *Morte*, truth and treason are contingent upon the particular relations of power that pertain to a chivalric society—the power of horse and armoured fighting man, the power of a king and his powerful need to hold the kingdom together. For Malory, truth and treason in their ideal forms recognize intentions and aspirations; the epistemology of discovering or constructing right and wrong ideally operates by taking into account the ends towards which an action is working, by paying heed to instrumentality rather than absolutes. Importantly, the machinery of truth and treason is something that Malory, like some contemporary romanciers and chroniclers, depicts—more comprehensively and insistently than earlier literature—as not secured from above and therefore in need of stabilization from within society. This perhaps represents a growing awareness or attitude of the age.

---

[109] Strohm, *Politique*, pp. 16–17; emphasis mine. Strohm persuasively locates a 'pre-Machiavellian moment' of unprecedented forms of 'pragmatic political discussion' between Richard of York's return to England in 1450 and the change of dynasty in 1485 (p. 1). While Strohm's analysis of the political tactics of princes is distinct from this study's focus on literary texts and the contemporary cultural imaginary to which they bear witness, his view of these decades' this-worldly focus is consonant with mine.

[110] Green, *A Crisis of Truth*, p. 9, details various late medieval ideas of truth.

[111] Louise Fradenburg and Carla Freccero, 'Introduction: Caxton, Foucault, and the Pleasures of History', in *Premodern Sexualities*, ed. by Louise Fradenburg and Carla Freccero (New York: Routledge, 1996), pp. xiii–xxiv (p. xvi); see Michel Foucault, *Archaeology of Knowledge*.

In mid- to late fifteenth-century texts such as the prose *Siege*s and Hardyng's *Chronicle* as well as the *Morte*, ideals of social behaviour are explored in ethical engagements with instances of unresolved treachery. In these texts, moreover, ideas of truth and/or knowledge as contingent are informed by a secularist attitude towards how good government and a stable community might be ensured. When we take these attributes into account, we see the *Morte* occupying a place in a wider generic and thematic late medieval English context. We see in the literature of this time some ideological strains and questioning modes of thinking about matters of truth, transgression, and providence; attitudes perhaps familiar in the early modern period, but that are also on display here in these texts' focus on treason and its relationship to good governance. When Malory's Launcelot hears the news of Arthur's passing, he throws 'hys armes abrode', saying 'Alas! Who may truste thys worlde?', and becomes a hermit (1254.11–12). The secular literary texts of the Wars of the Roses certainly recognize that the world is not to be trusted, and they agonize over it, but ultimately their response differs from Launcelot's: rather than figuratively washing their hands of their world, they seek to wrestle with it.

Malory and Company: Fifteenth-Century English Prose Romance

The first half of this chapter demonstrated that the *Morte*'s rhetoric about treason condemns underhanded actions and traitors by invoking an honour/shame ethos and the threat of the loss of community. Malory reworks matters of treason to create a pointedly current yet nostalgic representation of social and legal bonds, urging a renewal of personal loyalties and community-focused justice. The *Morte* imagines and valorizes a bipartite mode of chivalric conduct that involves loyalty and good will to both knightly equals and sovereign, but does so in a searchingly interrogative fashion. It is perhaps injudicious to overlook 'just how closely much Middle English romance connects with real life';[112] this chapter's assessment of the *Morte*'s attitudes towards treason emphasizes some of the ways in which Malory's romance is conditioned by history and encourages (future) history to follow romance. Offering an idealized world that is both tantalizingly similar to and separate from its readers' own, the *Morte* creates a nostalgic but forbiddingly admonitory dialectic that becomes more pronounced towards its end. Malory relates life to literature perhaps most

[112] Helen Cooper, 'When Romance Comes True', in *Boundaries in Medieval Romance*, ed. by Neil Cartlidge, Studies in Medieval Romance, VI (Cambridge: Brewer, 2008), pp. 13–27 (p. 13).

noticeably when writing that the usurper Mordred, seeking to capture Guenevere, 'layde a myghty syge aboute the Towre and made many assautis, and threw engynnes unto them, and shotte grete gunnes' (1227.23–5). This mention of 'grete gunnes' is not in Malory's sources, and is 'probably a conscious innovation', since Malory may have witnessed the Yorkists besieging the Lancastrian-held Tower of London in 1460, the only occasion on which cannons were used against the Tower prior to the completion of the *Morte*.[113] Here and when the narrator explicitly addresses 'ye all Englysshemen' (1229.6), the boundaries of the Arthurian world disintegrate; the golden age of Arthur's reign vanishes into the interstices of the text, but its problems are insistently those of late fifteenth-century England. By articulating anxieties about treason, the *Morte* bombards its contemporary readership with the correspondences between their lived and literary experiences.

The *Morte*'s emphasis on treason, as the unavoidable antithesis of fellowship, bespeaks a resonance for both its author and the contemporary English cultural imaginary. Malory's critique of increasingly institutional and unfeeling methods of determining identity was perhaps especially self-reflexive because he suffered for his own loyalties under such a regime. When he finished writing in 1469, Malory was in prison, and one of the crimes for which he was excluded from a general pardon may well have been involvement in a treasonous Lancastrian plot.[114] Malory increases the presence of legal procedures in treason episodes, but also critiques that legality. The ideological commentary that Malory's text offers with respect to treason seeks to define 'real' betrayal and admirable conduct based on personal intentions and relationships, rather than on the politically motivated notions of treason of which Malory himself seems to have been accused. It may not be inconsequential that Balyn, the character whom

---

[113] Field, 'Fifteenth-Century History', p. 65. While Field rightly cautions against searching for concrete historical parallels or straightforward partisanship in the *Morte* (as does Edward Donald Kennedy, 'Malory's *Morte Darthur*: A Politically Neutral English Adaptation of the Arthurian Story', in *Arthurian Literature XX*, ed. by Keith Busby (Cambridge: Brewer, 2003), pp. 145–69), Malory's curious mention of 'grete gunnes', particularly in light of Malory's independent blackening of Mordred, does read as a condemnation of the Yorkists' attack on the Tower. Malory favours a stable political order, championing kings rather than rebels; the Yorkists were rebels at the time of this bombardment but, of course, did not remain so.

[114] Suggested by Field, *Life and Times*, pp. 139–45; supported by Colin Richmond, 'Thomas Malory and the Pastons', in *Readings in Medieval English Romance*, ed. by Carol M. Meale (Cambridge: Brewer, 1994), pp. 195–208, and Felicity Riddy, 'Contextualizing *Le Morte Darthur*: Empire and Civil War', in *A Companion to Malory*, pp. 55–73 (p. 55). For an alternative view, see Anne F. Sutton, 'Malory in Newgate: A New Document', *The Library: The Transactions of the Bibliographical Society*, Seventh Series, 1.3 (2000), 243–62 (pp. 247–8).

the *Morte* most insistently (and desperately) proclaims to be without treason, had been incarcerated in a royal prison for ostensible ill-doing. To recognize that treason is a key word and concept in Malory's work is in part to appreciate another way in which the colourful Sir Thomas of Newbold Revel is an appropriate author figure for the *Morte Darthur*.[115]

In modern criticism, Malory the prose romancier stands head and shoulders above his anonymous English contemporaries. However, this perception of a difference in stature goes too far in assuming that the anonymous fifteenth-century English romances are entirely unlike the *Morte*, or are simply not worth a look. The *Morte*'s strategies of treating treason, and thus significant aspects of its style, themes, secular world view, and didactic modes and desires, are sometimes more sophisticated, but have a strong affinity with texts such as the prose *Siege of Thebes, Siege of Troy*, and *Melusine* (and its verse counterpart). Such anonymous romances parallel Malory in their concentration on moments of treachery, and in the legally mimetic character with which they imbue this material. The prose *Siege of Troy* and *Melusine* employ a lexicon for indicting traitors that is identical to Malory's, and to that of parliamentary attainders (as discussed in Chapters 2 and 3). That these romances' authors sought out, amplified, and created instances of treason and accompanying admonitions in a way that parallels Malory's composition indicates the resonance that such literary acts of interpretation and shaming would have carried for contemporary readers. Moreover, the fact that this performative rhetoric is in the prose *Troy* but not the prose *Thebes* suggests a nuanced appreciation of Malory's work: this use of a specific lexicon was neither an obscure nor an entirely commonplace mode of representation, but rather an evocative choice, connecting certain literary texts and incidents to contemporary political discourse.

The *Morte* and the *Thebes, Troy*, and *Melusine* romances are informed by the same cultural ontology of treason, one that, while often pointedly expressed in (and effective through) legal terms and procedures, is at least as reliant upon how the popular mind would define treason as it is on how the crown and its lawyers would do so. While, as discussed in Chapter 2, the institutionally codified conception of treason was hierarchical and could be committed only against someone to whom the traitor had been bound by an overt bond of subservient loyalty—that is, to one's king, master, husband, or prelate—the popular idea of treason included forms of underhanded harm such as covertly initiated armed robbery or assault that the

---

[115] For an insightful, and cautionary, discussion of critical attitudes towards Malory as author, see Andrew Lynch, 'A Tale of "Simple" Malory and the Critics', *Arthuriana*, 16.2 (2006), 10–15.

English crown would classify only as felony or trespass. The Malorian label of treason is certainly not restricted to acts perpetrated against persons of authority. In the *Morte*, a knight can be a traitor to another whom he has never met before, let alone sworn an oath to be loyal to, if the harm is done deviously—as when Garlon decapitates stranger knights while invisible (80–1), or when Gringamour absconds with the sleeping Gareth's dwarf (328–30). After Garlon slays Balyn's two successive knight companions (who cannot defend themselves against their unseen attacker), he is, like Gringamour, called 'traytoure knyght' by the offended party (81.11–12). Despite the disparity in the gravity of these offences, the text focuses on the shared treasonous nature of depriving a fellow knight of a dwarf and decapitating knights, because what is most important is the guileful nature of the (intended) injury. The outrage expressed by Malorian victims of treason shows that honourable conduct is expected even between people (of chivalric status) who have never previously met and whom no explicit bond binds. Gringamour and Garlon have neither taken the Round Table oath nor entered into any specific fellowship with those whom they betray; for Malory, the ethos of knighthood is a bond in itself. Likewise, in the prose *Troy*, while Hecuba's plot to kill Achilles is a breach of faith between members of different polities, it is emphatically termed treason because it is underhanded (284). By contrast, Eteocles' breach of faith with Polynices is not treason because, while uncommendable, it is openly announced rather than concealed. As discussed in Chapter 3, the prose author makes this distinction where Lydgate does not (since Lydgate's *Thebes*, like his *Troy Book*, is scattered with treason words in an undiscriminating and imprecise fashion, alternating with other terms such as falseness, malice, felony, and fraud). Moreover, in the prose romances, for example in the *Melusine*s, the reprehensibility and repercussions of betrayal acquire a legal force (even when, as in the prose *Thebes*, the treachery in question is not treason).

Contrasts with the anonymous contemporary romances also highlight some of the more distinctive achievements of the *Morte*'s representations of treachery. While accusations of treason are a primary feature of, say, the English *Melusine*s, Malory's treason rhetoric, as a result of being even more frequently deployed and occurring primarily within direct speech, is more profoundly performative and thus better able to affect an (aural) readership. The *Morte* is also more sophisticated and pointed in the realism of its procedures (such as appeals of treason), and in the social commentary thereby conveyed. For instance, as discussed above, in the articulation of the law of treason that condemns Guenevere (1174.19–29) and through his representation of the evidence and procedures surrounding her trial, Malory censures institutional laws as the potential enemy of chivalric community. Malory similarly supports older, more personal bonds against institutional ones in treatments of the treasons of Launcelot and Balyn, and in the text's construction of an implied bond for all persons of chivalric status. Malory represents treason as a deplorable phenomenon still present in his world, where it ought to be censured and avoided; his cultural work is more detailed and socially visionary than that of his anonymous fellow prose-romanciers. However, Malory, by writing in prose about secular ideals of conduct, and particularly by exploring these ideals in his ethical engagements with unresolved treachery, contributed to a wider contemporary English genre. This genre, at a time when England was particularly troubled by civil strife, operated as a culturally resonant mode of reshaping familiar romance material to both comment upon, and seek to renew, faltering social commitments.

Recent attempts to grapple with the *Morte*'s genre have varied in their verdict according to the degree to which they have taken its literary contexts into account. As mentioned in Chapter 1, Larry Benson has argued that Malory had no precedent for his style. Benson's primary reason for dismissing texts such as the prose *Thebes* and *Troy* seems to be their brevity;[116] however, it is both no more and no less just to call these texts 'redactions' of their sources than it is to call the *Morte Darthur* a redaction of its sources, since all three substantially reduce the verbiage of their sources while increasing emphasis on particular themes (a concentration also observed in the English *Melusine*s, though they are only a little shorter than their sources). More notably, Cooper has discussed the *Morte* alongside other fifteenth-century English prose romances as texts that all show a 'shift in the centre of gravity away from... the verse romances, with their calamities avoided or redeemed and political and familial order restored'.[117] Kevin Whetter, noting that the *Morte* has 'a somber and tragic outlook which is generically out of place in romance'—which he seems to consider an assertion opposed to Cooper's 'Counter-Romance' article—proposes that we view the *Morte* as 'a tragic-romance'.[118] Ideas of divergence from conventional romance are in fact the premise for both Cooper's argument and mine; such ideas are the basis upon which we can understand fifteenth-century prose romance as a genre that distinguishes itself in part by its response to earlier romance. While pushing the boundaries of insufficiently sophisticated assumptions of a stable or monolithic generic ethos for the *Morte*, Whetter unfortunately removes the text from its historical and literary milieu. James Simpson, like Whetter, argues that

---

[116] Benson, *Malory's 'Morte Darthur'*, p. 21.   [117] 'Counter-Romance', p. 145.
[118] Whetter, 'On Misunderstanding Malory's Balyn', pp. 150 and 162, and *Understanding Genre and Medieval Romance* (Aldershot: Ashgate, 2008), p. 148.

the *Morte* is not a romance because it does not have a happy ending: as a narrative 'of societal collapse', Simpson writes, it points 'in precisely the opposite direction from the comic resolutions of romance'.[119] Simpson elaborates his reasons for this opposition: romances

> are designed to address the internal, structural tensions of groups. The trag-edies...address the violence of external war, and the ways in which that vio-lence can produce civil destruction. Romances, by contrast, represent the ways in which the controlled expression of civil violence within social group-ings can serve finally to reintegrate them.[120]

In my view, Simpson has constructed a false dichotomy by privileging the overall arc of 'comedic' versus 'tragic' chivalric narratives at the expense of attention to the experience of reading through the text. Simpson's study is interested in the text's intentions in relation to its society. Such a focus on the work the *Morte* performs or seeks to perform should, however, produce a recognition that its representation of 'the violence of external war, and the ways in which that violence can produce civil destruction', through its admonitions, does in fact do work 'to address the internal, structural tensions of groups' in a manner that supports social cohesion.

We gain a better sense of how the generic ethos of the *Morte* would have been understood in its own time by attuning ourselves to the context of contemporary English romances. 'Prose romance' is in some senses a *faut de mieux* category for texts such as the *Morte* and the prose *Thebes* and *Troy*, but it allows us to see the intertextual connections and associations they exploit. The final section of Chapter 3 discussed the significance of prose's associations with chronicle and instructional writing for understanding these texts' affiliations and register; equally important for an understand-ing of these narratives is their connection to the romance genre. These texts, written for readers familiar with romance narratives, insist upon their ties to romance, requiring that romance 'horizons of expectation' be kept in mind when they are read,[121] even—or especially—in connec-tion with the expectations of romance that they confound, such as that of a happy ending. In their endings, as elsewhere, these texts exhibit the same concerns with secular ideals and 'human perfectibility within a social context' that characterize 'conventional' romances.[122] As Cooper remarks, 'romance, as the dominant secular literary genre of the period, was at the heart of [societal] self-representation, a means by which cultural values

---

[119] Simpson, *Reform and Cultural Revolution*, p. 263.
[120] Simpson, *Reform and Cultural Revolution*, p. 276.
[121] Hans Robert Jauss, *Toward an Aesthetic of Reception*, trans. by Timothy Bahti (Brighton: Harvester, 1982), pp. 76–109.
[122] Cooper, *English Romance*, p. 10.

and ideals were recorded and maintained and promulgated'.[123] These texts
certainly pursue the didactic role of a romance, but they employ different,
and more disturbing, means: they engage with cultural values and ideals,
but do so through instances of these ideals' negation, productively unsettling their readers' expectations. The mode of ethical narrative exhibited
by the *Morte* and contemporary English romances is, not insignificantly,
also shared by other Wars of the Roses texts (as discussed in Chapters 2 and
3), regardless of whether their form is prose or verse, their genre romance
or correspondence or polemic.

Thus, in designating Malory's *Morte* as fifteenth-century English prose
romance, the 'fifteenth-century' and the 'English' are from some angles
of approach the most salient adjectives; however, as argued here, there are
also compelling reasons to dwell upon the 'romance' and 'prose' distinc-
tions. On the one hand, thinking in terms of discourse allows a recognition of the widespread centrality of concerns about treason to the textual
culture of the Wars of the Roses; and, on the other hand, thinking in terms
of genre permits a deeper understanding of the cultural position and work
of a distinctive group of contemporary texts. We can thus view the *Morte*
as positioned at a nexus of hitherto neglected English traditions.

In order to reshape social conduct, the authors of mid- to late
fifteenth-century English versions of the stories of Arthur, Thebes, Troy,
and Melusine (and, as addressed in Chapter 5, Charlemagne) reformed
their legendary material. The protean malleability and lack of formal con-
straints of the medium of prose offered a way to tell stories related to but
distinct from the messages of the earlier verse romances; it constitutes a
socially symbolic narrative medium in which to reflect, refract, and reflect
upon the role of social bonds and their breach. It will come as no sur-
prise to the Malory scholar that the *Morte*'s complex social and ethical
proselytizing entwined with lamentation is unmatched in contemporary
English texts; however, we can productively complicate this awareness of
the *Morte*'s superiority by viewing the text as the foremost exemplar of
its genre rather than as a genre unto itself. Whether or not Malory was
familiar with such texts as the prose *Siege*s and the *Melusine*s, he was, by
writing in prose about social ideals through the issue of treason and within
a particularly secular framework, taking part in a wider fifteenth-century
English genre. Given the social and ethical focus of these texts, they seem
intended for a readership featuring gentry and merchants more centrally
than earlier romances. The way that Lydgate's *Siege of Thebes* and *Troy
Book* initially circulated primarily among an aristocratic audience, but

---

[123] Cooper, *English Romance*, p. 6.

by the 1450s also enjoyed widespread gentry circulation, testifies to the widening classes of people who wanted to read and/or had access to such texts.[124] The prose versions suggest which parts of Lydgate's texts may have most attracted gentry interest by omitting much of the Lydgate material pertaining to the 'mirror for princes' genre, and devoting greater attention to (gentry-related) concerns about interactions between chivalric equals. The intended readership of the prose *Sieges* and the *Melusines* likely matches Malory's readership, since the anonymous romances, in their concerns with worship, friendship, and fellowship, parallel the emphases on self-fashioning and community particular to the *Morte* and to contemporary gentry.[125] The following chapter broadens this context by considering further late fifteenth-century English prose romances that likewise circulated amongst gentry and merchants, but, unprecedentedly, did so in print.

---

[124] See Robert Edwards' introductions to the TEAMS editions of Lydgate's *Thebes* and *Troy*.
[125] These three concerns (along with good lordship) were those most central to gentry circles: Radulescu, *Gentry Context*.

5

Thinking Twice about Treason in Caxton's Prose Romances

Proper Chivalric Conduct and the English Printing Press

'It is the fouleste crafte that a knyght may for to doo treyson.'

'Ye have called me traytour / but ye lye falsly, for I never dide treison, nor never shall'.

'It were treson and vntrouth, and god forbede that I shold take suche hyre.'

'I reporte me to al knyghtes that euer haue knowen me, I ferd neuer with no treason, nor I loued neuer the felauship of no man that ferde with treson.'

'I swere and assure the that neuer while I lyue shal I be traytour to no man lyuyng.'[1]

Although Malory's *Morte Darthur*, when printed in 1485, entered wider circulation among a group of other prose romances likewise printed by William Caxton, it is rarely studied alongside them. Other prose narratives similarly treating distant or legendary history that Caxton's press imprinted in the 1480s include *Godeffroy of Boloyne* (1481) on the First Crusade, and *Charles the Grete* (1485) and *The Four Sonnes of Aymon* (1488)

---

[1] William Caxton, *The Right Plesaunt and Goodly Historie of the Foure Sonnes of Aymon*, ed. by Olivia Richardson, EETS ES 44 and 45 (London: Trübner, 1885), pp. 234.8–9 and 265.19–21; Caxton, *Godeffroy of Boloyne*, p. 236.7–8; *Caxton's Malory*, ed. by James W. Spisak (Berkeley: University of California Press, 1983), p. 546.7–9; Caxton, *The Lyf of the Noble and Crysten Prynce, Charles the Grete*, ed. by Sidney J. H. Herrtage, EETS ES 37 (London: Trübner, 1881), p. 58.24–6.

on the reign of Charlemagne. Because these understudied texts and others like them are Caxton's own translations, following their French sources more closely than Malory adheres to his, they have commonly been dismissed as Burgundian importations with little grounding in or relevance to English culture.[2] Moreover, the few critics who have allowed Caxton's prose romances to have connections to English literature and society have confined their analyses to the texts' construction of the reputations of the three Christian 'Worthies'—Arthur, Charlemagne, and Godfrey—and thus to the texts' treatment of crusading and hierarchical loyalties,[3] without addressing these texts' striking investment in other aspects of chivalric conduct. Caxton's prose romances of the 1480s, like Malory's *Morte*, devote a great deal of attention to horizontal chivalric bonds and to anxieties about trust and fellowships, anxieties shared by readers during the later stages of the Wars of the Roses. Again, as in the *Morte*, the mode of ethical narrative employed in *Godeffroy*, *Charles*, and *The Foure Sonnes* engages with ideologies of chivalry and troth by advocating proper social conduct through discussions of these concepts' opposites, negation, or breach.

The brief passages quoted above are paradigmatic of how, in these four texts, exemplary behaviour is defined, interrogated, urged, and elegized in part through the determination of chivalric paragons 'alweyes to flee treason' (92.32)—a stipulation of the Round Table oath unique to the *Morte*. Here Malory articulates a standard of conduct that, if less famously codified in Caxton's own prose romances, is equally espoused there, and in an equally admonitory and normative fashion. Moreover, although Caxton's prologues and other paratextual material supply an extra dimension to their didactic frame, his prose romances, again like the *Morte Darthur*, manifest anxiety about the ever-present possibility of treason even—or especially—in the ways that they seek to deny or forestall its inevitability. This chapter analyses these works' pervasive condemnations of treason as a crime with both hierarchical and horizontal dimensions, and one that can be committed between affinity groups, polities, and faiths, in order to explore the extent to which Caxton's romances and related chivalric tracts are cognate with other texts produced in and for mid- to late fifteenth-century

---

[2] Felicity Riddy, *Sir Thomas Malory*; Douglas Gray, *Later Medieval English Literature*, as discussed below. Dates of Caxton's prints are as in George D. Painter, *William Caxton: A Quincentenary Biography of England's First Printer* (London: Chatto, 1976).

[3] William Kuskin, *Symbolic Caxton: Literary Culture and Print Capitalism* (Notre Dame: University of Notre Dame Press, 2008); J. R. Goodman, 'Malory and Caxton's Chivalric Series, 1481–5', in *Studies in Malory*, ed. by James W. Spisak (Kalamazoo: Medieval Institute Publications, 1985), pp. 257–74; Joerg Fichte, 'Caxton's Concept of "Historical Romance" within the Context of the Crusades: Conviction, Rhetoric and Sales Strategy', in *Tradition and Transformation in Medieval Romance*, ed. by Rosalind Field (Cambridge: Brewer, 1999), pp. 101–13.

England. The *Morte* is by no means the sole English touchstone for Caxton's romances; like the *Morte*, Caxton's prose romances parallel the other English romances, poems, chronicles, and correspondence addressed in previous chapters. Paying heed to the role of treason in each text permits both a deeper understanding of how these texts reimagine and seek to regulate their society, and a reconsideration of the relationships between Caxton's canon of prose romances and contemporary English culture. It also raises broader questions about late fifteenth-century literary culture's position between 'medieval' and 'early modern' which are addressed at the end of this chapter and, more fully, in Chapter 6.

ENGLAND, BURGUNDY, AND BEYOND?

In an otherwise perspicacious study of Malory's context, Felicity Riddy argues that Caxton's prose romances did not connect with English culture and concerns because, she contends, they constituted 'Burgundian court culture' inappropriately transplanted onto English soil. Riddy dismisses Caxton's prose romances on the grounds that they lack longevity, observing that de Worde reprinted 'only three' of Caxton's own translations.[4] However, the way in which texts such as *The Foure Sonnes* were reprinted multiple times until after the midpoint of the sixteenth century indicates at least some ongoing popularity.[5] Moreover, their declining popularity in the early sixteenth century, when de Worde's printing press flourished, is of dubious value as an indicator of Caxton's texts' popularity in the late fifteenth century. Douglas Gray's recent survey sounds a slightly more receptive note, but Gray, like Riddy, characterizes the vogue for these texts as foreign and fleeting.[6] Yet to view transience as evidence that a literary movement or body of works was 'misguided' is to flatten out the fabric of history; it is to disregard the shape and substance of a historical moment. If Caxton's prose romances were popular with contemporary readers and less so with later ones, what made these texts particularly relevant to their own time?

The cultural position or power of Caxton's prose romances—that is, the extent to which these texts should be considered English rather than only Burgundian in their genre, themes, and work—is suggested by the way in which they match the aspects of 'English' character that Riddy rightly

---

[4] Riddy, *Sir Thomas Malory*, pp. 12–13.
[5] For the several further editions of *The Foure Sonnes of Aymon* between de Worde's, *c.*1505, and Copland's, *c.*1554, see A. W. Pollard and G. R. Redgrave, *A Short-Title Catalogue of Books Printed in England, Scotland, and Ireland and of English Books Printed Abroad, 1475–1640*, 2nd edn, 3 vols (London: British Library, 1976–91), I, 1007–11.5.
[6] Gray, *Later Medieval English Literature*, p. 205.

perceives in the *Morte*. Riddy reads the social significance of Malory's text in terms of its concerns with The British Past, Good Manners, Right Conduct, and Divisions.[7] Romances about Charlemagne's knights, such as Caxton's *Charles* and *The Foure Sonnes*, obviously do not address the British past directly; however, these texts, and *Godeffroy*, do manifest marked interest in good manners, right conduct, and divisions, and convey these concerns through narratives of Christian history or legendary French history comparable to those of Arthur and his knights. Caxton's are certainly not the only Middle English Charlemagne romances; there are also ten earlier verse romances and the anonymous prose *Pseudo-Turpin Chronicle*. Charlemagne romances would not likely have struck their English readers as inimically French; they are, as Thomas Crofts has argued, chivalric rather than nationalistic in interest and ordering principle.[8] Caxton's Charlemagne romances, then, were available—in a fashion more or less untroubled by their French origins—to English readers interested in didactic chivalric literature. Moreover, *unlike* the earlier verse versions, Caxton's *Charles* and *The Foure Sonnes*, along with the *Pseudo-Turpin Chronicle*, pursue a mode of didacticism that devotes more attention to negative examples than to positive ones, and that employs a particularly secular framework (as discussed in preceding chapters with respect to other contemporary English romances).[9]

This chapter does not contest that Caxton drew upon Burgundian literary traditions, but rather seeks to deepen our awareness of the ways in which his selection of romances and chivalric treatises was also acutely informed by English literary fashions and concerns. Accordingly, late fifteenth-century prints and manuscripts are treated here as complementary forms. While Cooper's convincing though tantalizingly skeletal adumbration of the genre of mid- to late fifteenth-century English prose romance includes the prose *Siege of Thebes, Siege of Troy, King Ponthus, Melusine*, and *Valentine and Orson*, and, of course, Malory's *Morte*—texts which, among others, are discussed elsewhere in this study—the only Caxtonian texts she admits are *Charles* and *The Foure Sonnes*. Cooper contends that the cultural and ideological context of Caxton's prints differed from that of manuscript romances, and that

---

[7] I leave to one side Riddy's remaining chapter ('The Next World') because it is primarily a discussion of Malory's 'Tale of the Sankgreal', whose religious focus is not paralleled elsewhere in the *Morte* any more than in other contemporary English romances.

[8] Thomas H. Crofts and Robert Allen Rouse, 'Middle English Popular Romance and National Identity', in *A Companion to Medieval Popular Romance*, ed. by Raluca L. Radulescu and Cory James Rushton, Studies in Medieval Romance, X (Cambridge: Brewer, 2009), pp. 79–95 (p. 95); see also Marianne Ailes and Phillipa Hardman, 'How English Are the English Charlemagne Romances?', in *Boundaries in Medieval Romance*, pp. 43–55 (pp. 53–5).

[9] For the *Pseudo-Turpin Chronicle*, see Chapter 3.

Caxton's 'generic assumptions were formed so extensively' by his prolonged exposure to Burgundian literature.[10] However, recent work has emphasized the codetermination of manuscript and print when Caxton's press was in operation. Kuskin cautions that early print does not constitute 'a fundamental break with the past' but rather 'reasserts this past by transforming it', and, as Wakelin writes, 'readers continued to consult both media as complementary forms of one thing (the book) rather than as opposed entities'.[11] Moreover, views of the importance of Burgundian influence on Caxton (as espoused by Cooper, Riddy, Gray, Gordon Kipling, and Diane Bornstein)[12] are tenable only when we recognize that Caxton's choice of texts capitalized upon a keen awareness of English tastes in order to provide 'Burgundian' texts whose genres and values paralleled those already popular with their intended readership.

While scholars such as Bornstein dwell on the fact that many of the romances translated and printed by Caxton were in the Duke of Burgundy's library, Norman Blake and Jennifer Goodman have downplayed Burgundian courtly influence on Caxton's printing decisions by looking at his connections in France and the Low Countries more broadly.[13] Goodman emphasizes the selectivity of Caxton's romances and demonstrates their cultural influences from other parts of the continent, such as Geneva and the northern margins of France.[14] This profitably widened lens, however, still neglects the influences of English culture on the reasons for and results of Caxton's choice of romances. The Caxton translations discussed here—*Godeffroy of Boloyne, Charles the Grete, The Foure Sonnes of*

[10] Cooper, 'Counter-Romance', pp. 144–5.

[11] Kuskin, *Symbolic Caxton*, p. 4; Wakelin, *Humanism, Reading, and English Literature*, pp. 129 and 157. See also David McKitterick, *Print, Manuscript, and the Search for Order* (Cambridge: Cambridge University Press, 2003); Alexandra Gillespie, *Print Culture and the Medieval Author: Chaucer, Lydgate, and Their Books, 1473–1557* (Oxford: Oxford University Press, 2006), esp. Chapters 1 and 2 (pp. 27–103); William Kuskin, 'Introduction: Following Caxton's Trace', in *Caxton's Trace: Studies in the History of English Printing*, ed. by William Kuskin (Notre Dame: University of Notre Dame Press, 2006), pp. 1–31.

[12] Diane Bornstein, 'William Caxton's Chivalric Romances and the Burgundian Renaissance in England', *English Studies*, 57 (1976), 1–10; Gordon Kipling, *The Triumph of Honour: Burgundian Origins of the Elizabethan Renaissance* (Leiden: Leiden University Press, 1977), p. 14; see also Benson, *Malory's 'Morte Darthur'*, pp. 21–4.

[13] Bornstein, 'Caxton's Chivalric Romances', p. 5; N. F. Blake, 'William Caxton Again in the Light of Recent Scholarship', *Dutch Quarterly Review of Anglo-American Letters*, 12.3 (1982), 162–82 (pp. 164 and 180–2); Lotte Hellinga, 'Caxton and the Bibliophiles', *Onzième congrès international de bibliophilie*, ed. by P. Culot and E. Rouir (Brussels: Société royale des bibliophiles et iconophiles de Belgique, 1981), pp. 11–38. Blake calls for a reconsideration of Caxton's influences in the light of *English* literary precedent, but does not pursue this promising angle beyond briefly comparing the strength of Caxton's didactic impulse to Lydgate's; yet Lydgate's didacticism is, as discussed in Chapter 3, of a rather more religious tenor than that of the romances (including Caxton's) produced thereafter.

[14] Jennifer R. Goodman, 'Caxton's Continent', in *Caxton's Trace*, pp. 101–23.

Aymon, The Game of Chess, The Book of the Ordre of Chyvalry, and *The Boke of the Fayttes of Armes and of Chyualrye* among them—show that the mode of addressing treason through admonitorily ethical narrative that these texts share is not exclusive to England or to the second half of the fifteenth century; however, they also testify to the way in which, in these decades of instability and internecine strife, English textual culture devoted especially intensive attention to producing, compiling, and incorporating such literature. Indeed, some recent criticism has begun to profitably explore the 'Englishness' of Caxton's romances. William Kuskin, productively arguing that the place of the fifteenth century in English literary history, and Caxton's place within both, are more important than commonly considered, sees Caxton's romances contributing to the ideologically complex project of 'unifying English identity'. Kuskin locates the significance of Caxton's Worthies series for his readers in how 'Caxton's critical program' developed 'a symbolic space in which to define individuals as participating in a larger imaginary community as secular subjects'.[15] Focusing only on the idea of central authority, however, Kuskin is silent on the aspects of Caxton's romances' ideological engagements with contemporary English society that are of interest here; these texts' 'implicit imagination of social relations' goes beyond the hierarchical forms he treats.[16]

The way in which Malory's *Morte* and other mid- to late fifteenth-century English romances increase emphasis on treason relative to their sources indicates that Caxton's decision to translate and print treason-filled narratives provided insular readers with more material in a resonant English mode. In *Godeffroy, Charles*, and *The Foure Sonnes*, Caxton did not increase emphasis on treason relative to his French sources as much as some contemporary English romanciers did;[17] arguably, however, he did not need to, since remaining faithful to his sources produced newly 'Englished' romances with a greater focus on treason than, for instance, Malory's French sources. To maintain focus on Caxton's presentation of romances, this chapter cites Caxton's edition of Malory; however, the Winchester and Caxton versions do not differ significantly in their treatment of treason. Caxton's edition of the *Morte* retains Malory's emphasis on treason and even adds to it slightly by inserting a few extra 'treson' and 'traytour' words to fill space at the bottom of a printed page, as when Winchester's 'sir Brewnys' is expanded into 'this false knyght and traitour Breuse saunce Pyte'.[18] This lexis thus served a pragmatic end for the purposes of printing, but it was presumably not the only available choice to fill the space.

[15] Kuskin, *Symbolic Caxton*, pp. 193 and 235.
[16] Kuskin, *Symbolic Caxton*, p. 194.   [17] See Chapters 3 and 4.
[18] *Works*, 684.30; Spisak, 352.8 (Book 10:53; the end of F2r in the Pierpont Morgan copy). For another example of this compositor's strategy, compare *Works*, 1125.14 with

Accordingly, these additions also show that Caxton too—like Malory and the authors of works such as the prose *Siege of Troy* and the *Melusine*— engaged in thematic accretion around issues of treason when given the opportunity.

Caxton's sense of the importance of treason to his didactic project is also demonstrated in his prologues to his own romances (discussed further below), as in his prologue to the *Morte*, where he writes that the text offers ethical instruction not only through positive examples, but also by recounting 'how they that were vycious were punysshed and ofte put to shame and rebuke' (2.38–9): in other words, by representing condemnations of 'traytours'. Furthermore, again like the *Morte*, Caxton's romances were probably intended in part for aural reception, wherein the person reading aloud might emphasize keywords such as treason (as discussed in Chapter 4).[19] More significantly in terms of intentionality, Caxton marketed his texts through user-friendly paratextual apparatuses that further highlight treason. Dividing the *Morte* into books and chapters, he provided a table of contents to point up the subject matter of each section.[20] Caxton's own prose romances are likewise presented with chapter divisions and extensive tables of contents (reproduced from his sources), in which treason is mentioned almost whenever the corresponding narrative contains it. Caxton's prologues and other paratextual elements thus serve as ways both of highlighting how his narratives are troubled by treason, and of seeking to reinforce the didactic framework of the texts.

Thus, Caxton's romances parallel the focus in other mid- to late fifteenth-century English literature on instruction about a universalized notion of treason, but sometimes do so in ways that more strongly suggest the tensions in the narrative material—between an admonitory frame and what escapes it. The following three sections address Caxton's *Godeffroy*, *Charles*, and *The Foure Sonnes*, demonstrating how they use treason to treat horizontal social relationships as well as hierarchical

Spisak, 541.21–3. While it could be argued that such differences between Winchester and Caxton are due to Caxton's exemplar, it is quite likely that, because they occur at the very end of a folio (Z3v) and a chapter (19.3), Caxton's expansions are inserted to fill the remaining space. Caxton's version has ninety-nine instances of 'traytour' and its variants and plurals to Winchester's ninety-seven, 134 instances of 'treson' to Winchester's 124, and eleven occurrences of 'traytourely' adverb forms to Winchester's nine: *A Concordance to Caxton's Morte Darthur (1485)*, ed. by Kiyokazu Mizobata (Osaka: Osaka Books, 2009); Chapter 4 discusses the *Morte*'s representations of treason more fully. Since treason is not substantially found in the Roman War or the Grail Quest, the changes made to produce Caxton's Book V (the Roman War) are irrelevant here.

[19] Joyce Coleman, 'The Audible Caxton: Reading and Hearing in the Writings of England's First Publisher', *Fifteenth-Century Studies*, 16 (1990), 83–109.

[20] Meale, 'The Hoole Book', pp. 7 and 11–12.

ones, and how their contents sometimes resist this didactic treatment or response. Each of these texts focuses on a horizontal community of knights bound to each other by loyalty and common interest—the barons of the First Crusade, Charlemagne's twelve peers, and Renaud's fellowship—none of them unlike Malory's knights of the Round Table. These romances are contextualized in a further section considering other Caxtonian prose treatises that similarly foreground the reprehensibility of treason between members of fellowships and between individuals and their enemies. As the final section shows, the centrality of these matters of treason to these texts both informs and is informed by the mutually reinforcing interests of the printing press and of Caxton's gentry and merchant readership.

'ENGLISHING' GODFREY

Caxton's *Godeffroy of Boloyne*, the only medieval English version of the popular William of Tyre crusade chronicle (*c.*1175), is based on a fifteenth-century French manuscript with a continuation to 1285.[21] Caxton followed his source closely but not entirely slavishly. By ending his translation with the death of the 'protagonist' Godfrey, omitting his source's chronicle of the kingdom of Jerusalem,[22] Caxton reshaped the text to fit a romance mould. A consideration of forms of chivalric interest in *Godeffroy* beyond the evident crusading zeal[23] will demonstrate the text's participation in contemporary English romances' mode of addressing concerns about treason and proper conduct. While Latin and French versions were known in England earlier, Caxton, by 'Englishing' the exemplary chivalric life of Godfrey of Bouillon and its narrative of the First Crusade, made the text linguistically and economically available to a new and wider insular readership.[24] Indeed, although Caxton's prologue dedicates *Godeffroy* to Edward IV and his two sons, whom Caxton hopes will 'see & here redde this symple book, by which they may be encoraged to deserue

[21] Colvin, 'Introduction', *Godeffroy*.

[22] Fichte, 'Caxton's Concept of "Historical Romance"', p. 105.

[23] N. F. Blake, for instance, writes that Caxton's *Godeffroy* 'reflects an attempt to capitalize on the interest shown in crusading at this time', made urgent by the Ottoman capture of Constantinople (1453) and siege of Rhodes (1480): *Caxton and His World* (London: Deutsch, 1969), p. 89.

[24] A. E. B. Coldiron, 'William Caxton', in *The Oxford History of Literary Translation in English*, ed. by Roger Ellis, 4 vols (Oxford: Oxford University Press, 2008), I, 160–9 (pp. 165–6); on Caxton's rhetoric of translation, see Laura L. Howes and Sarah McCollum, '"Reducing into English": Translation as Alchemy in the Prologues and Epilogues of William Caxton', *N&Q*, 57.3 (2010), 321–5.

lawde and honour' (5.22–4),[25] it also proffers the book to all classes: 'alle Cristen princes / Lordes / Barons / Knyghtes / Gentilmen / Marchanntes / and all the comyn peple of this noble royamme' (4.20–2). When Caxton points out that while there are many volumes *in English* about the first two Christian Worthies, Arthur and Charlemagne, there is as yet no parallel for the third, Godfrey (3), he acknowledges that Englishing the narrative, and producing it in cheaper and more plentiful copies, made it more accessible. The prologue also states that the text seeks to encourage readers '*teschewe and flee werkes vycious, dishonnest and vytuperable* / And for tempryse and accomplysshe enterpryses honnestes, and werkes of gloryous meryte' (1.5–8): *Godeffroy*, as Caxton advertises it, instructs through negative reinforcement, in no trifling fashion. Here Caxton's paratextual intervention attempts to reinforce *Godeffroy*'s admonitory containment of treason, but neither it, nor he, is entirely successful.

Godeffroy's narrative of the First Crusade is concerned with treason on more than one level. For instance, when the king of Hungary is overrun by pillaging Dutchmen travelling to the Holy Land, he 'lefte the force of bataylle / and toke hym to subtilite and falshed / as peple that is ful of barate decyte and trycherye' (60.19–21).[26] The Hungarians slaughter all the pilgrims except a few who, returning to their country, '*tolde this* meschyef and *trayson* / by which they *taught* alle the pylgryms…that they shold not truste to the peple of hongrye' (61.27–9). Here the text is not simply instructive; it is also *about* instruction, providing heuristic examples between characters as well as between narrator and readers. The text, that is, both shows and tells. This admonition produces another company of pilgrims, who enter Hungary seeking to 'auenge thoccision [slaughter] that was doon by falsehed and trayson…ffor the rumoure and speche was moche yet of that fowle and vylanous fayte thurgh out al the londe' (62.28–31). This impulse to tell of treason, to shame and dishonour perpetrators and warn others about it, is pursued not only by the Dutchmen, but also by the text, and by Caxton (in his prologue).

This impulse to publicize betrayal also provides insight into the types of acts that the text views as treason. As discussed in Chapter 2, late medieval English statute law defined treason in a strictly hierarchical sense as an act or thought harmful to one's king, master, husband, or prelate. *Godeffroy*'s representations of 'treason', however, primarily concern betrayals that

---

[25] On Edward IV as patron for some of Caxton's chivalric texts (including *Godeffroy*), see Margaret Kekewich, 'Edward IV, William Caxton, and Literary Patronage in Yorkist England', *Modern Language Review*, 66 (1971), 481–7 (p. 487).

[26] 'Barate', derived from Old French, usually means 'strife', 'turmoil', or 'trouble', but can also mean 'deception' or 'fraud' (*MED*).

cross polities and affinity groups, and/or reverse or disregard hierarchy. Although these acts could not be considered 'treason' according to institutional law, their labelling as treason is consistent with more communal and extra-national senses of justice surviving in late medieval English imagination and literature; that is, it appropriates the precision and power of legal language to reinforce accusations against, and punishments of, betrayers (as discussed in Chapters 3 and 4). *Godeffroy* discusses treason most frequently as a trait of figures on the margins of, or in opposition to, Western Christian (knightly) identity. Yet while the Hungarian incident constitutes a warning about the treason of others, to a late medieval English audience, this warning lands close to home, since in Middle English literature Hungarians are commonly aligned with the English and Western Christians.[27] The category of liminal Others more unambiguously includes the emperor of Constantinople and his 'Greeks', while Saracens occupy the oppositional category. For instance, the narrator comments that the pilgrims do not suspect that the emperor's actions 'myght come of ony trayson ne of euyl / They knewe not by experyence so moche thenne as they dyde afterward' (88.16–17). When the emperor orders his soldiers to attack the host of the Earl of Toulouse, his and his people's actions are called 'trayson' four times in one two-page chapter (88.27; 88.31; 89.9; 89.13), and 'desloyal felonnye' just once (90.8): here, betrayals perpetrated across polities and/or to subordinates are again explicitly termed treason. This vocabulary of treason is widespread, and when alternatives are used, a similar message is conveyed, for instance when a deserter (Latyns the Greke) is described as 'the moost fals, vntrewe man that euer was' (93.2). The text insistently labels reprehensible actions and agents as such.[28]

However, those who commit treason, and are accused and shamed for it, include not only obvious Others, but also Western crusaders. After the crusaders have taken Antioch and are themselves besieged there, some barons flee. The narrator names 'somme that thus departed shamefully' (190.8), shaming those who violate their commitments to both their beliefs and their comrades. More commendable crusaders 'swore alle that they shold not departe fro the companye, ne breke the commaundementes of Buymont' (190.20–1), a declaration of loyalty and cohesion that, while positive, is nonetheless articulated negatively. Likewise, Bohemond and 'grete plente of men' patrol at night 'to thende that no peryll shold happe ne trayson' (190.22–4)—*not* 'to keep the city and the crusaders safe'. These utterances refuse to allow *Godeffroy*'s readers to view their own relation to

[27] Norman Simms, 'Hungary and Hungarian Knights in Middle English Literature', *Parergon*, 8.1 (1990), 57–72.
[28] See also, for instance, 71.17–18, 93.8, and 127.11–12.

treason with complacency, invoking the need to avoid treasonous conduct in order to retain one's place in one's community. Moreover, Godfrey, the preeminent chivalric exemplar, explicitly eschews treason. When a bailiff of the caliph of Egypt seeks to bribe him to raise a siege, Godfrey 'wold in no wyse here thyse wordes / but sayde that it were treson and vntrouth, and god forbede that I shold take suche hyre' (236.6–8). Like Malory's Balin, who is called the knight 'moost of worship, withoute treson, trechery, or vylony' (64.5), Godfrey is defined as exemplary through his tensional relationship to treason. Treason, as the abjected yet ineradicable *extimité* of knightly identity,[29] shows that, when even the best cannot fully dissociate themselves from the possibility of committing treason, continual self-regulation is required, and worries cannot be assuaged.

While *Godeffroy* follows its source closely, Caxton does make some alterations that further testify to the significance of 'treason' words in Wars of the Roses literature. For instance, when the Turkish Balac deceitfully pretends to desire peace with the Christian leader Baldwin, Caxton's version states that Balac: 'as a *fals traytre* had hyd an honderd of his men, well armed' (223.34–5). Caxton's source instead reads: 'li *desloiaus* Turs auoit mis [et] ordonnes cent homes' ('the *disloyal* Turk had placed and arrayed a hundred men').[30] The switch from 'desloiaus' to 'as a fals traytre' is not a straightforward translation. Caxton sometimes uses 'disloyal' in this translation; moreover, the closest English synonyms for 'desloiaus', to judge from Caxton's translations here and elsewhere (as well as the translations of the Melusine romances discussed in Chapter 3), is 'false'.[31] The French source's words of disloyal(ty) become words of false(ness) in Caxton's texts in phrases such as 'ayenst this fals turk' (224.35). Thus Caxton's replacement of 'desloiaus' not only with 'false', but with 'as a fals *traytre*', is a conversion and intensification, resulting in an interpellative utterance that would be very much at home in Malory's *Morte* or the prose *Troy*. That Caxton does sometimes increase emphasis on treason suggests another way in which (in parallel with his prologues) he, as one fifteenth-century English reader, understood and 'pointed' the significance of the narratives he reproduced. *Godeffroy* condemns treason in terms and concepts familiar to Wars of the Roses readers, bearing witness to its relevance to contemporary English culture. This text evidently has its roots in the chronicle

[29] On my use of Lacan's concept of *extimité*, see Chapter 4, note 24.
[30] Paris, Bibliothèque Nationale, MS Français 68, f.87r.
[31] 'Disloyal' was foreign: the *MED* does not contain 'disloyal', and cites just one use of 'disloyally' in a letter of 1417, which itself survives only in a *c.*1600 copy, and thus may or may not be an accurate reflection of the original. Caxton was therefore a pioneer in using 'disloyal' in his translations (and the earliest mention of 'disloyal' as an adjective in the *OED* is in Caxton's *Jason* (1477)).

tradition, but the lines between medieval romance and chronicle were blurred.[32] *Godeffroy* concerns itself with similar deeds, modes of narration, and values as more unambiguous romances; it performs the same kind of work, as is shown by the parallel treatments of treason in the anonymous manuscript romances (Chapter 3), Malory's *Morte* (Chapter 4), and Caxton's other printed romances (below).

TREASON AS (INTER)TEXTUAL SUTURE IN *CHARLES THE GRETE*

On 1 December 1485, a few months after he printed Malory's *Morte*, Caxton printed *Charles the Grete*, with a prologue presenting the text 'for proufyte of euery man' (2.17) in 'folowyng the good and eschewyng the euyl' (1.11–12). Caxton articulates a further rationale for printing this text by linking it to *Godeffroy* and the *Morte*, stating that to his prints concerning Godfrey and Arthur he feels obliged to add one treating the remaining Christian worthy, Charlemagne, so that it will be available 'in our maternal tongue, lyke as...in latyn or in frensshe' (2.35–6). However, the French text Caxton chose to translate, a compilation by Jean Bagnyon,[33] is not exclusively, or even primarily, a life of Charlemagne; its three 'books' concern different narratives (and, to an extent, different genres), with a recurring focus on treason. The first book chronicles the kings of France, dwelling upon the conversion of King Cloys and Charlemagne's early career, and establishing Charlemagne's fellowship and the horizontal pledge its members swear to each other: 'the xij pyeres of fraunce, whyche al had *promysed fydelyte one to that other* for to Ieoparde theyr lyf for the crysten fayth' (25.2–4). The second book focuses on chivalric exploits: the interactions of the Saracen siblings Fierabras and Floripas with the peers of France, and the latter's struggle to overcome the siblings' father, Balan, ruler of Spain. The final book concerns Charlemagne's later crusades, and 'the treason made by ganellon' (230.2–3). Thus treason, in the strictly hierarchical sense, is only substantially present in the second half of the final book; however, the volume's contents cohere thematically through other types of treason, and through discussions of treason even where there is none. The episodes in *Charles* share interests in crusading, proselytizing, and conversion, but they are also linked and intertwined

---

[32] For a Caxton-specific discussion of such generic hybridity, see Fichte, 'Caxton's Concept of "Historical Romance"', pp. 101–2 and 106.

[33] An incunable of the French *Fierabras*, comparable with British Library, C.6.b.12: Herrtage, 'Introduction', *Charles*.

through an accretion of material concerning secular chivalric conduct. Goodman argues that Charlemagne's life is the organizing principle of Caxton's *Charles* and claims that it and other texts such as the *Morte* are characterized by a 'propensity to reorder older material within a compact biographical form';[34] however, the middle book devotes less attention to Charlemagne than to Fierabras, Floripas, and the peers. Furthermore, this book's recurring theme of treason connects it to the third book. I would argue that what is most characteristic about texts such as Malory's *Morte* and Caxton's *Charles* is not their tendency to have a biographical form, but rather their strategy of exploiting a biographical framework in order to organize and convey didactic material. Goodman views Charlemagne as the point of *Charles*; I view him as the platform.

Treason is ever-present as something to be avoided throughout the bulk of the volume; there is a robust didactic frame, but the material also threatens to escape from it, as treason becomes a sort of textual desire in itself. Awareness of the Roncesvalles episode overshadows the entirety of the two final and principal books. The text not only ends with Ganelon's treason, it lets the reader know (or makes sure that the reader cannot *not* know) that it is going to end with Ganelon's treason. When Charlemagne's twelve peers are listed at the beginning of the second book, eleven are either described solely by name or with a genealogy. Ganelon, however, is introduced as 'Ganellon whych dyd the treson *at the ende of the iij book* at rouncyuale' (39.29–31). This narratorial aside makes readers acquainted with Ganelon's tainted future; Ganelon is the traitor with whom they may be familiar from other contexts. This intertextual reference also serves as an *intra*textual reference regarding where to find treason in the volume that the reader holds in his or her hands. Soon afterwards, we are told of 'ganellon and Andrewe the traytres that dyd the trayson *as the laste book shall make mencyon*' (50.17–19). Here the reader is again invited to skip forward to read of treason, if s/he wishes; from one perspective, then, these directions collude with the possibility of treason, by encouraging readers to *choose* to turn to and consider it. Moreover, by means of these signposts, treason shapes the structure of the narrative. Such *intra*textual references do not occur for other characters, themes, or events.[35] *Charles*, then, gains coherence by adding reminders of treason where there is none, and by

---

[34] Goodman, 'Malory and Caxton's Chivalric Series', pp. 269–70, and *Chivalry and Exploration, 1298–1630* (Woodbridge: Boydell, 1998), pp. 28–9.

[35] There is, however, an *inter*textual reference to Jason and the golden fleece, 'as it is redde in the destructyon of troye almoost at the begynnyng' (91.1–2), which is similarly in the French source.

making its incorporation of romance (Book 2), otherwise extraneous to a history of Charlemagne, instead its centrepoint.

There are many other discussions of treason in the text, both present and absent, hierarchical and horizontal. When Fierabras comes to Charlemagne's court to challenge the peers, we see that Ganelon's treason is not confined to the prelude to the battle of Roncesvalles; when Oliver is preparing to fight Fierabras, the narrator comments that 'the traytre [Ganelon] sayd to hym self secretly: "God forbede that euer Olyuer retorne but that he haue hys heed smyton of"' (50.33–5). Ganelon's thought is treasonous not only to Charlemagne but also to Oliver, because, as the narrator stresses, the twelve peers swore an oath to each other (25.1–4). Book 2 also defines exemplary characters through lack of treason: Fierabras tells Oliver, 'I swere and assure the that neuer while I lyue shal I be traytour to no man lyuyng' (58.24–6). This concern to avoid a treasonous reputation is matched in contemporary England—as in a 1460 political poem that mentions 'þat noble prynce, Richard [of York] be name, / Whom treson ne falshod neuer dyd shame'[36]—and is expressed again in the Saracen barons' report of the duel to Balan: 'Fyerabras your sone…was taken vaynquysshed & dyscomfyted in loyal batayl *without doyng ony treson*' (86.13–17). Cross-polity horizontal treason is, then, as possible as the internecine variety—yet is, here at least, expressly eschewed.

When treason *is* attributed to characters, the accusation often leads to violent threats and/or punishment. For instance, when Guy is captured from the citadel defended by the French (and his betrothed, Floripas), Roland hastens to save him from hanging, scaring Saracens away by calling them traitors:

'ha! *trayters*, mastyns! It shal not be as ye thynk: ye haue begonne such a thynge wherof ye shal repente.' *Of thys bruyt* which was made so Impetuously, *the moost hardy of xxx that helde guye began to flee*; and they were so hastely poursyewed that xx of them were slayn. (136.4–9)[37]

Guy, rejoining the battle, 'sayd to the sarasyns: "O ye traytres mastyns, I shal shewe you in thys Iourney that I am escaped fro your handes"' (137.5–7). The violence with which Roland and Guy support their accusations indicates that the Saracens had good reason to be afraid when they were called traitors.[38] In the citadel, another peer, Ogier the Dane, motivates his comrades: '*O loyal companyons, replenysshed of fydelyte*, For ony

---

[36] 'Of all mennys disposicion naturall', lines 144–5.
[37] 'Mastyn', from Middle French, means 'mastiff', 'dog'; Caxton may be the first to use it in English (*OED*).
[38] See also 113.4–8.

payne or doubte of deth emonge vs, *late none be founde wyth ony treason*, ne suffre to entre in to hym ony euyl thought of Infydelyte and cowardyse' (183.21–4). Ogier's juxtaposition of a view of his fellows as chivalric exemplars with an admonition to avoid the opposite of loyal and honourable behaviour encapsulates the behavioural binary the text repeatedly offers to its readers: they are given the option of which identity they wish to claim, of whether they wish to contribute to the good of the community or risk its retaliation.

Ganelon cannot escape his label as a traitor, even when acting honourably before his principal treason. Throughout the campaign that Charlemagne and his knights undertake to rescue Roland, Oliver, and the other captured peers, Ganelon is called a traitor. The 'counceyl of ganellon traytour' (159.3), motivated by Ganelon's oath-breaking intention to bring about the deaths of Roland and Oliver, nearly causes Charlemagne to abandon his captured peers before battle is joined. Ganelon's insidious advice is supported by his faction, 'whyche al were parentes & traytres wyth Ganellon the moost parte' (160.25–6). This affinity group, termed 'the partye of the traytres' (161.12) and 'the companye of traytres' (162.26) by the narrator, privileges loyalty to kin above that to king and community in a fashion that resonates with the threatened disaster in *The Foure Sonnes* (see below), and with the downfall of Arthur's kingdom in the *Morte*, where the Orkney clan are responsible for many of the fractures in the Round Table community and where the fact that their divisive actions are performed in the interests of their kin group is emphasized (see Chapter 4). Soon, however, Charlemagne recognizes Ganelon for what he is: the king 'conceyued wel that Ganellon was a traytre and ful of wyckednesse' (164.24–5).[39] In one battle towards the end of Book 2, the narrator comments that 'Ganellon, whyche after was traytour, bare hym valyauntly... but the loyalte & trouthe of hym ne of hys kynnesmen endured not longe, as the laste book shal more playnly shewe' (170.25–9).[40] Ganelon's later tainted actions inform the text's understanding of his character throughout, indicating that traitorousness is to be understood as innate—not just colouring actions, but indelibly staining a figure's reputation. These achronological comments also betray anxieties about the ontology of knighthood and the unstable division between good and

---

[39] This parallels the way in which a fifteenth-century London chronicle discusses the duplicitous actions of 'that fals traytur thee Duke of Somersett' (221) and his supporters in the North in 1463: 'Gregory's Chronicle' remarks with relief that 'thenn the kynge, owre soverayne lorde Edwar[d] the iiij, hadde knowleche of hys fals dysposysycyon of thys fals Duke Harry of Somersett' (223), and 'God be thonkyd, hyr fals treson was aspyde and knowe' (223–4).

[40] See also 173.29–30.

bad: battlefield prowess was supposed to correspond with inward honour, but figures such as Ganelon reveal the fissures in this ideological conjunction. This anxiety about the correspondence between prowess and disposition is also expressed in the *Morte*, when the regicidal but valiant brothers Helyus and Helake are repeatedly referred to as 'these two traytours', 'tho traitours' (363.29, 363.39, 364.10, 364.23, 364.28, 364.33), and, like Ganelon, their treasonous deeds dog descriptions of their prowess: 'they were fals and ful of treason ... yet were they noble knyghtes of their handes' (366.21–2).

After the treason-filled narrative of Book 2, Charlemagne frees all prisoners in France prior to setting out on new crusades: 'to al them that shold haue ben delyuerd to deth for felonnye, murdre, or treason, he pardonned them & gaf to them theyr lyf' (215.3–5). It is as though the beginning of Book 3 seeks to forget treason and give the narrative a fresh start. This thematic clean slate is short-lived, however; treason is pervasively present both rhetorically and substantively in the final half-book. 'Ganellon, the traytre' (230.20) commits his famous betrayal for personal gain when he is sent to demand the surrender of Spanish Saracens. The narrator laments, 'O wycked Ganellon ... thou hast consented to trayson, and allone hast commysed Infydelyte ... was there noo persone that thou louedest whan *to al crysten men* thou hast ben traytre?' (231.10–23). Here as in other contemporary English literature, treason is a universal (horizontal) crime. After Roland and his companions fall in the ambush Ganelon arranged, Charlemagne:

> began tenquyre vpon the fayt of trayson ... he was enfourmed that Ganellon had made it, and that was the comune oppynyon of them alle. And emonge all other Thyerry accused and *appeled* hym of the treason ... kyng charles ordeyned a knyght for ganellon, named pynable, to fyȝt ayenst thyerry. And whan these ij champyons were in the lystes, anone pynalle was slayne by Thyerry; and as wel by thys moyen as by other, it appered clerely that ganellon had bytrayed them. (242.22–34)

This accusation and trial by combat effects the legal proof of a traitor's guilt. While the French *Fierabras* has 'thierry laccusa de la trayson' (o.ii.r), Caxton adds the specifically legal term (*not* near the bottom of a page or column of his print): 'Thyerry accused and *appeled* hym of the treason' (242.25–6). Appeals were not exclusive to English legal practice, but they were particularly Malorian;[41] this seems a sign of the affinities linking the *Morte* and *Charles* despite the Battle of Bosworth (22 August 1485) intervening between their publications. When Charlemagne orders Ganelon to

---

[41] See Chapter 4, notes 43 and 44.

be publicly drawn asunder by horses, we see that, for *Charles*, the traitor's 'end', in both senses of the word, is to be severely punished as an example and admonition for society.

GENERATIONS OF TREASON IN
THE FOURE SONNES OF AYMON

As the previous sections have argued, *Godeffroy* and *Charles* parallel Malory's *Morte* not least in their shared concern and work with representations of treason. Goodman argues that these three prose romances, published between 1481 and 1485, appeal 'urgently to the knights of England to conform to a standard of conduct marked out in' Ramon Lull's *The Book of the Ordre of Chyvalry* (which Caxton printed in 1484; discussed further below).[42] Goodman excludes *The Foure Sonnes of Aymon* from this group because its Charlemagne, 'unsympathetic' and 'senile', 'hardly shines as a Christian Worthy'.[43] The difference between *Charles'* and *The Foure Sonnes'* Charlemagnes is indeed pronounced, but the three romances Goodman singles out have much more than their connections with the Christian Worthies to recommend them as literary treatments of Lull's chivalric principles. The wider context of the texts' espoused standards of chivalric conduct—their shared interest in and anxieties about horizontal or broad-based social bonds—shows that *The Foure Sonnes* does not 'jar' with *Godeffroy, Charles*, and the *Morte*, but is rather a complementary, cognate text.

In 1488 Caxton translated and printed a fifteenth-century French prose version of the story of Aymon's four sons, resulting in a protracted narrative spanning nearly six hundred pages in the EETS edition.[44] Encompassing more than fifteen years of strife between Charlemagne and the four sons, the narrative reels from one instance, accusation, or admonitory utterance of treason to another, never seeming to find its balance except in the reiterative rhythm of these recriminations. *The Foure Sonnes'* concentration upon treason reflects even stronger anxieties than Caxton's other romances; here it is not only the possibility of treason that is disturbing, but also the difficulties of discerning what constitutes treason, and to whom.

---

[42] Goodman, 'Malory and Caxton's Chivalric Series', p. 271.

[43] Goodman, 'Malory and Caxton's Chivalric Series', p. 271. Goodman's more recent 'Caxton's Continent' reproduces this view of the alterity of *The Foure Sonnes.*

[44] The earliest extant version is a twelfth-century chanson de geste, and all versions remain in verse until the fifteenth century: Richardson, 'Introduction', *The Foure Sonnes.* For Caxton's source, see British Library, *Les Quatre Fils Aymon*, IB.42244 (printed at Lyons in 1480).

The fealty Duke Aymon and his family owe to Charlemagne is com-plicated by a blood feud when Aymon's brother, Duke Benes, refuses to pay homage to his overlord. Charlemagne sends his eldest son, Lohier, to Benes to tell him that he will be judged as 'a false traytour to thy souerayne lorde. for to be fleyen and hanged all quycke, thy wiffe brente, and thi children dystroyed and banysshed' (25.9–13). Benes kills Lohier, but afterwards submits and renews his fealty to Charlemagne. However, Benes is then murdered 'by trayson, and vnder the saufconduyt of the kynge Charlemayne' (51.14–15), who reveals an amoral streak by pursuing this revenge despite recognizing its reprehensibility. Charlemagne declares that to kill Benes 'were traison, for we haue gyuen to hym tryewes' (51.32–3), and reiterates: ' "Certes", sayd the kyng, "it were trayson" ' (52.10–11)—treason, that is, in a counter-hierarchical sense. The doomed Benes, lament-ing 'the false enterpryse of Charlemayne and of the erle Guenellon / that soo cruelly and *by grete trayson* shalle this daye make me Inhumaynly for to deye' (54.12–15), articulates one of the text's abiding questions: 'how myght one kepe hym frome traytours[?]' (53.23–4). This incident, which repeats 'treason' and 'traitor' at least eight times over the next four pages of the EETS edition, exemplifies both the text's persistent unease about the possibility and nature of treason, and its interest in emphatically con-demning it. Although Aymon's sons initially serve Charlemagne against their uncle, after Benes' death the eldest son, Renaud, is provoked by Charlemagne's nephew Berthelot during a chess match and kills him with the chess board. Fearing reprisals, Renaud and his brothers flee the court and prepare for Charlemagne's assaults; what follows is a prolonged strug-gle saturated, both discursively and diegetically, with treason.

Those who fit the mould of chivalric exemplar in the ensuing feud do not do so easily or unambiguously. The four sons' castle in the forest of Ardennes is eventually overcome by treason in an episode peppered with accusations and interpellations of traitors.[45] Before making their escape, the four sons hang, draw, and quarter those Charlemagne sends to infiltrate their stronghold, for, as Renaud puts it, 'traitours ben good to overcom' (95.35). The narrator supports this admonitory punishment: 'ye maye see how the traytours that wolde betraye Reynawde, were deed and slayne. For they were punysshed as they had deserved' (96.31–97.3). Aymon sup-ports Charlemagne against his sons because, as another of Charlemagne's supporters, Esmenfray, reminds Aymon, 'a man of your age shoulde rather deye than he sholde doo ony treyson' (105.28–9). This curious age depend-ency suggests that it is less reprehensible for the four sons to fight against

---

[45] For instance, 81.21, 90.20, 91.12, 91.19, 92.18, 94.4, 95.3, 96.11, and 98.8.

their overlord than for an established chivalric figure to do so, allowing a valorization of the young, newly made knights' conduct by viewing their 'rebellion' as, perhaps, a phase of their chivalric self-fashioning later to be subsumed by their loyalty to Charlemagne once they have established their prowess. Indeed, whether the four sons' resistance is a 'rebellion' is uncertain; the text does not assign blame to either side for the instigation of the strife. Renaud kills Berthelot when defending himself against an insult to his honour, and afterwards Charlemagne sets out to avenge the killing of his nephew, a blood-debt for which he, as king and paterfamilias, must seek retribution. The potential for treason between these two opposing forces only really exists afterwards. Are Renaud and his brothers' actions really treason, or are Charlemagne's more treasonous, despite the fact that the latter is the king to whom the former owe their allegiance? The text seems to invite such questions in its presentation of events, challenging readers to navigate the accusations of treason hurled by both sides.[46]

The closest the text comes to an unproblematic definition of who is or is not a traitor is in reminders that it is not what one does, but how one does it, that determines whether behaviour is exemplary or transgressive. The text displays a powerful interest in the *how* of the conflict, and in lauding or condemning conduct and characters as deserved. For example, Renaud defends his character and actions to Yon, the king of Gascony who offers the four sons shelter: 'I had moche lever deye an evyll deth amonge the turkes / than that I *sholde* thinke treyson vpon you nor vpon no other' (148.11–13). Renaud continues, 'sire, thinke you by cause I am enmye to charlemagn, my soverayn lord / that I *sholde* be therfore a traytour', rejecting the label of treason for his killing of Charlemagne's nephew (148.16–18). Here Balin is again a useful analogue: although he has killed a relative of King Arthur's, the *Morte Darthur* nonetheless repeatedly terms Balin the least treasonous knight. Treason, then, to Renaud as to *The Foure Sonnes*, entails an *underhanded* breach of a loyalty, either a formalized one, as in the case of fealty to overlord, or an informal but expected one, as between family members and comrades in arms. For instance, in response to a demand that he yield up his youngest brother, Richard, Renaud tells Charlemagne's messenger, 'I am not the man that shall doo ony trayson / For *if I sholde* doo it he hym self [Charlemagne] *sholde* blame me for it' (189.31–3). This demonstrates both what Renaud deems to be treason, and his determination to avoid such actions. Similarly, Roland refuses Charlemagne's command to hang Richard because, Roland explains, '*yf I dyde this, I shold be* taken for a traytour / For I have answered Richarde a fore that I toke hym, that he

---

[46] For instance, Charlemagne accuses the brothers as 'the traytoures' (212.3) whom he wishes to hang, and Renaud's side view Charlemagne's actions as 'mortalle trayson' (213.23).

shold have noo harme of his body' (326.15–19). The fact that Roland must disobey his overlord in order to avoid (another) treason reveals the inclusive yet conflicted nature of treason. The italicized words in quotations in this paragraph constitute hypothetical phrasing; that is, a sort of subjunctive treason that universalizes the standards of conduct and repercussions for transgression as a system applicable to everyone. These articulations also acknowledge the ineradicable possibility—the ever-present 'yf'—of falling prey to either treason or treasonousness.

The mode of defining exemplary characters negatively, through the explicit negation of the attribution of treason, is prevalent in this romance as in the others. Yon vouches for Renaud to his own barons not by praising Renaud's good conduct, but by stressing his avoidance of bad conduct: 'he shall never thynke vpon no treyson nor to no shame in no maner of wyse' (150.32–151.2). Aymon similarly defends his sons' conduct, declaring, 'my children be no theves, traytours, nor no murdrers' (435.17–18). Treason cannot be forgotten, even when absent; as extimate, abjected and expelled but not eliminated, its possibility never recedes to a comfortable distance, in this society as in that of late fifteenth-century England. The characters' caution in not easily bestowing their trust, manifested in their concern to establish the reliability of associates, would resonate for Caxton's contemporary readership—as would the wish to avoid receiving the reputation or punishment of a traitor expressed by, among others, Yon's barons, who advise their king against underhandedly breaking his alliance with Renaud because 'if ye doo it . . . ye shall be taken and holden for a traytour' (206.30–1). An awareness that traitors should expect to lose their social position and reputation pervades the text as it would Wars of the Roses society: after deceitfully sending the four sons into a death trap, Yon says, in recognition of his own culpability, 'a man that betrayeth his frende, oughte never to have honoure' (217.11–12).[47] This is why, when Ogier hears Charlemagne 'call . . . hym traytour afore all his barons' (251.27–8), he must defend himself vigorously against the public shame it threatens, declaring, 'I never dide treison, nor never shall' (265.20–1). There is perhaps no better gloss for this exchange than the accusations that Malory's Gawain utters when Launcelot is estranged from Arthur:

> where arte thow now, thou fals traytour Syre Launcelot? Why hydest thow thyself within holes and walles lyke a coward? . . . thow fals traytour knyghte . . . I shal reuenge vpon thy body the dethe of my thre bretheren! All this langage herd Sir Launcelot euery dele.

---

[47] For another such articulation specific to traitor kings, see 207.29–31. Yon's status as a traitor is frequently repeated in the text: for instance, he is 'full of evyll trayson' (215.24), and 'the traytour kyng Yon' (219.18–19); see also 218.17 and 218.26.

> And his kyn and his knyghtes drewe about hym, and alle they sayd at
> ones . . . Sir Launcelot, now muste ye defende yow lyke a knyghte or els ye
> be shamed foreuer, for now ye be called vpon treason. It is tyme for yow to
> stere. (580.3–9)

The members of these chivalric communities share an awareness that public accusations of treason cannot be ignored. For the knights in *The Foure
Sonnes* and the *Morte* as for fifteenth-century English gentry,[48] fear of the
dire consequences meted out to those convicted of treason encourages
proper conduct. Ogier, like Launcelot and his kin, has to continually strive
to distinguish himself from treason, and to worry about what might hap-
pen if he does not succeed.

The Foure Sonnes also resonates with contemporary ideas regarding how
both the order of knighthood as a whole and individual knights should
regulate themselves (as in Caxton's *Book of the Ordre of Chyvalry*, discussed further below). Roland shows that it is the duty of all righteous
knights to police treason even if the treason committed has advantageous
results for them. After Yon's affinity betrays Renaud and his brothers to
Charlemagne, Roland—who is on Charlemagne's side—declares, 'I shall
avenge Reynawde and his brederne . . . For *I never loved tratours nor never
shal*' (280.27–30). Hatred of traitors is universal, even, in some cases,
articulated by the traitor, who knows what he deserves and can expect for
his transgression: Yon acknowledges, 'Alas . . . I consented to this mortalle
trayson / Now oughte I well to deye ten tymes yf it myghte be soo / For
I have well deserued deth' (283.4–7). That a traitor to one is a traitor
to all within the commonweal of a kingdom or of Christendom is further stressed by comparisons between particular traitors and Judas. Yon
laments that because he has committed treason, 'I well say that I shall be
lykened to Iudas from hens forthe' (215.34–216.1).[49] Roland, moreover,
terms him not only 'the falseste traytour of the world' (281.32–3), but also
'that devyll the kynge Yon, whiche is the brother of Iudas' (282.10–11).
Comparing traitors to the readily intelligible touchstone of (a secularized)
Judas makes their treason of universal relevance and maintains a focus on
actively responding to traitors with all the worldly repercussions available.

The end to the romance's principal strife re-establishes proper order, but
rather contingently or superficially. Throughout the feud, Renaud continually tries to make peace with Charlemagne, who is finally compelled
to accept Renaud's renewed fealty by the peers' threat to forsake him unless
he does so. Renaud and his brothers submit to their inferior position,

---

[48] See Radulescu, *Gentry Context* (as discussed in Chapters 3 and 4) on correspondences
between the interests of Malorian knights and English gentry.
[49] Yon makes similar self-recriminations at 209.22–3, 279.10–12, and 283.15–19.

but not because they have to. After clearly and consistently demonstrating their superior prowess, courtesy, and honour across fifteen years, they insist on regaining their ordained place in the sociopolitical hierarchy. They act according to the same scruples that Malory's Launcelot expresses when Arthur declares war on him: Launcelot's loyalty remains, as he says, 'I wille neuer see that most noble kynge that made me knyghte neyther slayn ne shamed' (570.15–16). The results are more fortunate in *The Foure Sonnes*, yet this fantasy of a happy ending does not last long. Even when Renaud and his cousin Maugis journey to the Holy Land to fulfil one of Charlemagne's stipulations for peace, their pilgrimage becomes a tale of battles against traitorous Others to regain Jerusalem (497.28–498.2). This channelling of Renaud's prowess towards combatting non-Christians does make the fight against treason 'productive' for Christianity; however, the text proceeds to discuss further major episodes of internecine (Christian) treason. The peace gives way to new accusations of treason and reminders of old strife in the next generation, intertwining an uneasy awareness that treason will recur with a hope that it can be dealt with when it does.

The text demonstrates that continued vigilance is required by concluding with two additional horizontal treasons and by dwelling on the ultimate treason committed by Ganelon. When Renaud's sons are well received at Charlemagne's court, the sons of Foulques 'layd treison vpon reynaud their fader' (540.9–10). Here, as in the main narrative, the accusations of both sides are presented. Constans and Rohars, within hearing of Renaud's sons Aymonet and Yonnet, accuse Renaud of treason against both their father, Foulques, and Charlemagne, a public threat to reputation that must be countered. Renaud's progeny are not slow to respond: Yonnet tells Constans that while the latter has claimed that Charlemagne knows that 'our fader slewe yours by treyson ... I wylle ye wyte that ye lie falsly / but your fader dyde assaylle our by treyson / as a traytour / come of the linage of traytours' (545.8–11). This delightfully overdetermined (yet not entirely repetitious) counter-challenge prompts a trial by combat, with kinship fostering wider division: 'the traytour guenellon' and his family act as sureties for Constans and Rohars because, as Ganelon states, 'they be of our linage' (546.19–20), while Roland and Oliver stand surety for Aymonet and Yonnet, who eventually achieve a righteous victory. Afterwards, the text gestures towards a treasonous disaster that it does not itself relate: Ganelon, watching Foulques' two sons hang after they have lost the judicial contest, is called 'the traytour' who 'betrayed afterwarde the xii peres of fraunce / and made theim all deye at the bataylle of rouncevals' (569.15–18). The text strives to rebuke and therefore contain treason throughout, but it also gestures towards a future in which treason eludes such checks or responses.

Lastly, and similarly, the text generates yet more treason when Renaud is killed by the horizontal treason of the fellowship of church-building labourers to which he belongs after he renounces the chivalric life. The narrator explains that 'whan the traytours' saw Renaud sleeping, one 'traitour wyth the hamer' struck Renaud (581.17–24). Then, 'whan the traytours had thus slayn reynawd' (581.30), they put him in a sack in the river, whence he is recovered and canonized. Despite combatting against his king, Renaud remains the text's principal exemplary figure throughout because he strives to do the best he can by those to whom he owes faith. In a world of complex loyalties and murky politics not unlike that of the Wars of the Roses, Renaud instructs some fellow knights that 'it is the fouleste crafte that a knyght may for to doo trey-son' (234.8–9); it is continually made clear that treason ought to be avoided, but the text's unease about contested definitions of treason indicates that finding the best course of action is no easy matter. In *The Foure Sonnes* as in *Godeffroy* and *Charles*, the narratives, it seems, cannot be trusted to speak for themselves; the labels 'traitor' and 'treason' and attendant intensifying adjectives ('false', 'evil', 'great') are insistently provided, perhaps not least because they seek to define something that is hard to define.

A CAXTONIAN CANON?

Other prose romances that Caxton translated and printed—the *Recuyell of the Histories of Troy* (1475), *Blanchardine and Eglantine* (1488), and *Eneydos* (1490)—also treat treason, though less intensively than *Godeffroy*, *Charles*, and *The Foure Sonnes*. *Troy*, Caxton's first translation, demonstrates Caxton's interest in reproducing tales of treason and destruction from the start of his printing, an interest that deepened after Caxton relocated from Bruges to Westminster: intriguingly, though he printed from 1475 until 1491/2, his romances manifesting the strongest preoccupation with treason were all printed in the volatile decade of the 1480s. In this decade, Caxton also produced a set of handbooks propounding tenets of ideal interpersonal conduct: *The Game of Chess* (second edition 1482), *The Book of the Ordre of Chyvalry* (1484), *The Book of Fayttes of Armes and of Chyualrye* (1489). These treatises parallel and provide commentaries on the romances' representations of treason.[50]

---

[50] Caxton printed another conduct book, *The Book of the Knight of the Tower* (1484; closely translating a 1370s French source), which comments that some people are 'tray-tours and backbyters' (61.4; when listing common sins), but does not focus on treason very

Caxton's *Troy*, translated from the 1460s French version written by Raoul Lefèvre, Philip of Burgundy's chaplain, treats treason in similar ways to the other prose romances discussed thus far, but less extensively. While Caxton printed *Troy* on the continent, he specifies that one of his reasons for translating it into English was so that 'hyt myght be had as well in the royame of Englond as in other landes'; he connects the text to the strife of the time by specifying the contemporary 'grete devysions' in England.[51] The first two books include several shaming accusations of treason for homosocial betrayals,[52] and the third book is concerned with the troubles and divisions leading to the final destruction of Troy. Calchas' defection to the Greeks receives attention as an act of treason, and he is accused as a traitor by both characters and text: the Trojans 'callid hym euyll and fals traytre' (601.30–602.2); Briseyda accuses him of having 'ben trayttre thou that oughtest to haue... deffended thy contree vnto the deth' (604.28–30); and the narrator punctiliously labels him as 'the false traytour Calcas / whiche was traytour to the troians' (632.18–19). Later, Hecuba exhorts her son Paris to avenge Hector's and Troilus's deaths by reminding him, 'this trayttre Achilles hath slayn by trayson forseen thy brethern... And for as moche as he hath so slayn hem by trayson / me semeth good and also Iuste and right that he be slayn by trayson' (641.13–18). This logic, and the lack of reference to providence concerning punishment for traitors, aligns Caxton's *Troy* with the prose *Siege of Troy* and distinguishes it from Lydgate's *Troy Book*. Caxton locates the moral of 'the generall destruccion of that noble cyte of Troye and the deth of so many... kynges, dukes, erles, barons, knyghtes and comyn peple' in the secular admonition these events offer as an 'ensample to all men duryng the world how dredefull and jeopardous it is to begynne a warre and what harmes, losses and deth foloweth' (*Own Prose*, 101.34–40).

Blanchardyn and Eglantine likewise condemns as treason betrayals that are horizontal and/or cross-polity, as when Blanchardyn fights a single combat against a Saracen giant who treacherously calls in reinforcements.[53] Treason is treated elsewhere in this text, but not extensively.[54] *Eneydos* also

much, perhaps in part because it is directed towards women. While the text has plenty of examples of *wicked* women, when it comes to *crime*, there is much more emphasis on urging women to inculcate moral virtue in 'an euylle and felon husbond' than on discussing women themselves as potential felons or traitors: *The Book of the Knight of the Tower*, ed. by M. Y. Offord, EETS SS 2 (London: Oxford University Press, 1971), p. 133.4–5.

[51] *Caxton's Own Prose*, ed. by N. F. Blake (London: Deutsch, 1973), pp. 97.11–17 and 99.10–15.

[52] For instance, *Recuyell of the Historyes of Troye*, ed. by H. O. Sommer, 2 vols (London: Nutt, 1894), pp. 33.17–21 and 103.22–6.

[53] *Blanchardyn and Eglantine*, ed. by Leon Kellner, EETS ES 58 (London: Trübner, 1890), p. 87.1–5.

[54] For instance, p. 23.24–5 and a scattering in pp. 175.21–199.3–5.

features some homosocial accusations of treason in a prologue to Aeneas'
arrival in Carthage,[55] and thereafter concerns itself primarily with betrayals in love, which are discussed in the language of treason: for instance,
Dido bewails, 'eneas...how haste thou had the herte so vntrue, to thynke
so grete a treason / as for to wyll departe out of my lande sodaynly' (66.23–
6). In the same vein, Dido elsewhere calls Aeneas 'this euyll man / & a
traytour' (72.2–3).[56] This use of legalistic accusations of treason to condemn the betrayal of lover by lover in the 1490 *Eneydos* is reminiscent
of the anonymous *Melusine* romances (discussed in Chapter 3), similarly
'Englished' towards the close of the fifteenth century. This may suggest
that the early Tudor era, perhaps due to deflection from and/or diminish-
ment of concern with homosocial treason, had more room for condemning gender betrayals than did the literature of the more central years of the
Wars of the Roses; however, matters of political alliance also inflect these
gendered accusations, especially in the case of Dido and Aeneas.

Caxton's remaining prose romances, the *History of Jason* (1477) and *Paris
and Vienne* (19 December 1485), treat treason minimally; for instance, it
is mentioned only once in the latter, where it is strictly hierarchical.[57] In
Jason, Mirro accuses Jason as 'dysloyall and vntrewe false lyer where as ye
haue not holden ne fayth ne trouth' because he does not keep his promise to marry her.[58] Yet even compared to *Eneydos*, there is little mention
of treason in this text, despite an uncle's intentions to murder Jason and
usurp his throne, and Jason's betrayal of a string of women. This lack of
treason is due to Caxton's source, the *Histoire de Jason* of Raoul Lefèvre,
who, writing *c.*1460 to celebrate the chivalric Order of the Golden Fleece
founded by his employer Duke Philippe le Bon of Burgundy, elided the
reprehensibility of Jason's betrayal of Medea and other women to present a
more attractive image of the order's hero.[59] That making *Jason* 'Burgundian'
involved writing treason *out* of the narrative, and that this Burgundian
move is an exception among Caxton's prose romances, serves as another

[55] William Caxton, *Eneydos*, ed. by M. T. Culley and F. J. Furnivall, EETS ES 57
(London: Oxford University Press, 1890), pp. 13.1–2, 19.15–19, and 19.25–6.

[56] Dido further condemns Aeneas' actions at 72.26–8, 76.15, 86.31, 93.5, 99.16,
105.17, and 101.15–16. On Dido's central role in Caxton's *Eneydos* (though not in terms of
treason), see Marilynn Desmond, *Reading Dido: Gender, Textuality, and the Medieval Aeneid*
(Minneapolis: University of Minnesota Press, 1994), pp. 167–76.

[57] *Paris and Vienne*, ed. by MacEdward Leach, EETS OS 234 (London: Oxford
University Press, 1957), p. 42.13–15.

[58] Caxton, *The History of Jason*, ed. by John Munro, EETS ES 111 (London: Oxford
University Press, 1913), p. 178.29–30.

[59] Ruth Morse, 'Problems of Early Fiction: Raoul Lefèvre's "Histoire de Jason" ', *Modern
Language Review*, 78.1 (1983), 34–45 (pp. 35–7).

warning against viewing his romance printing as primarily influenced by Burgundian literary models.

More significant here are the three tracts of the 1480s that complement the prose romances' attitudes towards treason. The first of these, *The Game of Chess*, which Caxton translated from a mid-fourteenth-century French version of the Latin *Liber de ludo scaccorum*, was initially printed in Bruges in 1475 and dedicated to Edward IV's brother George of Clarence. However, since Clarence was executed for treason in 1478, Caxton's second edition of *The Game of Chess*, printed at Westminster in 1482, is packaged with new paratextual comments to serve a different readership. Caxton does not dedicate the second edition to a specific patron; instead, he writes, 'thys sayd book is ful of holsom wysedom and requysyte vnto euery astate and degree'.[60] Moreover, Caxton specifies its didactic purpose: 'late euery man of what condycion he be that redyth or herith this litel book redde. take therby ensaumple to amende hym' (L6r). This text articulates the integral role that all estates must play to ensure social order; Caxton further sharpens this focus through interpolations in the text (in both editions), and by the new stress he places on its broad relevance when reissuing it in England in 1482.

In late medieval literary texts and political treatises alike, chess games, as Jenny Adams observes, 'encoded anxieties about political organization' and 'civic community', because chess modelled political order;[61] therefore a treatise on the roles of the various chess pieces as overt social allegory seems an especially appropriate forum for Caxton's meditations on treason and societal decline. In a discussion of oath-breaking, the text states that Alexander the Great 'had leuer not to do his wyll than to be periured and forsworn and doo ageynst his oth' (B1v). Caxton then remarks, in a passage not found in his source, 'Alas who kepe the prynces their promyses in thyse dayes / not onely her promyses but their othes her sealis and wrytynges and signes of theyr propre handes' (B1v). Moreover, the text, and Caxton's additions, by no means confine their negative admonitions and lamentations regarding proper conduct to rulers; elsewhere, the text declares that 'now a dayes there is no thynge ellis in the world but / barate treson / deceit falsenes and trecherye men kepe not their couenauntes / promyses. othes. writynges / ne trouth' (D4r). Knights are singled out for attention in a chapter that confirms the importance of chivalric fellowship: 'Thus ought the knyghtes to loue to gyder. and eche to put his lyf in

---

[60] Caxton, *Jacobus de Cessolis, The Game of Chess*, ed. by N. F. Blake (London: Scolar Press, 1976), a.ii. References to this facsimile are cited by quire and leaf signatures.

[61] Jenny Adams, *Power Play: The Literature and Politics of Chess in the Late Middle Ages* (Philadelphia: University of Pennsylvania Press, 2006), p. 2.

auenture for other. ffor so been they the strenger and the more doubted'
(C6r). However, this chapter also details the shameful loss of status that
those who exhibit a lack of loyalty will suffer (C5r).[62]

In *The Game of Chess*, Caxton also inveighs against the lack of social
cohesion in England:

> Alas what habundaunce was somme tymes in the royames. and what pros-
> perite / In whiche was Justice. and euery man in his offyce contente /...how
> was renomed the noble royame of englond alle the world dradde hit and
> spake worshyp of hit. How hit now standeth...I reporte me to them that
> knowe hit yf ther ben theuys wyth in the royame or on the see. they knowe
> that laboure in the royame / and sayle on the see / I wote well the fame is
> grete therof / I pray god saue that noble royame. and sende good trewe and
> polletique counceyllours to the gouernours of the same. (I8v–K1r)

Here Caxton expresses anxieties about social stability that have no full
or comforting answer, but also redeploys the age-old topos of worldly
decline in contemporary armour to militate against the evils and instabilities caused by civil war and grasping magnates. His concern to ameli-
orate England's security and well-being includes a prayer, but the solution
he requests of God is a very secular and pragmatic one: better and more
honest counsellors, better governance. The deictic 'now a dayes' recurs
insistently in this text's lamentations and critiques; the 'ubi sunt' topos
germane to Caxton's view of society is not 'Hwaer cwom mearg? Hwaer
cwom mago? Hwaer cwom maþþumgyfa?',[63] but rather, hwaer cwom
troth, fidelity, friendship, and perhaps especially, commitment to the commonweal. This last receives an elegy of its own:

> the verray trewe loue of the comyn wele and proffyt now a dayes is selde
> founden / where shal thou fynde a man in thyse dayes that wyl expose hym
> self for the worshyp and honour of his frende / or for the comyn wele / selde
> or neuer shal he be founden. (C6v)

As discussed in Chapter 2, in the English textual culture of this period—in
literary texts, treatises such as this one, correspondence, chronicles, and
political poems and proclamations alike—treason is often configured
as an act that contravenes the commonweal in particular. The imagined
community in which Caxton invites all English people to participate by
buying his book and following its instruction is a community organized
around the secular, civil, egalitarian concept of the commonweal. His texts

---

[62] The text similarly criticizes lawyers (f.ii.v–f.iii.r), and Caxton denounces the dishonest,
disloyal behaviour of men of law in England specifically (f.iii.r).

[63] 'The Wanderer', in *The Exeter Anthology of Old English Poetry*, ed. by Bernard J. Muir,
2 vols (Exeter: University of Exeter Press, 1994), I, 218–22 (line 92).

repeatedly deploy treason to articulate this more horizontal or holistic idea of social cohesion.[64] Because the commonweal as an idea of governance began to obtain in England with York and other malcontents *c.*1450, Caxton's publishing of literature that concentrates on and worries about the commonweal would have special resonance for contemporary English readers.

Caxton's *Book of the Ordre of Chyvalry*, another cultural grammar-book that meditates upon the sorts of treason manifested in the romances, similarly presents the commonweal as an ideal of social organization and a focus for loyalty. This text asserts that 'thordre of chyulary is moche necessary as touchyng the gouerneme[n]t of the world' (115.7–8), and that chivalry should preserve and advance the commonweal: 'To a knyght apperteyneth / that he be louer of the comyn wele / For...the comyn wele is gretter and more necessary than propre good and specyall'.[65] Part handbook, part philosophical treatise, Caxton's print is the only medieval English rendering of Ramon Lull's manual of chivalry.[66] In the text's narrative frame, an old knight educates an aspiring squire by giving him a book to read and to offer to 'euery noble man that wold be in thordre of chyalry' (14.4–5); understanding how to be a good knight requires not just practical skills, but also textual authority and firm ideological foundations. This text-within-a-text provides definitions, injunctions, and admonitions regarding proper knightly behaviour and its antithesis, treason. It specifies that knights (and clerks) are to be models of ideal conduct to all people in order to counteract stability-threatening treasonous tendencies: 'yf ther were none errour in the clerkes and in the knyghtes / vnneth shold ther be ony in other peple /...by the knyghtes they shold doubte to doo wronge / trayson and barate the one to another' (23.3–8). Here the preeminence of the chivalric and educated classes is stressed, but avoiding treason is also a norm to which everyone should aspire.

---

[64] The concerns with lateral community in *Godeffroy, Charles*, and *The Foure Sonnes* are addressed in the previous sections; concern with the commonweal also inflects Caxton's *Troy* and *Eneydos*. In *Troy*, Hercules' exemplary pursuit of the common good is set against fifteenth-century behaviour: 'The men at this day fyght oon ayenst another And make conquestes ynowhe / but they attrybue them vnto their synguler proffit. They resemble not vnto hercules / that neuer fought but for the comyn wele of the world' (428). In *Eneydos*, Dido instructs her citizens that 'he is right *vnhappy*, that for his partyculer wele wyll leue ye publike & comyn wele / & contrary wyse, he is blessyd that Ieopardeth hym to the deth for ye comen wele of his countrey' (33.26–9). Here 'unhappy' seems to carry the same connotations of lamentable misfortune as when it describes Malory's Mordred, whose behaviour is similarly antithetical to ideals.

[65] William Caxton, *The Book of the Ordre of Chyvalry*, ed. by Alfred T. P. Byles, EETS OS 168 (London: Oxford University Press, 1926), p. 113.1–5.

[66] There is, however, a mid-fifteenth-century Scottish translation, by Sir Gilbert Hay.

The *Book of the Ordre of Chyvalry* emphasizes an exclusionary demarcation of the order of knighthood. The text repeatedly moves from a negative to a positive model in an admonitory dialetic. For instance, knights are supposed to be active proponents of social cohesion and stable hierarchy: 'the euyl knyght whiche...wold put doun his lord fro the seignory...he foloweth not thoffyce by which he is called a knyȝt / By the knyȝtes ouȝt to be mayntened & kept justyce' (30.2–7).[67] Oath-breaking, not unsurprisingly, receives repeated attention, including parallels drawn between spiritual and secular troth: 'by cause that god and chyualry concorde to gydre / hit behoueth / that fals swerynge and vntrewe othe / be not in them that mayntene thordre of chyualrye' (43.1–4; see also 32.15–33.3). Yet these parallels between secular and spiritual obligations also show that the former are not solely subordinate components of the latter, but should be honoured for their own sake and within their own framework. Part of the text allegorizes chivalric accoutrements, encircling the knight with tangible admonitory reminders of what he must not do: for example, 'By the gau[n]telots is also sygnefyed / that he ought not to lyfte vp his hond / in makyng a fals othe / ne handle none euylle' (82.15–83.1). Knights and oath-breakers are, in fact, mutually exclusive groups: 'he is not that periureth hym worthy to be in thordre of chyualry' (54.14–15). Exhortations to police or purge traitors offer the same message: 'Thoffyce of a trewe knyȝt is to accuse a traytour / & to fyght ageynst hym' (51.16–17). Knighthood, then, is defined not only in opposition to but by explicit regulatory exclusion of treachery; for if an aspiring squire 'euer dyd ony falsenesse or trechery...he is not worthy that chyualry shold receyue hym in to his ordre / ne that he be made felawe of them / that mayntene thordre of chyualrye' (64.5–10). Caxton writes in his epilogue that this text is not for 'euery comyn man' but for 'noble gentylmen that by their vertu entende to come and entre in to the noble ordre of chyulary' (123.7–9); this encourages virtuous conduct (and increased sales) by aligning worship with possessing a copy of his book. Here Caxton also advertises his other publications by accompanying his recrimination, 'O ye knyghtes of Englond where is the custome and vsage of noble chyualry that was vsed in tho dayes' (122.8–9), with a prescription to read romances—such as his own—as a corrective to the decline in chivalric conduct.

Another of Caxton's chivalric tracts, his 1489 translation of Christine de Pisan's *Book of Fayttes of Armes and of Chyualrye*, further illuminates the prose romances' understanding of treason. Written in 1408–9, Christine's treatise on military strategy and standards was compiled from works by Roman authors (such as Vegetius, Frontinus, and Valerius Maximus),

---

[67] See also 39.11–15.

Honoré Bouvet, and anonymous medieval contemporaries, and woven together with her own comments.[68] The first of the four books treats the justification and preparation for war, and the second concerns tactics; the latter two, drawn from the cleric Honoré Bouvet's 'L'Arbre des batailles' (*c.*1387), concern 'the ryghtes of armes after the lawes',[69] and discuss how to navigate the ambiguities of troth and treason. The third book specifies that deceit is allowed as long as a state of war is openly declared: 'men ought to vaynquysshe his enemye or may ouercome hym by barat / cawtelle and engyne without wronge of armes *syth that the werre is Iuged and notyfyed betwyx bothe partyes*' (214.2–5). Ambushes are permissable too, if a leader can 'ordeyne busshementes there as hys ennemye muste passe...or alle suche other maneres of cawteles / so that they be not ayenst feyth promysse nor ayenst thassuraunce that men had made' (214.26–32). However, it is quite a different matter if one's enemy has cause to expect good faith. *Fayttes of Armes* defines treason as a subset—the forbidden subset—of 'barates',[70] or deceptions: if

> I sholde assure som body for to come to me in a place where as I shulde be for to speke with hym / and...vndre myn assuraunce he cometh there where as I shulde doo hym to be taken and slayne / *Suche as thynge were a ryght euylle treason* / Or ellis yf by feyned trewes or peas I shulde aspye my tyme for to hurte som other body that...weneth to be sauffe / and all suche other maners of wayes / wherof I shulde doo euill and grete dyshonoure and repreef shulde come to me therby...And therfore *the lawe* saythe / that syth the fayth is youen to hys ennemye / men ought to kepe it to hym. (214.11–26)

By definition, this 'law' can apply to people who are not hierarchically related or even part of the same polity; its regulation of 'treason' accords with the international military law (discussed in Chapter 2), and this same 'law' informs the prose romances' judgements concerning treason. Book 4 of *Fayttes of Armes* adds to this ideology in its treatment of safe conducts, which should be given and kept in good faith (and without deceptive wording) because otherwise 'it shulde be treason that ouer gretly were to be blamed' (244.38–245.2): this is again inclusive of cross-polity trust and contracts. Here Christine offers a negative social commentary (not found in her source) that makes concerns about treason relevant to people of all stations: it

> semeth me grete merueylle seeyng the lytel trouthe and fydelyte that this day renneth thrughe al the worlde / how *a prynce or a lorde or som other*

---

[68] Bornstein, 'Military Manuals in Fifteenth-Century England', pp. 475–7.

[69] William Caxton, *The Book of Fayttes of Armes and of Chyualrye*, ed. by A. T. B. Byles, EETS OS 189 (1932; London: Oxford University Press, 1937), p. 1.

[70] For a definition of 'barate', see note 26.

gentylman & namely what soeuere man that it be dare truste hym self vndre a
saufconduyt…where his enemyes be more myghty and more stronge than he.
(247.35–248.5)

Thus, in his 'faithful' rendering of Christine's version, Caxton codified
for contemporary England one of the discourses concerning treason that
shapes the standards of conduct urged in his, and other, Wars of the Roses
romances.

READING TREASON IN THE CIVIC AND CHIVALRIC LITERATURE OF THE LATE FIFTEENTH CENTURY

This chapter has argued that, in the mid- to late fifteenth century, insular literary culture selectively availed itself of continental cognates as contributions to its fund of romances preoccupied with treason. Caxton's
romances such as *Godeffroy, Charles*, and *The Foure Sonnes* are able to repay
more attention than the slim share they have received, both for their own
sake and for the light they shed upon Malory's *Morte* and contemporary
literary culture. Caxton printed these four prose romances and a series
of handbooks on chivalry across the 1480s, a decade that witnessed four
kings and two dynasties on the English throne. That Caxton intended
these works to be read together, regardless of whether each was issued
under the aegis of the Yorkist Edward IV and Edward V, or Richard III,
or their Tudor successor Henry VII, is implied both by the explicit connections made between the texts in their prologues' discussions of the
Worthies, and by the texts' shared cultural work. Indeed, it is a testament
to the continuity of Caxton's readership and their interests that Caxton
did not interrupt his printing even at times of particular crisis that caused
him to omit his customary mention of the regnal year in a prologue, as
when he printed the *Morte* without mention of Richard three weeks before
Bosworth.[71] Bornstein maintains that Caxton's romances, in the tradition
of Burgundian chivalric writings, 'only portray the positive aspects of the

---

[71] Painter, *William Caxton*, pp. 146–7. Caxton did not print any chivalric romances
for two years after 1485, but this was due to him having nearly exhausted his list before
Bosworth rather than to extended disruption; it took some time to find new patrons, but
Caxton did secure both royal and noble patronage after the Tudor succession: Painter,
pp. 150–2; Louise Gill, 'William Caxton and the Rebellion of 1483', *English Historical
Review*, 114 (1997), 105–18 (p. 116). That readers still wanted the same sorts of books
after the regime change is confirmed by Caxton's 1488–9 printing of *The Foure Sonnes,
Blanchardyn and Eglantine, Fayttes of Arms*, and *Eneydos*.

chivalric code'.[72] However, while these texts certainly render themselves available as chivalric manuals, the general tenor of their engagements with the chivalric code is not 'positive' per se, but is, rather, admonitory in order to be aspirational. The reader of these texts is directed to emulate the treason-eschewing conduct of Godfrey, Launcelot, Tristram, Oliver, Roland, and Renaud. Like these figures, Caxton's romances transcend partisan ties, remaining a viable mode across their decade's political tensions and regime changes by constituting a sort of literary canon unto themselves, informed by and informing contemporary English concerns.

As a publisher, then, Caxton remained loyal not only to this material, but also to the expectations of readers of manuscript romances; such continuities and overlaps between manuscript and print culture in the late fifteenth century[73] further testify to the relevance of Caxton's printed prose romances and their concerns with treason to contemporary English literary culture. The printing press certainly had specific implications for the romances it produced and the readers who purchased them. Because printing presses had much greater productive capacity than scribes, speculative production had to be made viable in order for a press to maximize profits; therefore, greater demand for books had to be created. Yet while Caxton's romance publishing was motivated by mercantile interests, because Caxton had to develop a book list that would convince potential consumers that 'they wanted what he could make',[74] this does not imply that his texts were selected on the basis of different characteristics than those of manuscript romances. Malory and contemporaries such as the author of the prose *Thebes* and *Troy* wrote manuscript romances that engaged with the concerns of their intended audiences; Caxton was evidently aware of texts and interests of this nature, and sought to produce books with a similar appeal.[75] Thus the fact that he chose books that seemed likely to sell—and packaged them with paratextual material foregrounding their thematic and didactic interests in treason—does not contradict but should rather add to our awareness of the extent to which his books belonged to a type of texts already popular in England.

Caxton's texts, however, made this literature about treason relevant and available to more people than before. Caxton's romance readership was

---

[72] Bornstein, 'Caxton's Chivalric Romances', p. 6.   [73] See note 11.

[74] David R. Carlson, 'A Theory of the Early English Printing Firm: Jobbing, Book Publishing, and the Problem of Productive Capacity in Caxton's Work', in *Caxton's Trace*, pp. 35–68 (pp. 52 and 57–8).

[75] Similar arguments are made for the selectivity of Caxton's publishing (with respect to other components of his print corpus) by R. F. Yeager, 'Literary Theory at the Close of the Middle Ages: William Caxton and William Thynne', *Studies in the Age of Chaucer*, 6 (1984), 135–64 (p. 139 and p. 146), and by Desmond, *Reading Dido*, p. 170.

drawn from the widening social classes desiring and able to take advantage of the cheaper, more plentiful printed copies he produced. On the evidence of contemporary signatures and annotations, Yu-Chiao Wang has shown that '[c]ourtiers, merchants, clerics, lawyers, state officials, male and female members of the landed families, and gentlewomen at court—rather than aristocrats—seem to have formed the major readership' for Caxton's romances.[76] Many of these groups belonged to the expanding gentry class, and as such they parallel the likely gentry readership for that other romance printed by Caxton, the *Morte*. The four concerns most central to gentry circles—worship, friendship, fellowship, and good lordship—are preoccupations of the *Morte*,[77] and, as we have seen, they are central preoccupations of Caxton's *Godeffroy, Charles*, and *The Foure Sonnes* as well. The 'grete books' compiled for Sir John Astley, Sir John Paston, and Sir Gilbert Hay in the 1450s–1470s (along with two royal manuscripts containing related texts), each including 'a treatise on warfare, on chivalric ethics, on princely behaviour, and sometimes on knightly ceremonial', show the interests in chivalric instruction that members of the gentry would have brought to a reading of Malory's *Morte* and Caxton's own prose romances,[78] particularly since, alongside the romances, Caxton published chivalric handbooks that feature in the 'grete books', such as Lull's *Ordre of Chyvalry* and Christine de Pisan's *Fayttes of Armes*.

Moreover, Caxton presented his romances to appeal not only to the gentry but also to merchants, who were beginning to own and read books in greater numbers and who could find a positive identity for themselves in Caxton's literary models. Caxton was, of course, a merchant himself, and in the prologue to a text he printed in 1484, he identifies himself as a citizen of London and a member of 'the fraternyte and *felauship* of the mercerye',[79] evincing the analogous function and conception of civic guilds and chivalric fellowships. Recent scholarship has drawn attention to the direct relevance of some of Caxton's texts to merchant readerships.[80] However, the

---

[76] Yu-Chiao Wang, 'English Romance in Print from 1473 to 1535: Reception and the History of the Book' (unpublished doctoral thesis, University of Cambridge, 2008), p. 74.

[77] Radulescu, *Gentry Context*, p. 84 (as discussed in Chapter 4).

[78] Karen Cherewatuk, ' "Gentyl" Audiences and "Grete Bookes": Chivalric Manuals and the *Morte Darthur*', in *Arthurian Literature XV*, ed. by James P. Carley and Felicity Riddy (Cambridge: Brewer, 1997), pp. 205–16 (pp. 213–15), and 'Sir Thomas Malory's "Grete Booke" ', in *The Social and Literary Contexts of Malory's Morte Darthur*, ed. by D. Thomas Hanks, Jr and Jessica G. Brogdon (Cambridge: Brewer, 2000), pp. 42–67 (pp. 43 and 51–2). For the full contents of one such compilation, see G. A. Lester, *Sir John Paston's 'Grete Boke'* (Cambridge: Brewer, 1984).

[79] *Caton*, in *Caxton's Own Prose*, p. 63.14–15. Caxton dedicates this book to the city of London.

[80] A. F. Sutton, 'Caxton was a Mercer: His Social Milieu and Friends', in *England in the Fifteenth Century: Proceedings of the 1992 Harlaxton Symposium*, pp. 118–48; Mark Addison

connections between the *chivalric* interests of late fifteenth-century merchants and the type of chivalric literature they were increasingly beginning to read invite further attention. Late medieval London citizens 'developed their own brand of chivalric spectacle...influenced by chivalric tournaments and romances' but with 'a distinct, possibly bourgeois, character of its own'.[81] These civic–chivalric displays included a ceremonial marching of the Watch at midsummer (which began to incorporate pageants during the fifteenth century) and another public procession every autumn when the new mayor (accompanied by more pageantry and a swordbearer by the fifteenth century) rode from London to Westminster to swear his oath to the king. Moreover, aldermen were knighted in greater numbers in the reigns of Edward IV and Henry VII.[82] Chivalric display, then, was a form of aspirational performative identity for fifteenth-century London merchants. While Londoners' wills from 1300 to 1450 frequently bequeath religious books but rarely chivalric ones, by contrast, records from the later 1400s show that many copies of Caxton's romances, such as *Troy* and *Godeffroy*, were held by London merchants.[83] In this merchant context for the production and reception of Caxton's chivalric prints, it is important that late fifteenth-century citizens believed civic society was weakening. London's administrative system 'depended on being able to locate citizens in resident communities of sworn householders who, as neighbours, would know and pledge each other to keep the peace', but this system was destabilized by the increasing numbers of outsiders or 'foreigners' who were, by the late fifteenth century, in London and refusing to abide by the rules.[84] By making romances more widely available, particularly ones strongly concerned with secular and horizontal fellowships and the commonweal, Caxton's printing press offered not only landed society, but also members of urban society, a type of reading material with which they could identify themselves and their anxieties.[85] Indeed, by including a merchant readership in his prologues' and epilogues' urgings that readers emulate the good and eschew the bad in his books, Caxton shows merchants how to read texts that are

Amos, 'Disciplining Women and Merchant Capitalists in *The Book of the Knyght of the Towre*', in *Caxton's Trace*, pp. 69–100.

[81] Caroline Barron, 'Chivalry, Pageantry and Merchant Culture in Medieval London', in *Heraldry, Pageantry and Social Display in Medieval England*, ed. by Peter Coss and Maurice Keen (Woodbridge: Boydell, 2002), pp. 219–41 (p. 228).

[82] Barron, 'Chivalry, Pageantry and Merchant Culture', pp. 228–30.

[83] Barron, 'Chivalry, Pageantry and Merchant Culture', pp. 223–4 and 240.

[84] Jones, 'Thomas More's *Utopia* and Medieval London', p. 127.

[85] The importance, in late medieval London political culture, of the common good, secular ceremony, and exemplary history is addressed by Caroline Barron, 'The Political Culture of Medieval London', in *Political Culture in Late Medieval Britain*, pp. 111–33.

ostensibly addressed to an aristocratic public but that focus on types of virtue as 'learned behaviour' that 'could be performed by the willing reader' of any status.[86]

In seeking to evaluate the 'what' and 'why' of these texts, however, it is also important not to single them out too much. Caxton's prose romances do not function identically either with each other or with other contemporary English texts; for instance, while all three attitudes are present in each, *Godeffroy, Charles*, and *The Foure Sonnes* can be seen respectively as othering, admonishing, and agonizing about treason (and this sequence perhaps charts their progression through their decade's unrest). However, these texts do share a mode of operating, and with respect to the same concerns. The extent to which Caxton's own translations are cognate to the *Morte Darthur* is demonstrated perhaps especially well by what appears to be a self-reflexive cross-canon reference in *Charles*, where Fierabras asks that he be sent, as opponent, 'Rolland or olyuer or one of thother *knyghtes of the rounde table*' (56.12–13). In Caxton's French source, Fierabras asks only to be sent 'rolla[n]t ou oliuier ou lung des aultres' ('Roland or Oliver or one of the others');[87] in context, this evidently implies a reference to 'one of the other peers of Charlemagne', and Round Table knights are, unsurprisingly, not mentioned here. This is the copy of the French version against which the EETS edition of Caxton's *Charles the Grete* was collated, yet the editor, usually scrupulous in detailing Caxton's minor deviations from his source, does not note that 'knyghtes of the rounde table' is original to Caxton's version. Since this interpolation occurs in the middle of a page in Caxton's print, it is unlikely to be a compositor's error or filler. The printing of *Charles* was finished on 1 December 1485, but Caxton specifies that he finished translating it on 18 June 1485; thus he was working on it at the same time as the printing of the *Morte*, which was not finished until 31 July 1485.[88] Given this overlap, we may view this surprising

---

[86] Tracy Adams, ' "Noble, wyse and grete lordes, gentilmen and marchauntes": Caxton's Prologues as Conduct Books for Merchants', *Parergon*, 22.2 (2005), 53–76 (pp. 55–6 and 73–6). Whether or not all readers were so willing is a different matter. While 'Caxton's readers sometimes shared views similar to his in terms of those characteristics and moral lessons of the romances that Caxton identifies in his paratexts', his romances 'were sometimes read as lascivious tales, and at other times as romances, historical accounts, moral exempla, travel guides, religious treatises, or crusading propaganda' (Wang, 'English Romance in Print from 1473 to 1535', pp. 103 and 76). To read according to the plot and/or to Caxton's directions is to be more or less 'faithful' to the text; to read in anticipation of treason (following foreshadowing remarks such as those concerning Ganelon in *Charles*) perhaps involves a disloyal complicity in the betrayal, but to read in anticipation of traitors' accusation and punishment manifests loyalty.

[87] British Library, C.6.b.12, *c*.8v.

[88] Painter, *William Caxton*, p. 148.

insertion to *Charles* as a (likely unconscious) slip of Caxton's pen that bears witness to an association both between the two volumes in their material production, and between the stories and partially synonymous horizontal fellowships upon which they focus.

Texts such as the anonymous prose *Siege of Thebes*, *Siege of Troy*, *King Ponthus*, *Pseudo-Turpin Chronicle*, and *Melusine*, which parallel Caxton's and Malory's prose romances in their mode of treating chivalry and treason (as discussed in Chapters 3 and 4), parallel or predate Caxton's printing activity in England (1476–92) by between one and three decades, constituting touchstones for our understanding of manuscript copies of Malory's work—of which only the Winchester manuscript has survived but of which there may once have been others from 1469 onwards. The discourses of treason in contemporary correspondence, poetry, and drama (discussed in previous chapters) likewise confirm that this interest was not confined to one or two individuals or initiated by Caxton, but rather a more widespread expression of English culture in the mid- to late fifteenth century that Caxton tied together with the use of new technology. Caxton's translated romances offer their English readerships an addition to their bookshelves and libraries (actual or conceptual) that could be shelved and catalogued adjacent to Malory's *Morte* and a set of other fifteenth-century English texts that all display a desire, manifested through censure and repetition, to make their audiences 'think twice' about treason.

These texts' mode of exemplary narrative, then, separates them from both what precedes them and what follows them. Yet what also makes the romances of this period distinctive are the ways in which they can be separated from neither. Discussing the way in which Caxton's prologues for both chivalric and 'classical' works foreground the interest of the commonweal and the 'efficacy of history', Wakelin asks 'whether chivalry and humanism are distinct categories in the 1480s',[89] but does not further pursue possible intersections of humanist and chivalric literature. As argued here and elsewhere, the way in which late fifteenth-century romances engage with chivalric loyalties is striking in its embodiment of anthropocentrism and secularity. Eschewing the providential frame of earlier romances, these romances instead evince this-worldly frameworks of regulation to construct an ethic of social conduct that privileges legal reasoning and communal accountability. That is, they avail themselves (in a fashion not entirely dissimilar from humanist praxis) of a historicity, classical or Christian, imagined or real, in which ideals can be situated, tested, and

---

[89] Wakelin, *Humanism, Reading, and English Literature*, pp. 154–5.

disseminated for emulation in the pursuit of secular moral virtue. That these texts fell out of fashion later should not obscure their participation in a nascent ideological strain, their reconfiguration of romance to collocate and fuse chivalric and civic projects in a way that indexes the late fifteenth century's continuities and fissures alike.

6

Post Script

Writing of/off Treason after 1500

As the previous chapters have shown, treason haunts the textual culture of the Wars of the Roses. Yet treason is more than a spectre, more solid than a ghost; it is the reader's sinister guide and constant companion. When the *Squire of Low Degree* asserts that 'treason walketh wonder wyde' (520), it summons an image of treason as a long-legged, far-travelling menace. This image of striding ubiquity may well have had proverbial status. In a similar vein, Malory's Round Table oath instructs the knights 'allwayes to fle treson' (120.18), as though treason were a hunter—a dark force or figure shadowing its prey, waiting for its chance to strike. This idea of treason as something that walks, something that stalks, also animates another feature of Launcelot's declaration, 'I fared never wyth no treson, nother I loved never the felyshyp of hym that fared with treson' (1134.17–19). Here Launcelot registers the intimate nature of treason by figuring it not only as a predator, but also as a companion. This persistent touch of anthropomorphism in mid- to late fifteenth-century representations of treason testifies to its hold on the contemporary cultural imaginary.

In addition to personifications of treason, individuals also stand for treason itself. In contrast to late fourteenth-century Langlandian allegory, where the attributes False and Fikel are personified as wicked men, in Malory's and Caxton's prose romances, named figures prompt the opposite cognitive process: characters typify treason. We have seen this in King Yon's recognition that for his treason he will be 'taken all my lyffe as a Iudas' (*Four Sonnes of Aymon*, 209.22–3). Here Judas is a symbolic marker, a signifier calling up a host of damning connotations; he and Mordred, as the arch-traitors of the Christian and English traditions, are metaphors in themselves. As Paul de Man describes, symbol is 'always a part of the totality that it represents'. That is, while allegory alludes to 'a meaning that it does not itself constitute', symbol operates to incorporate signification into itself; a symbol is a concretized metaphor that works *from within* rather than pointing outwards.[1] Accordingly, the way in which, in fifteenth-century England, Mordred, Judas, and words of treason alike operate as concretized metaphors, as shorthands evoking mentalities of which they are a part, is a particularly appropriate and powerful way of figuring treason—since treason is, after all, about action *from within*: within the individual, within the affinity group, within the social body. In Wars of the Roses mentalities, treason is inherently metaphorical; accusatory labels of 'Judas' or 'traitor' serve as touchstones for concerns about social maladies, for a discourse on cultural values and chronic manifestations of their abject, unacceptable opposites. Indeed, the need to 'flee' treason articulated in the Round Table oath also construes the crime as akin to both disease and sin; just as important to avoid was succumbing to another's treason, or spreading the infection by committing or inciting treason oneself.[2]

Yet while treason plagues mid- to late fifteenth-century literary culture and its characters much as it plagues contemporary society, it is both the contagion which must be cured and, as admonitory literature, itself the offer of a cure. As part of a contemporary discourse about treason, the condemnations of treason in Wars of the Roses romances act to interpellate traitors not only within their diegetic bounds, but also among their readership—a readership whose concerns about the prevalence and unpredictability of treason are evinced in gentry letters and civic chronicles. When John Paston II wrote to his brother in 1473 that despite the Yorkist magnates' outward show of unity, 'som men thynke þat vndre thys ther sholde be som other thynge entendyd and som treason conspyred',[3] such uncertainty and fears about 'som treason' speak to the parallels and intersections between the various genres addressed in this study. While the literary texts seek to contain treason by constructing a didactic, admonitory frame, similarly, non-literary texts such as parliamentary attainders, bills, letters, and political verses often seek to contain treason within the legal frameworks available in mid- to late fifteenth-century England. Yet both sets of texts reveal anxious awareness

---

[1] Paul de Man, 'The Rhetoric of Temporality', in *Blindness and Insight: Essays in the Rhetoric of Contemporary Criticism*, 2nd edn (1971; London: Methuen, 1983), pp. 187–228 (pp. 189–91).

[2] A 1472 tract by John Alcock, Bishop of Rochester—which may have been delivered as a speech to Parliament—shows the associative nature of disease and sociopolitical division. Alcock warns against 'discencion and discorde' and asserts that 'every man of this land that is of resonable age hath knowen what trouble this reame hath suffred, and it is to suppose that noon hath escaped but att oo tyme or other his part hath be therein', reasoning metaphorically that 'suche is the condicion of every body that the discrase of oo membre distempereth all the other' (quoted in Strohm, *Politique*, p. 144).

[3] *Paston Letters*, I, 281.2–8.

that treason cannot be entirely contained within such reactionary struc-tures during a time of civil war, in ways that speak to a recognition of the ever-present need to think twice about treason.

This study has sought to offer a more contextualized and thorough understanding of the secular literary culture of the second half of the fifteenth century: in itself, as it relates to preceding literary culture, and (below) as it relates to subsequent literary culture. The cultural imagin-ary of the mid- to late fifteenth century is connected to that of the four-teenth and early fifteenth century by a shared penchant for didactic, chivalric romance; and it is connected to that of the 'early modern' by the secular attitude both frequently manifest. However, what distinguishes the literary culture of the second half of the fifteenth century from both what went before and what went after is its tendency to combine the two: that is, to produce didactic chivalric romances that elide or inter-rogate a providential framework. This secularism of literary world view is not visible much before the mid- to late fifteenth century, and it is conveyed pragmatically *through treason and in romance* much less both before and after.

ROMANCE AND TREASON AFTER 1500?

Paul Scanlon claims that, from the end of the fourteenth century until the beginning of the Elizabethan age, the genre of prose romance 'is essentially of a piece'.[4] However, as the previous chapters have shown, looking for-ward from the initial stages of this temporal sweep—and as is argued here, looking backward from the later stages—this is certainly not the case. The new English 'romances' of the early sixteenth century differ in interest and mode from the romances produced by the preceding generation or two. Moreover, while some chivalric romances translated post-1500 continue the mid- to late fifteenth-century romances' mode of treating treason *qua* underhanded harmful action, others focus only on hierarchical treason and contain a degree of emphasis on providence and spiritual didacti-cism more in keeping with Lydgate's writings than with those of the inter-vening sixty years. Overall, in the romances produced during the early sixteenth century, the scope of secular pragmatism narrows and treason content diminishes, and inclination towards or tolerance of unhappy end-ings also decreases. These trends do suggest certain chronological distinc-tions between literary moments, but do not encourage reliance on period

---

[4] Paul A. Scanlon, 'Pre-Elizabethan Prose Romances in English', *Cahiers Élisabéthains: Études sur la pré-renaissance et la renaissance anglaises*, 12 (1977), 1–20 (p. 1).

binaries—because these are not the distinctions we may expect for the year 1500.

Romance after 1500 includes, not least, new prints of texts from the second half of the fifteenth century, such as the *Squire of Low Degree, Melusine*, and at least three of Caxton's romances (*Recuyell, Morte Darthur*, and *Foure Sonnes*): these are addressed in the preceding chapters in the context of their first (English) appearances, but their reproduction shows that they were still sufficiently popular to claim a readership in the early 1500s (and sometimes, as with the *Recuyell*, long afterwards too). However, the phenomenon of these sixteenth-century (re)printings resembles the way in which Lydgate was recopied (in both manuscript and print) through the second half of the fifteenth century: each generation recopied the previous generation's literature, but the tenor of the *new* texts differed, as literary interests, styles, and modes in part overlapped and in part diverged. Moreover, many of the romances de Worde printed are the sort of earlier English verse romances that Caxton had eschewed,[5] and that do not (as demonstrated in the first section of Chapter 3) devote sustained attention to treason.

Stephen Hawes' romances exemplify early sixteenth-century literary culture's divergence from the preoccupations of mid- to late fifteenth-century romances. That both the *Example of Vertu* (1503–4) and the *Pastime of Pleasure* (1505–6) are in verse constitutes a departure from the primary mode of secular literature written in the preceding sixty years, as does the allegorical nature of Hawes' 'romances', partly modelled on the 'Pilgrimage of Life' genre (originating in fourteenth-century France with Guillaume de Deguileville), on allegories of love, and on encyclopedic poems.[6] In the *Example of Vertu*, a dream vision furnishes allegorical figures who offer the narrator both spiritual and secular instruction. Here 'Discretion' advises the narrator to avoid treason:

> Be to thy kynge euer true subgete
> …
> Without ony spot of euyll treason
> And be obedyent at euery season
> Vnto his grace without rebellyon
> That thou with trouth may be companyon.[7]

    [5] Carol Meale, 'Caxton, de Worde, and the Publication of Romance in Late Medieval England', *The Library: Transactions of the Bibliographical Society*, Sixth Series, 14.4 (1992), 283–98.

    [6] A. S. G. Edwards, *Stephen Hawes* (Boston: Twayne, 1983), pp. 29 and 60; Daniel Wakelin, 'Stephen Hawes and Courtly Education', in *The Oxford Handbook of Tudor Literature*, pp. 53–68 (pp. 56–8).

    [7] *The Example of Vertu*, in *The Minor Poems of Stephen Hawes*, ed. by Florence W. Gluck and Alice B. Morgan, EETS OS 271 (London: Oxford University Press, 1974), lines 92–8.

However, this injunction is one facet of the poem's general advice rather than a central preoccupation. Moreover, in this poem, treason can be committed only against the king, a definition of the crime that is much narrower than that of the fifteenth-century romances. Hawes' rhyme royal provides an up-to-date reflection of England during Henry VII's reign, under a monarch exerting increasing authority to counter the potential danger of rebellions—as when 'Dame Hardynes' explains that 'a realme is vpholden' chiefly by:

> the swerd
> Whiche causeth it to be in good suerte
> And other realmes of it to be aferd
> By whiche the vsurpers be dyfferd
> From theyr wyll with treason knyte
> And by me slayn for theyr fals fyte. (610–16)

While the idea of enforcement of hierarchical loyalty as paramount for England's security is strongly topical for Henry VII's reign, Hawes' specification of hierarchical treason also mirrors the idea of treason found in earlier Middle English literature (as discussed in Chapter 3), passing over the mid- to late fifteenth-century romances' preoccupation with horizontal treason much as he overlooked their possibilities as literary models. Moreover, focusing here on the limited amount of treason in Hawes' poems should not give the impression that the poems themselves focus on treason.[8] Hawes' work is typical of early Tudor literature in harking back to Chaucer, Gower, and perhaps especially Lydgate for literary models, jumping over the space between in a way that modern criticism has tended to emulate.[9]

A number of the prose romances translated from French after 1500 likewise differ from the previous generation of romances, in this case by relying upon a providential framework and urging compliance with divine precepts rather than maintaining a focus on secular pragmatism or human regulation of social stability. For instance, in *Robert the Devil*, printed by de Worde in 1500 and again in 1517, hierarchical treason is certainly

---

[8] Similarly, in the two dozen English poems of Hawes' contemporary John Skelton, 'treson' is mentioned in only one poem, and that briefly: 'Upon the Dolorus Dethe and Muche Lamentable Chaunce of the Mooste Honorable Erle of Northumberlande', in *John Skelton: The Complete English Poems*, ed. by John Scattergood (Harmondsworth: Penguin, 1983), pp. 29–35 (lines 6 and 151).

[9] Spearing, *Medieval to Renaissance*; Peter C. Herman, 'Introduction: Rethinking the Henrician Era', in *Rethinking the Henrician Era*, pp. 1–15; Pincombe, 'Introduction—Tudor Literature: Drab or Tarnished?', p. 4; Deanne Williams, 'Medievalism in English Renaissance Literature', in *A Companion to Tudor Literature*, ed. by Kent Cartwright (Oxford: Wiley-Blackwell, 2010), pp. 213–27 (pp. 214–19).

condemned, but the text is essentially a moral *exemplum* rather than a secular admonition; it warns against spiritual sin, and shows that even the worst of sinners, such as the fiendish Robert, can—or must—repent. Robert does penance for his gross violence and discourtesy through pilgrimage and a canine existence in the hall of the emperor of Rome until he is absolved of his murders and misdeeds. Treason figures briefly after Robert, incognito, wins a battle for the emperor: the disloyal seneschal who has secretly raised an army of Saracens against Rome claims that *he* is the saviour knight, and is praised by the emperor, who suspects 'no treason nor deceyte'.[10] The true story is revealed by the emperor's previously dumb daughter, who, given voice by a divine miracle, tells her father not to believe what 'this proude folysshe traytoure [the seneschal] telleth you' (200). Yet the main focus is on Robert's fulfilment of his penance. This emphasis on religious content instead of chivalry characterizes de Worde's romances in contrast to Caxton's; as Paul Scanlon remarks, some of de Worde's seem to be 'religious tracts using romance machinery'.[11] Another such 'romance', *Oliver of Castile*—translated by Henry Watson shortly after 1500 from a French source of the 1450s, and printed by de Worde in 1518—displays a similar tendency by placing treason firmly and purposefully within a providential framework. As in *Amis and Amiloun*, the two young near-identical protagonists pursue knightly adventures together and rescue each other when required, including through the sacrifice (and miraculous resuscitation) of Oliver's two children to heal the diseased Arthur. Arthur rescues Oliver from a more chivalric danger when the latter is treacherously imprisoned by a 'fals traytour kynge' of Ireland. The text's rationale for the inclusion of the Irish king's treason emphasizes God's agency:

> Where as it toucheth that Olyuer was taken by one of the kynges of Irlande / and retayned prysoner / and after delyuered out of pryson by Arthur / *god caused all this* / to the ende that the kynge of Irlande that vniustely and without cause was enemye of his herte and traytour / . . . abode not vnpunysshed

[10] *Robert the Devil*, in *Early English Prose Romances*, ed. by William J. Thoms, rev. edn (1858; London: Routledge, 1906), p. 199. The French source was printed at Lyon (1496) and at Paris (1497).

[11] Scanlon, 'Pre-Elizabethan Prose Romances', pp. 12–13. Scanlon, like Carol Meale (see note 4), argues that de Worde continues Caxton's project of printing both Middle English texts and continental romances, but does so 'to meet quite different demands' (p. 11). The previously unprinted romances that de Worde printed after Caxton's death in 1491–2 and before his own in 1534 include: *Robert the Devil, Melusine, Squire of Low Degree, King Ponthus, Apollonius of Tyre, Valentine and Orson, Helyas Knight of the Swan, William of Palermo, Oliver of Castile*, and *Huon of Bordeaux*, a representative selection of which are discussed here.

in this same worlde of his euyll and traytourous wyll / *to the ende that all traytours take ensample by hym / and kepe them from falsynge of theyr othe.*[12]

Here the text defends its decision to represent treason because it exemplifies God's provision of justice. This justification occurs in the text's 'Epilogue', which is not found in the Burgundian original but appears first in the French text printed in 1492–4, whence Watson reproduced it.[13] Watson evidently chose to include this moralizing gloss, and others like it; unlike the English romance writers, redactors, or translators of the previous generation or two, sixteenth-century romancers often did *not* omit or interrogate such statements about providence.

Other prose romances translated from French after 1500 do carry on the mode of treating treason as a source of secular didacticism; however, treason does not predominate as much in these later texts as it does in their late fifteenth-century English precursors. In this vein are two close translations of French romances, produced *c.*1515 by John Bourchier, Lord Berners. *Huon of Burdeux* begins in the aftermath of the 'grete treason done and ymagenyde / by Duke Ganelon' that resulted in the loss of eleven of the twelve peers.[14] Huon and his brother, travelling to Paris to perform fealty to Charlemagne, are attacked by Charlemagne's malicious son and his accomplice Amaury. When he reaches Paris, Huon *asks God* to

confounde the kynge whome I se there syttyng / for there was neuer harde of a greter treason then the kyng hath purchasyd for vs / seynge that by his messengers and his letters patentes he hath sent fore vs to do hym seruyce / the which commaundement we haue obbeyed as to our souerayne lorde / but by false treason & a wayte hath layde asspyall fore vs, and a grete busshement, for to haue murderyd vs by the way. (26.22–30)

Here Huon accuses not his direct attackers, but rather Charlemagne, of treason, because Huon and his brother had journeyed under Charlemagne's

[12] Henry Watson, *The History of Oliver of Castile*, ed. by Robert Edmund Graves (London: Blades, 1898), f.U2v.

[13] Elizabeth Williams, 'England, Ireland and Iberia in *Olyuer of Castylle*: The View from Burgundy', in *Boundaries in Medieval Romance*, pp. 93–102. The text's mention of the attempted usurpation by a duke of Gloucester, while referring to Humphrey (d. 1447), would be a topical reminder, for an early Tudor readership, of the treason of a more recent duke of Gloucester, Richard III: see Helen Cooper, 'Romance after Bosworth', in *The Court and Cultural Diversity*, ed. by Evelyn Mullally and John Thompson (Cambridge: Brewer, 1997), pp. 149–57 (p. 153).

[14] John Bourchier, *Duke Huon of Burdeux*, ed. by S. L. Lee, EETS ES 40, 41, 43, and 50 (London: Trübner, 1882–7), pp. 2.26–3.1. The French prose version was written in the 1450s and printed by Michel le Noir at Paris in 1513 and 1516. A date of *c.*1515 is probable for the first edition of *Huon*: see N. F. Blake, 'Lord Berners: A Survey', *Medievalia et Humanistica*, NS, 2 (1971), 119–32; updated by Joyce Boro, 'The Textual History of *Huon of Burdeux*: A Reassessment of the Facts', *N&Q*, 48.3 (2001), 233–7.

safe conduct; this broad understanding of treason is familiar from late fifteenth-century romances and chivalric tracts, but the way in which Huon calls upon God for his redress is not. Charlemagne, who had no knowledge of the ambush, defends himself in a fashion reminiscent of Malory's Launcelot and the heroes of Caxton's prose romances (as quoted at the beginning of Chapter 5): 'neuer of all my lyfe I nother dyde nor consent any treason' (27.15–17). When we are told that Earl Amaury, the 'felon traytour' (5.4), is 'son to on of the neuewse of the traytour Ganelon' (5.7–8), we are invited to infer that he is predisposed to be a traitor by blood.[15] In this episode, as in texts such as Caxton's *Foure Sonnes of Aymon*, 'traitor' accusations fly both ways.[16] However, the bulk of the text is concerned with Huon's eastward travels and the bond he forges with Oberon, king of the fairies, which allows him to perform otherwise impossible tasks while learning lessons about proper conduct. Like fifteenth-century romances, this text includes treason, horizontal as well as hierarchical; however, *unlike* the fifteenth-century romances, it emphasizes neither aspect as much as it emphasizes *positive* rather than negative didacticism,[17] such as when Huon is advised by one of Oberon's servants, Malabron, to 'always be trew & say ye trouthe' (113.1–2) on pain of losing Oberon's favour and assistance.[18] Lord Berners' second prose romance, *Arthur of Lytell Brytayne*, concerns the son of a Duke of Brittanny descended from Lancelot's family; the story follows the tribulations of this post-Arthurian Arthur and his beloved, Florence. 'Treason' in this romance likewise denotes harmful intentions manifested through deceit, yet there is even less of it than in *Huon of Burdeux*.[19] These texts show only a weakened and subsumed continuation of the interests of fifteenth-century romances.

[15] The idea of genetic treasonousness is a recurring axiom in *Huon*. For instance, the traitorous inclinations of the duke of Vienna (who wants to kill Huon and claim his wife, Esclaramond, for himself) are traced as follows: 'this duke Raoull was the vntrewest traytoure that euer lyued: the which ylnes procedyd by ye duches his mother / who was doughter to . . . the moost vntrewest and falsest traytour' (315.21–5). Similarly, the actions of a certain Brohart, who drowns the protector of Huon and Escaramond's daughter Clariet because he wants to marry her, are explained along genetic lines: 'the lyngnage and parentes issued of ye blode of Brohart . . . alwayes they haue bene full of treason' (617.28–30).

[16] Amaury calls Huon 'traytoure' (35.26, 41.26), and Amaury is called the same by the abbot of Cluny (36.13, 36.16), by Huon (37.7, 40.2, 42.3, 43.25, 44.23), by the narrator (37.20, 39.8, 42.2, 44.18), by the people (38.30), and in a chapter heading (41.11).

[17] Elizabeth Archibald, 'The *Ide and Olive* Episode in Lord Berners's *Huon of Burdeux*', in *Tradition and Transformation in Medieval Romance*, pp. 139–51 (p. 141).

[18] Another instance of this positive reinforcement occurs when all of Huon's men are separated from Huon: Gerames tells the others that they should seek news of Huon, because 'we shall do lyke trew men' (130.11)—and 'yf we do thus, then we do as trew men ought to do' (130.16–17).

[19] Arthur's first wife's mother seeks to deceive him by sending a maiden to bed with him on his wedding night to disguise the fact that his new wife is not a virgin; there are a few other underhanded attempts at harm and/or self-gain. The French source was printed by

Valentine and Orson, translated by Henry Watson and printed by de Worde in the first decade of the sixteenth century, also demonstrates this continued, yet diffused and relegated, interest in didacticism through treason. As in Berners' translations and the late fifteenth-century romances, treason in *Valentine and Orson* is primarily a mode of acting rather than a contravention of a specific feudal loyalty; to act 'by treason' is to accomplish or attempt something harmful to another in a devious, dishonourable fashion. For instance, when an archbishop seeks retaliation after his advances were rejected by a married lady, he accuses her of infidelity, and 'the gracious lady Bellyssant... *by treason and false accusacion* was casten in exyle'.[20] Likewise, when Bellisant laments that the 'cursed Archebysshop /... hathe separed me *by treason* from my lorde and husbande the Emperoure' of Constantinople (30.16–17), treason is at least as much, if not more, about *how*, rather than *what*. Bellisaunt's twin sons both become members of the court of King Pepin: Valentine is raised there to exemplary young knighthood, and Orson, as his name suggests, is raised by bears (before becoming his brother's bodyguard). Pepin's illegitimate sons Haufray and Henry concoct a series of treasonous plots to try to destroy Valentine, or sometimes Orson, against whom 'they ymagyned mortall treason... with all their puyssaunce' (205.13–14). Yet the treasons in this text are mostly averted, or, failing that, revenged, and a providential framework is invoked to support these outcomes. *Valentine and Orson* makes a Lydgate-like reference to divine providence that would be out of place in texts such as Malory's and Hardyng's: the narrator declares that in the 'battayll' between the treasonous archbishop and the heroic merchant who defends the wronged Bellisaunt, 'God that is ryghtfull Iudge, shewed before euery body that treason and falshode retourned euer to their maisters, as you shall here' (43.32–4). Here the maxim that 'treason and falshode retourn... euer to their maisters' *does* in fact seem to be the case. Such a maxim is usually not articulated in the fifteenth-century romances, or in the rare case where it is, it is shown to fail.[21] *Valentine and Orson*'s traitor archbishop is boiled alive in oil after he loses his trial by combat to the merchant (52.24–5); Haufray and Henry's suitable

---

Michel le noir at Lyon (1496) and Paris (1502); Berners' version, written before 1533, was printed *c.*1555 and *c.*1582.

[20] Henry Watson, *Valentine and Orson*, ed. by Arthur Dickson, EETS OS 204 (London: Oxford University Press, 1937), p. 14.1–2. The late fifteenth-century French source was printed in 1489.

[21] See the mid-fifteenth-century prose *Siege of Troy*, where, as discussed in Chapter 3, while the final sentence declares 'alwey the ende of euery tresoun and falsenes to sorowe and myschef at the last' (285), no such habitual result is visible in the narrative proper, which repeatedly demonstrates the failure of providence.

'dystruccyon' is ensured for their attempts on Valentine's and Orson's lives and their assassination of King Pepin and Queen Berthe (309.32–3); and other, more minor traitors also meet painful ends.[22] Moreover, although Valentine goes unpunished after killing his father, he by no means knew he was fighting, or wished to fight, his father. Thus, wherever evil will or treasonous *intentions* occur, the actors are punished and shamed accordingly. Treason in *Valentine and Orson* is more contained, less dangerous, than in the fifteenth-century prose romances, where traitors are likewise shamed, but justice is less frequently obtained, and worries cannot be written out. Moreover, the fact that treason does not cause the climactic disaster in *Valentine and Orson* is *not* like the earlier romances.

UNHAPPY ENDINGS?

In contrast to the way in which happily ending romances confirm a 'providential ordering', unhappy endings entail 'a shaking loose of the genre from its customary grounding in a providential and poetic justice'.[23] Fifteenth-century romances with unhappy endings—from the *Siege of Thebes* and *Siege of Troy* to *Melusine* and the *Morte Darthur*—suggest divine justice is no longer ensuring that right order prevails in the temporal world, and devote their attention to instances of treason as the most concerning 'wrongs' in an unprovidential world. In these texts, it is not arbitrary fate that is blamed for unhappy endings, but rather human inability or unwillingness to keep faith, placing the emphasis on a secular didacticism: everyone should act loyally and honestly to ensure good governance and social cohesion. For Cooper, the parricide in *Valentine and Orson* constitutes an unhappy ending that makes the text 'a story of thwarted expectations—of personal and political treachery and disaster: the very opposite of what its...romance motifs had promised'.[24] However, while the parricide in *Valentine and Orson* does indeed suggest that 'God does not necessarily support the good', the fact that this parricide is *accidental* distinguishes it from the father-killings or other forms of unhappy ending of the pre-1500 prose romances, which are effected through malevolence or adversity rather than bad luck. Immediately after discovering who he

---

[22] However, although Valentine and Orson do not keep their oaths to women (one is unfaithful to his wife and the other reneges on his promise to marry), they are not admonished for treason (or anything else) for these betrayals, unlike Raymond in the late fifteenth-century *Melusines*.

[23] Cooper, *English Romance*, p. 363.

[24] Cooper, 'The Strange History of *Valentine and Orson*', in *Tradition and Transformation in Medieval Romance*, pp. 153–68 (pp. 156 and 158); Cooper, *English Romance*, pp. 364–7.

has killed, Valentine calls himself 'the moost cursed, vnhappy, and euil for-tuned' (308.30), but, appropriately, he refrains from calling himself a trai-tor. *Valentine's* unwitting parricide is tragic, but, unlike the climax of the *Morte Darthur* when Mordred kills and is killed by his father, Arthur, its tragedy is not caused by treason, and its ending is at least partially happy. Moreover, although the prose *Siege of Thebes* contains Oedipus' accidental parricide, this occurs in the brief beginning of the text that gives way to the more emphasized events of the next generation's *intentional* betrayal. The fifteenth-century prose romances, which not only condemn, but also have their unhappy endings constituted by, treason, question providence in a way that *Valentine and Orson's* accidental parricide does not. The latter, as unfor-tunate happenstance, unsettles a providential framework, but, unlike the for-mer, does not imply that all would be well (and providence would not *need* to show itself) if only people would conduct themselves ethically.

In the early sixteenth century we see movement away from the mode of treating treason and simultaneously interrogating divine providence pursued by late fifteenth-century literary culture; moreover, the partial post-1500 continuance of this mode becomes even more fragmented after de Worde's generation. When *Valentine and Orson* was reshaped into the metrical form appearing in the Percy Folio Manuscript (*c.*1600) as *The Emperour and the Childe*, its unhappy ending was supressed. In this later version, the emperor is not killed by his son, but is instead reconciled with his estranged wife.[25] Moreover, as the sixteenth century progressed, the production of and respect for chivalric romances slumped significantly. There were no more romances with unhappy endings, and, while there was not quite an unhappy ending for romance itself, the genre changed signifi-cantly under Iberian influence.[26] William Copland, active at mid-century, was 'the last major early printer of romance'.[27] Copland's contemporary printers and their successors eschewed chivalric romance.[28] In addition, in

---

[25] Cooper, 'History of *Valentine and Orson*', p. 163.

[26] Paul Scanlon, 'Pre-Elizabethan Prose Romances', p. 15; Alexandra Gillespie, 'Caxton and After', in *Companion to Middle English Prose*, pp. 307–25 (p. 319). The shift in the mid-sixteenth century to a taste for 'sentimental and humanist' romances, originating in Spain, is addressed by Joyce Boro, 'All for Love: Lord Berners and the Enduring, Evolving Romance', in *The Oxford Handbook of Tudor Literature*, pp. 87–102 (pp. 89–91); see, simi-larly, Richard Cooper, '"Nostre histoire renouvelée": The Reception of the Romances of Chivalry in Renaissance France', in *Chivalry in the Renaissance*, pp. 175–238.

[27] A. S. G. Edwards, 'William Copland and the Identity of Printed Middle English Romance', in *The Matter of Identity in Medieval Romance*, ed. by Philippa Hardman (Cambridge: Brewer, 2002), pp. 139–47 (pp. 140 and 147). Copland, influenced by de Worde, printed prose romances including Malory's *Morte*, Caxton's *Troy* and *Foure Sonnes, Valentine and Orson*, and *Arthur of Lyttel Brytayne*.

[28] Scanlon, 'Pre-Elizabethan Prose Romances', p. 17. There was, however, a tempor-ary resurgence of interest in medieval romance in the 1580s and 1590s when the warring

the early Tudor period and especially after the Reformation, some humanists denounced romance as a base and frivolous genre.[29] Roger Ascham
famously scorned the *Morte Darthur* (as published posthumously in
1570) as offering only 'open mans slaughter, and bold bawdrye... This is
good stuffe, for wise men to laughe at.'[30]

Yet such early modern critics, reviling romance as simple, foolish, and
sometimes amoral, seem not to have noticed a secularism and interrogative
spirit akin to their own in mid- to late fifteenth-century prose romances
such as the sieges of *Thebes* and *Troy* and the *Morte Darthur*. Cooper posits
that 'the secular focus of Renaissance humanism was needed before writers
dared to imagine a world in which humankind was left to act independently of divine control' and claims that *Valentine and Orson* makes 'a first
gesture in that direction';[31] however, while *Valentine and Orson* does make
such a gesture, it is by no means the first one, or the strongest. Because we
find this secular focus throughout the second half of the fifteenth century,
the period binary between late medieval and early modern that Cooper
appears to support by aligning 'secularism' and 'humanism' only with the
latter does not hold. Strohm has shown the secularity of Wars of the Roses
political discourse; Wakelin has shown that secular humanism was established in mid- to late fifteenth century England;[32] this study has shown
that secularism imbues the English romances of the same decades. Thus
Cooper's claim that the disastrous climax of *Valentine and Orson*, by considering a non-providential world, marks 'a symbolic moment more usually *dated* to the high Renaissance' invites further query.[33] If we have not
been accustomed to detecting such attitudes earlier, is it because they are

---

Elizabethan state required models of chivalric conduct for its gentlemen to emulate: Michael
L. Hays, *Shakespearean Tragedy as Chivalric Romance: Rethinking Macbeth, Hamlet, Othello,
and King Lear, Studies in Renaissance Literature, XII* (Cambridge: Brewer, 2003), p. 57;
Goran V. Stanivukovic, 'English Renaissance Romances as Conduct Books for Young Men',
in *Early Modern Prose Fiction: The Cultural Politics of Reading*, ed. by Naomi Conn Liebler
(New York: Routledge, 2007), pp. 60–78.

[29] Early Tudor humanists such as Erasmus, More, and Vives were opposed to romances,
and 'denunciations became more frequent and bitter' during the second quarter of the sixteenth century, when humanism was joined by 'a Protestant suspicion of pre-Reformation
culture': Scanlon, 'Pre-Elizabethan Prose Romances', p. 16. The early sixteenth-century
humanists' opposition to romance is also addressed, though in the form of an apologia, in
Robert P. Adams, ' "Bold Bawdry and Open Manslaughter": The English New Humanist
Attack on Medieval Romance', *Huntingdon Library Quarterly*, 23 (1959–60), 33–48.

[30] Ascham, *Scholemaster*, in *English Works*, ed. by W. A. Wright (Cambridge: Cambridge
University Press, 1904), pp. 230–31; see A. S. G. Edwards, 'The Reception of Malory's
Morte Darthur', in *Companion to Malory*, pp. 241–52.

[31] Cooper, 'History of *Valentine and Orson*', p. 162.

[32] Strohm, *Politique*; Wakelin, *Humanism, Reading, and English Literature*.

[33] Cooper, 'History of *Valentine and Orson*', p. 168; emphasis mine.

not there, or because we do not expect to find them there—and have not been looking in the right places?

A function of romance, whether its ending is happy or not (whether it is aligned with comedy or with tragedy), is to explore and promote moral values and social cohesion. In late fifteenth-century romance, as in Shakespeare's *King Lear* more than a century later (*c.*1605), we see a more secular, admonitory, and interrogative exploration and promotion of these ideals than in most chivalric romance. While Shakespeare's examination of the downfall of a king and the associated collapse of social order on the heath undermines the idea of a providential anchoring of justice and order, the play nonetheless affirms the good of, and the need for, a moral order—just one that is put in place and regulated by humans rather than by the divine. In connection with the resurgence of popularity for chivalric romance from *c.*1580 to *c.*1605, Michael Hays has argued convincingly that Shakespeare's major tragedies such as *King Lear* are influenced by chivalric romance.[34] For Shakespeare as for late fifteenth-century romancers, tragedy and romance can go together, because both entail 'a morally ordered universe embracing human experience': 'the "once upon a time" of romance and the "what might have been" of tragedy are compatible—indeed, virtually indistinguishable—measures of what was, and imply what can and should be'.[35] It is to Shakespeare that we owe the popularization, anachronistic as it may be, of the idea of the wars between the white rose and the red, and to end this study of the fifteenth century with a glance forward to Shakespeare is to remember the extent to which he looked back to the fifteenth century for both subject matter and literary models for his plays. It is also to remember that the ending of a text does not necessarily indicate the type of cultural work that it seeks to do, though it can contribute to its performance of that work. God does not have to be actively involved for a text to be supporting a moral order (and thus to be a romance); romances such as the *Morte Darthur* place their didactic energy in the *wish* for everything to work out, for everyone to get their just deserts. The fact that such a morally ordered result does not eventuate implies ideological interrogation, but it does not constitute a negation of the values of romance.

However, we certainly do not find 'high Renaissance' writers using *romance* as a forum for such an ideological interrogation. *Valentine and*

---

[34] Hays, *Shakespearean Tragedy as Chivalric Romance*; see also Alex Davis, *Chivalry and Romance in the English Renaissance* (Cambridge: Brewer, 2003), esp. pp. 28–31. For a more wide-ranging survey of Shakespeare's debts to medieval media, including romance, see Cooper, *Shakespeare and the Medieval World*.

[35] Hays, *Shakespearean Tragedy as Chivalric Romance*, pp. 19 and 97.

Orson and *Huon of Burdeux* are the exceptions that prove the rule that
the romancing of treason was on the wane after the end of the fifteenth
century. The dwindling of the production of English secular literature
strongly concerned with treason after 1497, like its relative absence before
1437, indicates grounds on which the intervening decades can productively be distinguished. As a demarcation point, the turn of this century
should be used with some caution, because it brings unbidden in its train
a host of progressivist literary and historical value judgements. The present
study, by scrutinizing the decades adjacent to 1500 rather than contrasting
literatures a half-century or more to either side of it, uses a *c.*1500 demarcation point not to reify a larger boundary between 'medieval' and 'early
modern', but to address a sixty-year literary practice that cannot easily
be classified as either—thereby calling the binary into question. Cooper
takes 'somewhere around 1500' as the end point for the English Middle
Ages in a similarly ambivalent fashion, remarking that 'a date, even one as
approximate as that, cuts a good many Gordian knots, however interesting
they might be to untie'.[36] It is important to look to both sides of this point
together as well as separately, and this study, while focused primarily on
pre-1500 texts, emphatically engages, by implication, with understandings of the early modern. Rather than supporting standard views of rupture and renewal, this study has sought to show that the era we term 'late
medieval' was, to an extent, challenging and interrogating providence in
similar ways to the 'early modern', though through a different medium—a
medium that the latter era scorned, much as it scorned many of its cultural
debts to the centuries that directly proceeded it. In demonstrating that
some attitudes we associate with the early modern, such as secularism and
a civic spirit, took literary form in the fifteenth century, I hope both to
have picked apart one of the knotty tangles regarding the trajectory from
medieval to early modern, and to have shed light on other knots, joining
the premodern across the 1500 frontier, that cannot be so easily untied.

---

[36] *Shakespeare and the Medieval World*, p. 7. Others date this transition to the Reformation
instead: Simpson, *Reform and Cultural Revolution*; Greg Walker, 'When Did "The Medieval"
End?: Retrospection, Foresight, and the End(s) of the English Middle Ages', in *The Oxford
Handbook of Medieval Literature in English*, ed. by Elaine Treharne, Greg Walker, and
William Green (Oxford: Oxford University Press, 2010), pp. 725–38.

APPENDIX

Chronology

Contexts*		Texts	
1422	Death of Henry V; accession of his son Henry VI aged 9 months	1420	Lydgate's *Troy Book*
		1422	Lydgate's *Siege of Thebes*
1437	End of Henry VI's minority	*c.*1422	Lydgate's *Serpent of Division*
1447	Death of Duke of Gloucester when charged with treason	1438/9	Lydgate's *Fall of Princes*
		*c.*1450	Prose *Siege of Thebes* and *Siege of Troy; King Ponthus and the Fair Sidone*; prose *Life of Alexander*
1450	Impeachment of Suffolk; loss of Normandy; Jack Cade's Rebellion; Duke of York's discontent		
		1450–80s	*Paston Letters* concerning the Wars of the Roses
1453	Loss of Gascony; insanity of Henry VI		
1455	First Battle of St Albans	1457	Hardyng's *Chronicle* (1st edn)
1459	Confrontation at Ludlow from which Yorkists flee abroad; attainder of Yorkist lords	1459	*Somnium Vigilantis*
		*c.*1460	*Pseudo-Turpin Chronicle; Knyghthode and Bataile*
1460	Battle of Wakefield (Duke of York killed)	*c.*1460–71	Ashby's *Active Policy of a Prince*
1461	Battle of Towton (Edward of York victorious; accession as Edward IV)	*c.*1464	Hardyng's *Chronicle* (2nd edn)
		1469	Malory's *Morte Darthur*
1461–4	Lancastrians battle for the north	1470/1	*Chronicle of Rebellion in Lincolnshire*
1468	Treason trials of prominent citizens		
1469	Robin of Redesdale's rising; Edward IV imprisoned by Warwick	1471/2	*Historie of the Arrivall of Edward IV*
1470	Lincolnshire rising; Warwick flees to France and returns to reinstate Henry VI; Edward IV in exile	1475	Caxton's *Recuyell of the Historyes of Troye*
		1480s	*John Vale's Book*; 'Warkworth's' *Chronicle*
1471	Battles of Barnet and Tewkesbury (Warwick and Prince Edward of Lancaster killed); Edward IV reigns again; Henry VI killed	1481	Caxton's *Godeffroy of Boloyne*
		1482	Caxton's *Game of Chess* (2nd edn)
		1484	Caxton's *Book of the Ordre of Chyvalry*
1478	Duke of Clarence executed for treason		
1483	Death of Edward IV; usurpation by Richard III	1485	Caxton's print of *Morte Darthur*; Caxton's *Charles the Grete*
1485	Battle of Bosworth (Richard III killed; Henry Tudor accedes)	1488	Caxton's *Foure Sonnes of Aymon* and *Blanchardine and Eglantine*
1487	Battle of Stoke (Yorkist pretender Lambert Simnel defeated)	1489	Caxton's *Book of Fayttes of Armes*
		1490	Caxton's *Eneydos*
1495	First invasion by Perkin Warbeck	Late 15th C.	Prose *Melusine*; verse *Melusine*; *Squire of Low Degree*
1497	Rebellion in Cornwall; Yorkist pretender Warbeck captured		
		1500	De Worde prints *Robert the Devil*
1509	Death of Henry VII; accession of Henry VIII	1500s	De Worde prints *Valentine and Orson*
		1503/4	Hawes' *Example of Vertu*
		1505/6	Hawes' *Pastime of Pleasure*
		*c.*1515	Berners' *Huon of Burdeux*

*This timeline of events follows Watts, *Henry VI*; Ross, *Edward IV*; Hicks, *Wars of the Roses*; and Chrimes, *Henry VII*.

Bibliography

PRIMARY SOURCES

Manuscripts

London, British Library, MS Lansdowne 204 [John Hardyng's *Chronicle*, first version]

Oxford, Bodleian Library, Rawlinson D82 [prose *Siege of Thebes* and *Siege of Troy*]

Paris, Bibliothèque Nationale, MS Français 68 ['William of Tyre' crusade chronicle]

Incunables

London, British Library, *Fierabras*, C.6.b.12

London, British Library, *Les Quatre Fils Aymon*, IB.42244

Editions

The Armburgh Papers, c.1417–c.1453, ed. by Christine Carpenter (Woodbridge: Boydell, 1998).

d'Arras, Jean, *Mélusine*, ed. by M. Ch. Brunet (Paris: Jannet, 1854).

Ascham, Roger, *Scholemaster*, in *English Works*, ed. by W. A. Wright (Cambridge: Cambridge University Press, 1904).

Ashby, George, *George Ashby's Poems*, ed. by Mary Bateson, EETS ES 76 (London: Paul, Trench, Trübner, 1899).

Barr, Helen, ed., *The Digby Poems: A New Edition of the Lyrics* (Exeter: University of Exeter Press, 2009).

Beadle, Richard, ed., 'Fifteenth Century Political Verses from the Holkham Archives', *Medium Aevum*, 71.1 (2002), 101–21.

Beadle, Richard, ed., *The York Plays*, EETS SS 23 (Oxford: Oxford University Press, 2009).

Benson, Larry D., ed., *King Arthur's Death: The Middle English 'Stanzaic Morte Arthur' and 'Alliterative Morte Arthure'* (Kalamazoo: Medieval Institute Publications, 1994).

Bourchier, John (Lord Berners), *Duke Huon of Burdeux*, ed. by S. L. Lee, EETS ES 40, 41, 43, and 50 (London: Trübner, 1882–7).

Bower, Walter, *Scotichronicon*, ed. by D. E. R. Watt, 9 vols (Aberdeen: Aberdeen University Press, 1993).

Braswell, Mary Flowers, ed., *Ywain and Gawain*, in *Sir Perceval of Galles and Ywain and Gawain* (Kalamazoo: Medieval Institute Publications, 1995).

Brie, Friedrich W. D., ed., *The Brut, or, the Chronicles of England*, EETS OS 131 and 136 (London: Paul, Trench, Trübner, 1906–8).

Brie, Friedrich W. D., ed., 'Zwei mittelenglische Prosaromane: *The Sege of Thebes* und *The Sege of Troy*', *Archiv für das Studium der neueren Sprachen und Literaturs*, 130 (1913), 40–52 and 269–85.

Caxton, William, *Blanchardyn and Eglantine*, ed. by Leon Kellner, EETS ES 58 (London: Trübner, 1890).

Caxton, William, *The Book of Fayttes of Armes and of Chyualrye*, ed. by A. T. B. Byles, EETS OS 189 (1932; London: Oxford University Press, 1937).

Caxton, William, *The Book of the Knight of the Tower*, ed. by M. Y. Offord, EETS SS 2 (London: Oxford University Press, 1971).

Caxton, William, *The Book of the Ordre of Chyvalry*, ed. by Alfred T. P. Byles, EETS OS 168 (London: Oxford University Press, 1926).

Caxton, William, *Caxton's Own Prose*, ed. by N. F. Blake (London: Deutsch, 1973).

Caxton, William, 'The Eighth Book of the Polychronicon', in *Polychronicon Ranulphi Higden*, ed. by Joseph Rawson Lumby, 9 vols (London: Longman, 1865–86), VIII, 522–87.

Caxton, William, *Eneydos*, ed. by M. T. Culley and F. J. Furnivall, EETS ES 57 (London: Oxford University Press, 1890).

Caxton, William, *Godeffroy of Boloyne, or The Siege and Conqueste of Jerusalem*, ed. by Mary Noyes Colvin, EETS ES 64 (London: Paul, Trench, Trübner, 1893).

Caxton, William, *The Golden Legend, or Lives of the Saints*, ed. by F. S. Ellis, 7 vols (London: J. M. Dent, 1900).

Caxton, William, *The History of Jason*, ed. by John Munro, EETS ES 111 (London: Oxford University Press, 1913).

Caxton, William, *Jacobus de Cessolis, The Game of Chess,* reproduced in facsimile from the copy at Trinity College, Cambridge, with an introduction by N. F. Blake (London: Scolar Press, 1976).

Caxton, William, *Lyf of the Noble and Crysten Prince Charles the Grete*, ed. by Sidney J. H. Herrtage, EETS ES 37 (London: Trübner, 1881).

Caxton, William, *Paris and Vienne*, ed. by MacEdward Leach, EETS OS 234 (London: Oxford University Press, 1957).

Caxton, William, *Recuyell of the Historyes of Troye*, ed. by H. O. Sommer, 2 vols (London: Nutt, 1894).

Caxton, William, *The Right Pleasaunt and Goodly Historie of the Foure Sonnes of Aymon*, ed. by Octavia Richardson, 2 vols, EETS ES 44 and 45 (London: Trübner, 1884–5).

The Cely Letters, 1472–1488, ed. by Alison Hanham, EETS OS 273 (London: Oxford University Press, 1975).

Chaucer, Geoffrey, *The Riverside Chaucer*, ed. by Larry D. Benson, 3rd edn (Boston: Houghton Mifflin, 1987).

Chestre, Thomas, *Sir Launfal*, in *The Middle English Breton Lays*, ed. by Anne Laskaya and Eve Salisbury (Kalamazoo: Medieval Institute Publications, 1995).

Conlee, John, ed., *Prose Merlin* (Kalamazoo: Medieval Institute Publications, 1998).

Craigie, W. A., ed., 'The Scottis Originale', in *The Asloan Manuscript*, 2 vols (Edinburgh: Blackwood, 1923), I, 185–96.

Crécy, Marie-Claude de, ed., *Le Roman de Ponthus et Sidoine* (Genève: Droz, 1997).

Dockray, Keith, ed., *Three Chronicles of the Reign of Edward IV* (Gloucester: Sutton, 1988).

Donald, A. K., ed., *Melusine*, EETS ES 68 (London: Paul, Trench, Trübner, 1895).

Dyboski, R., and Z. M. Arend, eds, *Knyghthode and Bataile*, EETS OS 201 (London: Oxford University Press, 1935).

Flenley, Ralph, ed., *Six Town Chronicles of England* (Oxford: Clarendon Press, 1911).

Fordun, John of, *Johannis de Fordun chronica gentis Scotorum*, ed. by William F. Skene (Edinburgh: Edmonston and Douglas, 1871).

Foster, Edward E., ed., *Amis and Amiloun*, in *Amis and Amiloun, Robert of Cisyle, and Sir Amadace* (Kalamazoo: Medieval Institute Publications, 1997).

Frappier, Jean, ed., *La Mort le roi Artu*, 2nd edn (1936; Genève: Droz, 1954).

Furnivall, F. J., ed., *The Three Kings Sons*, EETS ES 67 (London: Paul, Trench, Trübner, 1895).

Gairdner, James, ed., 'Gregory's Chronicle', in *Historical Collections of a Citizen of London in the Fifteenth Century*, Camden Society, NS, 17 (London: Nichols, 1876), 57–239.

Gairdner, James, ed., *Three Fifteenth-Century Chronicles*, Camden Society, NS, 18 (London: Nichols, 1880).

Gilson, J. P., ed., 'A Defense of the Proscription of the Yorkists in 1459', *English Historical Review*, 26 (1911), 512–25.

Given-Wilson, Chris, and others, eds, *The Parliament Rolls of Medieval England*, 16 vols (Woodbridge: Boydell, 2005).

Gower, John, *The Complete Works of John Gower*, ed. by G. C. Macaulay, 4 vols (Oxford: Clarendon Press, 1899–1902).

Hardyng, John, *The Chronicle of Iohn Hardyng*, ed. by Henry Ellis (London: Rivington, 1812).

Harington, John, *Epigrams, 1618* (London: Scholar Press, 1970).

Hawes, Stephen, *The Example of Vertu*, in *The Minor Poems of Stephen Hawes*, ed. by Florence W. Gluck and Alice B. Morgan, EETS OS 271 (London: Oxford University Press, 1974).

Hawes, Stephen, *The Pastime of Pleasure*, ed. by William Edward Mead, EETS OS 173 (London: Oxford University Press, 1928).

Herzman, Ronald B., Graham Drake, and Eve Salisbury, eds, *Four Romances of England* (Kalamazoo: Medieval Institute Publications, 1999).

Hoccleve, Thomas, *The Regiment of Princes*, ed. by Charles R. Blyth (Kalamazoo: Medieval Institute Publications, 1999).

Idley, Peter, *Peter Idley's Instructions to his Son*, ed. by Charlotte D'Evelyn (London: Oxford University Press, 1935).

Innes, C., ed., *The Acts of the Parliaments of Scotland, 1124–1707*, 12 vols (Edinburgh: 1814–75).

Kekewich, Margaret Lucille, and others, eds, *The Politics of Fifteenth-Century England: John Vale's Book* (Stroud: Sutton, 1995).

Kingsford, Charles Lethbridge, ed., 'Cotton Cleopatra C IV', in *Chronicles of London* (Oxford: Clarendon Press, 1905), pp. 117–52.

Kingsford's Stonor Letters and Papers, 1290–1483, ed. by Christine Carpenter (Cambridge: Cambridge University Press, 1996).

Kooper, Erik, ed., *The Squire of Low Degree*, in *Sentimental and Humorous Romances* (Kalamazoo: Medieval Institute Publications, 2006).

Love, Nicholas, *The Mirror of the Blessed Life of Jesus Christ*, ed. by Michael G. Sargent (Exeter: University of Exeter Press, 2005).

Luders, A., and others, eds, *Statutes of the Realm, 1101–1713*, 11 vols (London: Record Commission, 1810–28).

Lumiansky, R. M., and David Mills, eds, *The Chester Mystery Cycle*, 2 vols, EETS SS 3 and 9 (London: Oxford University Press, 1974–86).

Lydgate, John, *The Fall of Princes*, ed. by Henry Bergen, EETS ES 121–4, 4 vols (London: Oxford University Press, 1924).

Lydgate, John, *John Lydgate's Serpent of Division*, ed. by Henry Noble MacCracken (London: Oxford University Press, 1911).

Lydgate, John, *John Lydgate: The Siege of Thebes*, ed. by Robert R. Edwards (Kalamazoo: Medieval Institute Publications, 2001).

Lydgate, John, *Troy Book*, ed. by Henry Bergen, EETS ES 97, 103, 106, and 156 (London: Paul, Trench, Trübner, 1906–35).

Lydgate, John, *Troy Book: Selections*, ed. by Robert R. Edwards (Kalamazoo: Medieval Institute Publications, 1998).

Malory, Thomas, *The Works of Sir Thomas Malory*, ed. by Eugène Vinaver, 3rd edn, rev. by P. J. C. Field, 3 vols (Oxford: Clarendon Press, 1990).

Mannyng, Robert, *Handlyng Synne*, ed. by Frederick J. Furnivall, EETS OS 119 and 123 (London: Paul, Trench, Trübner, 1901–3).

Marx, William, ed., *An English Chronicle, 1377–1461* (Woodbridge: Boydell, 2003).

Mather, Frank Jewett, ed., *King Ponthus and the Fair Sidone* (Baltimore: Modern Language Association of America, 1897).

Matheson, Lister, ed., *Death and Dissent: Two Fifteenth-Century Chronicles* (Woodbridge: Boydell, 1999).

Ménard, Philippe, and others, eds, *Le Roman de Tristan en prose*, 9 vols (Genève: Droz, 1987–97).

Micha, Alexandre, ed., *Lancelot: Roman en prose du XIIIe siècle*, 9 vols (Genève: Droz, 1978–83).

Micha, Alexandre, ed., *Merlin: Roman du XIIIe siècle* (Genève: Droz, 1980).

Monro, Cecil, ed., *Letters of Queen Margaret of Anjou and Bishop Bekynton and Others*, Camden Society, LXXXVI (Westminster: Nichols, 1863).

Morris, Matthew W., ed., *A Bilingual Edition of Couldrette's Mélusine or Le Roman de Parthenay*, Mediaeval Studies, XX (Lewiston, NY: Edwin Mellen Press, 2003).

Muir, Bernard J., ed., 'The Wanderer', in *The Exeter Anthology of Old English Poetry*, 2 vols (Exeter: University of Exeter Press, 1994), I, 218–22.

Paston Letters and Papers of the Fifteenth Century, Parts 1 and 2 ed. by Norman Davis, Part 3 ed. by Richard Beadle and Colin Richmond, EETS SS 20–2 (Oxford: Oxford University Press, 2004–5).

The Plumpton Letters and Papers, ed. by Joan Kirby (Cambridge: Cambridge University Press, 1996).

Pronay, Nicholas, and John Cox, eds, *The Crowland Chronicle Continuations, 1459–1486* (London: Richard III and Yorkist History Trust, 1986).

Rawcliffe, Carole, ed., 'Richard, Duke of York, the King's "Obeisant Liegeman": A New Source for the Protectorates of 1454 and 1455', *Historical Research*, 60 (1987), 232–9.

Robbins, Rossell Hope, ed., *Historical Poems of the XIVth and XVth Centuries* (New York: Columbia University Press, 1959).

Robbins, Rossell Hope, ed., *Secular Lyrics of the XIVth and XVth Centuries* (1952; Oxford: Oxford University Press, 1955).

Rous, John, *Antiquarii warwicensis historia regum Angliae*, ed. by Thomas Hearne (Oxford: Fletcher, 1745).

Roussineau, Gilles, ed., *La Suite du roman de Merlin*, 2 vols (Genève: Droz, 1996).

Scott, W., and others, eds, 'The Cronycle of Scotland in a Part', in *The Bannatyne Miscellany*, 3 vols (Edinburgh: Ballantyne, 1855), III, 35–42.

Shepherd, Stephen H. A., ed., *Turpines Story: A Middle English Translation of the 'Pseudo-Turpin Chronicle'*, EETS OS 322 (Oxford: Oxford University Press, 2004).

Shuffelton, George, ed., *Lybeaus Desconus*, in *Codex Ashmole 61: A Compilation of Popular Middle English Verse* (Kalamazoo: Medieval Institute Publications, 2008).

Skeat, Walter W., ed., *The Romans of Partenay, or of Lusignen*, EETS ES 22 (London: Paul, Trench, Trübner, 1899).

Skelton, John, *John Skelton: The Complete English Poems*, ed. by John Scattergood (Harmondsworth: Penguin, 1983).

Spector, Stephen, ed., *The N-Town Play*, EETS SS 11–12 (Oxford: Oxford University Press, 1991).

Spisak, James W., ed., *Caxton's Malory* (Berkeley: University of California Press, 1983).

Stevens, Martin, and A. C. Cawley, eds, *The Towneley Plays*, 2 vols, EETS SS 13–14 (Oxford: Oxford University Press, 1994).

Thoms, William J., ed., *Robert the Devil*, in *Early English Prose Romances*, rev. edn (1858; London: Routledge, 1906).

Tolkien, J. R. R., and E. V. Gordon, eds, *Sir Gawain and the Green Knight*, rev. by Norman Davis (1925; Oxford: Clarendon Press, 1967).

Vegetius, Flavius Renatus, *Epitoma rei militaris*, ed. and trans. by Leo F. Stelten (New York: Lang, 1990).

Watson, Henry, *The History of Oliver of Castile*, ed. by Robert Edmund Graves (London: Blades, 1898).

Watson, Henry, *Valentine and Orson*, ed. by Arthur Dickson, EETS OS 204 (London: Oxford University Press, 1937).

Westlake, J. S., ed., *The Prose Life of Alexander*, EETS OS 143 (London: Oxford University Press, 1913).

Wyntoun, Andrew of, *The Original Chronicle of Andrew of Wyntoun*, ed. by F. J. Amours, 6 vols (Edinburgh: Blackwood, 1903–14).

SECONDARY SOURCES

Adams, Jenny, *Power Play: The Literature and Politics of Chess in the Late Middle Ages* (Philadelphia: University of Pennsylvania Press, 2006).

Adams, Robert P., ' "Bold Bawdry and Open Manslaughter": The English New Humanist Attack on Medieval Romance', *Huntingdon Library Quarterly*, 23 (1959–60), 33–48.

Adams, Tracy, "'Noble, Wyse and Grete Lordes, Gentilmen and Marchauntes": Caxton's Prologues as Conduct Books for Merchants', *Parergon*, 22.2 (2005), 53–76.

Ailes, Marianne, and Phillipa Hardman, 'How English are the English Charlemagne Romances?', in *Boundaries in Medieval Romance*, ed. by Neil Cartlidge, Studies in Medieval Romance, VI (Cambridge: Brewer, 2008), pp. 43–55.

Alexander, Flora, 'Late Medieval Scottish Attitudes to the Figure of King Arthur: A Reassessment', *Anglia*, 93 (1975), 17–34.

Althusser, Louis, 'Ideology and Ideological State Apparatuses', in *Lenin and Philosophy and Other Essays*, trans. by Ben Brewster (London: NLB, 1971), pp. 121–73.

Amos, Mark Addison, 'Disciplining Women and Merchant Capitalists in *The Book of the Knyght of the Towre*', in *Caxton's Trace: Studies in the History of English Printing*, ed. by William Kuskin (Notre Dame: University of Notre Dame Press, 2006), pp. 69–100.

Archibald, Elizabeth, 'Arthur and Mordred: Variations on an Incest Theme', in *Arthurian Literature VIII*, ed. by Richard Barber (Cambridge: Brewer, 1989), pp. 1–27.

Archibald, Elizabeth, 'Beginnings: *The Tale of King Arthur and King Arthur and Emperor Lucius*', in *A Companion to Malory*, ed. by Elizabeth Archibald and A. S. G. Edwards, Arthurian Studies, XXXVII (Cambridge: Brewer, 1996), pp. 133–51.

Archibald, Elizabeth, 'The *Ide and Olive* Episode in Lord Berners's *Huon of Burdeux*', in *Tradition and Transformation in Medieval Romance*, ed. by Rosalind Field (Cambridge: Brewer, 1999), pp. 139–51.

Archibald, Elizabeth, 'Malory's Ideal of Fellowship', *The Review of English Studies*, NS, 43 (1992), 311–28.

Austin, J. L, *How to Do Things With Words*, ed. by J. O. Urmson and Marina Sbisà, 2nd edn (1962; Cambridge, MA: Harvard University Press, 1975).

Baker, John H., *An Introduction to English Legal History*, 3rd edn (1971; London: Butterworths, 1990).

Barber, Richard, 'Malory's *Le Morte Darthur* and Court Culture under Edward IV', in *Arthurian Literature XII*, ed. by James P. Carley and Felicity Riddy (Cambridge: Brewer, 1993), pp. 133–55.

Barron, Caroline, 'Chivalry, Pageantry and Merchant Culture in Medieval London', in *Heraldry, Pageantry and Social Display in Medieval England*, ed. by Peter Coss and Maurice Keen (Woodbridge: Boydell, 2002), pp. 219–41.

Barron, Caroline, 'The Political Culture of Medieval London', in *Political Culture in Late Medieval Britain*, ed. by Linda Clark and Christine Carpenter (Woodbridge: Boydell, 2004), pp. 111–33.

Barron, W. R. J., *English Medieval Romance* (London: Longman, 1987).

Barron, W. R. J., *'Trawthe' and Treason: The Sin of Gawain Reconsidered* (Manchester: Manchester University Press, 1980).

Batt, Catherine, *Malory's 'Morte Darthur': Remaking Arthurian Tradition* (New York: Palgrave, 2002).

Beadle, Richard, 'Private Letters', in *A Companion to Middle English Prose*, ed. by A. S. G. Edwards (Cambridge: Brewer, 2004), pp. 289–306.

Bellamy, J. G., *The Law of Treason in England in the Later Middle Ages* (Cambridge: Cambridge University Press, 1970).

Benson, David C., 'Chaucer's Influence on the Prose "Sege of Troye"', *Notes and Queries*, 18.4 (1971), 127–30.

Benson, David C., 'The Ending of the Morte Darthur', in *A Companion to Malory*, ed. by Elizabeth Archibald and A. S. G. Edwards, Arthurian Studies, XXXVII (Cambridge: Brewer, 1996), pp. 221–38.

Benson, Larry D., *Malory's 'Morte Darthur'* (Cambridge, MA: Harvard University Press, 1976).

Bex, Tony, *Variety in Written English. Texts in Society: Societies in Text* (London: Routledge, 1996).

Black, Antony, *Political Thought in Europe, 1250–1450* (Cambridge: Cambridge University Press, 1992).

Blake, N. F., *Caxton and His World* (London: Deutsch, 1969).

Blake, N. F., 'Lord Berners: A Survey', *Medievalia et Humanistica*, NS, 2 (1971), 119–32.

Blake, N. F., 'William Caxton Again in the Light of Recent Scholarship', *Dutch Quarterly Review of Anglo-American Letters*, 12.3 (1982), 162–82.

Blamires, Alcuin, *Chaucer, Ethics, and Gender* (Oxford: Oxford University Press, 2006).

Boardman, Steve, 'Late Medieval Scotland and the Matter of Britain', in *Scottish History: The Power of the Past*, ed. by Edward J. Cowan and Richard J. Finlay (Edinburgh: Edinburgh University Press, 2002), pp. 47–72.

Bornstein, Diane, 'Military Manuals in Fifteenth-Century England', *Mediaeval Studies*, 37 (1975), 469–77.

Bornstein, Diane, *Mirrors of Courtesy* (Hamden, CT: Archon, 1975).

Bornstein, Diane, 'William Caxton's Chivalric Romances and the Burgundian Renaissance in England', *English Studies*, 57 (1976), 1–10.

Boro, Joyce, 'All for Love: Lord Berners and the Enduring, Evolving Romance', in *The Oxford Handbook of Tudor Literature, 1485–1603*, ed. by Mike Pincombe and Cathy Shrank (Oxford: Oxford University Press, 2009), pp. 87–102.

Boro, Joyce, 'The Textual History of *Huon of Burdeux*: A Reassessment of the Facts', *Notes and Queries*, 48.3 (2001), 233–7.

Bunt, Gerrit, 'The Art of a Medieval Translator: The Thornton Prose Life of Alexander', *Neophilologus*, 76 (1992), 147–59.

Burrow, Colin, 'The Experience of Exclusion: Literature and Politics in the Reigns of Henry VII and Henry VIII', in *The Cambridge History of Medieval English Literature*, ed. by David Wallace (Cambridge: Cambridge University Press, 1999), pp. 793–820.

Burrow, J. A., 'The Fourteenth-Century Arthur', in *The Cambridge Companion to the Arthurian Legend*, ed. by Elizabeth Archibald and Ad Putter (Cambridge: Cambridge University Press, 2009), pp. 69–83.

Burrow, J. A., *Ricardian Poetry: Chaucer, Gower, Langland, and the 'Gawain' Poet* (London: Routledge, 1971).

Butler, Judith, *Excitable Speech: A Politics of the Performative* (New York: Routledge, 1997).

Cannon, Christopher, 'Malory's Crime: Chivalric Identity and the Evil Will', in *Medieval Literature and Historical Inquiry: Essays in Honour of Derek Pearsall*, ed. by David Aers (Cambridge: Brewer, 2000), pp. 159–83.

Carlson, David R., 'A Theory of the Early English Printing Firm: Jobbing, Book Publishing, and the Problem of Productive Capacity in Caxton's Work', in *Caxton's Trace: Studies in the History of English Printing*, ed. by William Kuskin (Notre Dame: University of Notre Dame Press, 2006), pp. 35–68.

Carpenter, Christine, 'Henry VII and the English Polity', in *The Reign of Henry VII*, ed. by Benjamin Thompson (Stamford: Watkins, 1995), pp. 11–30.

Carpenter, Christine, *Locality and Polity: a Study of Warwickshire Landed Society, 1401–1499* (Cambridge: Cambridge University Press, 1992).

Carpenter, Christine, 'Political and Constitutional History: Before and After McFarlane', in *The McFarlane Legacy: Studies in Late Medieval Politics and Society*, ed. by R. H. Britnell and A. J. Pollard (Stroud: Sutton, 1995), pp. 175–206.

Carpenter, Christine, 'The Stonors and their Circle in the Fifteenth Century', in *Rulers and Ruled in Late Medieval England*, ed. by Rowena E. Archer and Simon Walker (London: Hambledon, 1995).

Carpenter, Christine, *The Wars of the Roses: Politics and the Constitution in England, c. 1437–1509* (Cambridge: Cambridge University Press, 1997).

Cavill, P. R., *The English Parliaments of Henry VII, 1485–1504* (Oxford: Oxford University Press, 2009).

Chartier, Roger, 'Histoire des mentalités', in *The Columbia History of Twentieth-Century French Thought*, ed. by Lawrence D. Kritzman (New York: Columbia University Press, 2006), pp. 54–8.

Chaytor, H. J., *From Script to Print: An Introduction to Medieval Vernacular Literature* (1945; London: Sidgwick & Jackson, 1966).

Cherewatuk, Karen, '"Gentyl Audiences" and "Grete Bokes": Chivalric Manuals and the *Morte Darthur*', in *Arthurian Literature XV*, ed. by James P. Carley and Felicity Riddy (Cambridge: Brewer, 1997), 205–16.

Cherewatuk, Karen, 'Sir Thomas Malory's "Grete Booke"', in *The Social and Literary Contexts of Malory's Morte Darthur*, ed. by D. Thomas Hanks, Jr and Jessica G. Brogdon (Cambridge: Brewer, 2000), pp. 42–67.

Cherewatuk, Karen, *Marriage, Adultery, and Inheritance in Malory's 'Morte Darthur'*, Arthurian Studies, LXVII (Cambridge: Brewer, 2006).

Chilton, Paul, *Analysing Political Discourse: Theory and Practice* (London: Routledge, 2004).

Chrimes, S. B., *Henry VII* (1972; London: Methuen, 1977).

Chrimes, S. B., *Lancastrians, Yorkists and Henry VII* (1964; London: Macmillan, 1967).

Chrimes, S. B., 'The Reign of Henry VII', in *Fifteenth-Century England, 1399–1509: Studies in Politics and Society*, ed. by S. B. Chrimes, C. D. Ross, and R. A. Griffiths (Manchester: Manchester University Press, 1972), pp. 67–85.

Clanchy, M. T., *From Memory to Written Record: England, 1066–1307*, 2nd edn (1979; Oxford: Blackwell, 1993).

Cohen, Jeffrey Jerome, *Of Giants: Sex, Monsters, and the Middle Ages* (Minneapolis: University of Minnesota Press, 1999).

Coldiron, A. E. B., 'William Caxton', in *The Oxford History of Literary Translation in English*, ed. by Roger Ellis, 4 vols (Oxford: Oxford University Press, 2008), I, 160–9.

Coleman, Joyce, 'The Audible Caxton: Reading and Hearing in the Writings of England's First Publisher', *Fifteenth-Century Studies*, 16 (1990), 83–109.

Coleman, Joyce, 'The Making and Breaking of Language in Sir Thomas Malory's *Morte Darthur*', in *To Make his Englissh Sweete upon his Tonge*, ed. by Marcin Krygier and Liliana Sikorska (Frankfurt: Lang, 2007), pp. 93–110.

Coleman, Joyce, *Public Reading and the Reading Public in Late Medieval England and France*, Cambridge Studies in Medieval Literature, XXVI (Cambridge: Cambridge University Press, 1996).

Coleman, Joyce, 'Reading Malory in the Fifteenth Century: Aural Reception and Performance Dynamics', *Arthuriana*, 13.4 (2003), 48–70.

Combellack, C. R. B., 'The Composite Catalogue of *The Sege of Troye*', *Speculum*, 26.4 (1951), 624–34.

Cooper, Helen, 'The Book of Sir Tristram de Lyones', in *A Companion to Malory*, ed. by Elizabeth Archibald and A. S. G. Edwards, Arthurian Studies, XXXVII (Cambridge: Brewer, 1996), pp. 183–201.

Cooper, Helen, 'Counter-Romance: Civil Strife and Father-Killing in the Prose Romances', in *The Long Fifteenth Century*, ed. by Helen Cooper and Sally Mapstone (Oxford: Clarendon Press, 1997), pp. 141–62.

Cooper, Helen, *The English Romance in Time: Transforming Motifs from Geoffrey of Monmouth to the Death of Shakespeare* (Oxford: Oxford University Press, 2004).

Cooper, Helen, 'Introduction', in *The Long Fifteenth Century*, ed. by Helen Cooper and Sally Mapstone (Oxford: Clarendon Press, 1997), pp. 1–14.

Cooper, Helen, 'Prose Romances', in *A Companion to Middle English Prose*, ed. by A. S. G. Edwards (Cambridge: Brewer, 2004), pp. 215–29.

Cooper, Helen, 'Romance after 1400', in *The Cambridge History of Medieval English Literature*, ed. by David Wallace (Cambridge: Cambridge University Press, 1999), pp. 690–719.

Cooper, Helen, 'Romance after Bosworth', in *The Court and Cultural Diversity*, ed. by Evelyn Mullally and John Thompson (Cambridge: Brewer, 1997), pp. 149–57.

Cooper, Helen, *Shakespeare and the Medieval World* (London: Methuen Drama, 2010).

Cooper, Helen, 'The Strange History of *Valentine and Orson*', in *Tradition and Transformation in Medieval Romance*, ed. by Rosalind Field (Cambridge: Brewer, 1999), pp. 153–68.

Cooper, Helen, 'When Romance Comes True', in *Boundaries in Medieval Romance*, ed. by Neil Cartlidge, Studies in Medieval Romance, VI (Cambridge: Brewer, 2008), pp. 13–27.

Cooper, Richard, '"Nostre histoire renouvelée": The Reception of the Romances of Chivalry in Renaissance France', in *Chivalry in the Renaissance*, ed. by Sydney Anglo (Boydell: Woodbridge, 1990), pp. 175–238.

Crofts, Thomas H., *Malory's Contemporary Audience: The Social Reading of Romance in Late Medieval England*, Arthurian Studies, LXVI (Cambridge: Brewer, 2006).

Crofts, Thomas H., and Robert Allen Rouse, 'Middle English Popular Romance and National Identity', in *A Companion to Medieval Popular Romance*, ed. by Raluca L. Radulescu and Cory James Rushton, Studies in Medieval Romance, X (Cambridge: Brewer, 2009), pp. 79–95.

Cummings, Brian, and James Simpson, 'Introduction', in *Cultural Reformations: Medieval and Renaissance in Literary History*, ed. by Brian Cummings and James Simpson (Oxford: Oxford University Press, 2010), pp. 1–9.

Cunningham, Sean, *Henry VII* (London: Routledge, 2007).

Cuttler, S. H., *The Law of Treason Trials in Later Medieval France* (Cambridge: Cambridge University Press, 1981).

Davis, Alex, *Chivalry and Romance in the English Renaissance* (Cambridge: Brewer, 2003).

Desmond, Marilynn, *Reading Dido: Gender, Textuality, and the Medieval Aeneid* (Minneapolis: University of Minnesota Press, 1994).

Doutrepont, Georges, *Les Mises en prose des epopees et des romans chevaleresques du XIVe au XVIe siecle: Memoires de l'Academie royale de Belgique*, Classe des lettres, 2, vol. 40 (Brussels: Palais des académies, 1939).

Edlich-Muth, Miriam, *Malory and his European Contemporaries: Adapting Late Arthurian Romance Collections* (Cambridge: Brewer, 2014).

Edwards, A. S. G, 'Gower in the Delamere Chaucer Manuscript', in *The Medieval Book and a Modern Collector: Essays in Honour of Toshiyuki Takamiya*, ed. by Takami Matsuda, Richard A. Linenthal, and John Scahill (Cambridge: Brewer, 2004), pp. 81–6.

Edwards, A. S. G, 'The Influence of Lydgate's *Fall of Princes, c.* 1440–1559: A Survey', *Mediaeval Studies*, 39 (1977), 424–39.

Edwards, A. S. G, 'The Manuscripts and Texts of the Second Version of John Hardyng's *Chronicle*', in *England in the Fifteenth Century: Proceedings of the 1986 Harlaxton Symposium*, ed. by Daniel Williams (Woodbridge: Boydell, 1987), pp. 75–84.

Edwards, A. S. G, 'The Reception of Malory's *Morte Darthur*', in *A Companion to Malory*, ed. by Elizabeth Archibald and A. S. G. Edwards, Arthurian Studies, XXXVII (Cambridge: Brewer, 1996), pp. 241–52.

Edwards, A. S. G, *Stephen Hawes* (Boston: Twayne, 1983).

Edwards, A. S. G, 'Tradition and Innovation in Fifteenth-Century Poetry', *Modern Language Quarterly*, 53 (1992), 1–4.

Edwards, A. S. G., 'William Copland and the Identity of Printed Middle English Romance', in *The Matter of Identity in Medieval Romance*, ed. by Philippa Hardman (Cambridge: Brewer, 2002), pp. 139–47.

Edwards, A. S. G., and Carol M. Meale, 'The Marketing of Printed Books in Late Medieval England', *The Library: Transactions of the Bibliographical Society*, Sixth Series, 15.2 (1993), 95–124.

Edwards, Elizabeth, *The Genesis of Narrative in Malory's Morte Darthur* (Cambridge: Brewer, 2001).

Ellis, Deborah S., 'Balin, Mordred, and Malory's Idea of Treachery', *English Studies*, 68.1 (1987), 66–74.

Ferguson, Arthur B., *The Articulate Citizen and the English Renaissance* (Durham, NC: Duke University Press, 1965).

Ferguson, Arthur B., *The Indian Summer of English Chivalry* (Durham, NC: Duke University Press, 1960).

Ferster, Judith, *Fictions of Advice: The Literature and Politics of Counsel in Late Medieval England* (Philadelphia: University of Pennsylvania Press, 1996).

Fichte, Joerg, 'Caxton's Concept of "Historical Romance" within the Context of the Crusades: Conviction, Rhetoric and Sales Strategy', in *Tradition and Transformation in Medieval Romance*, ed. by Rosalind Field (Cambridge: Brewer, 1999), pp. 101–13.

Field, P. J. C., 'Fifteenth-Century History in Malory's *Morte Darthur*', in *Malory: Texts and Sources*, Arthurian Studies, XL (Cambridge: Brewer, 1998), pp. 47–71.

Field, P. J. C., *The Life and Times of Sir Thomas Malory*, Arthurian Studies, XXIX (Cambridge: Brewer, 1993).

Field, P. J. C., 'Malory's Minor Sources', *Notes and Queries*, 26.2 (1979), 107–10.

Field, P. J. C., 'Malory's Mordred and the *Morte Arthure*', in *Malory: Texts and Sources*, Arthurian Studies, XL (Cambridge: Brewer, 1998), pp. 89–102.

Field, P. J. C., 'Malory's Own Marginalia', *Medium Aevum*, 70.2 (2001), 226–39.

Field, P. J. C., *Romance and Chronicle: A Study of Malory's Prose Style* (London: Barrie & Jenkins, 1971).

Field, P. J. C., 'The Source of Malory's *Tale of Gareth*', in *Aspects of Malory*, ed. by Toshiyuki Takamiya and Derek Brewer, Arthurian Studies, I (Cambridge: Brewer, 1981), pp. 57–70.

Field, Rosalind, 'Romance', in *The Oxford History of Literary Translation in English*, ed. by Roger Ellis and others, 4 vols (Oxford: Oxford University Press, 2008), I, 296–331.

Fletcher, Lydia, '"Traytoures" and "Treson": The Language of Treason in the Works of Sir Thomas Malory', in *Arthurian Literature XXVIII*, ed. by Elizabeth Archibald and David F. Johnson (Cambridge: Brewer, 2011), pp. 75–88.

Fletcher, Robert Huntington, *The Arthurian Material in the Chronicles* (Boston: Ginn, 1906).

Foucault, Michel, *The Archaeology of Knowledge*, trans. by A. M. Sheridan Smith (1969; London: Routledge, 2002).

Fowler, Alastair, *Kinds of Literature: An Introduction to the Theory of Genres and Modes* (Oxford: Clarendon Press, 1982).

Fowler, Elizabeth, and Roland Greene, eds, *The Project of Prose in Early Modern Europe and the New World* (Cambridge: Cambridge University Press, 1997).

Fradenburg, Louise, and Carla Freccero, 'Introduction: Caxton, Foucault, and the Pleasures of History', in *Premodern Sexualities*, ed. by Fradenburg and Freccero (New York: Routledge, 1996), pp. xiii–xxiv.

Furrow, Melissa, *Expectations of Romance: The Reception of a Genre in Medieval England*, Studies in Medieval Romance, XI (Cambridge: Brewer, 2009).

Gayk, Shannon, and Kathleen Tonry, eds, *Form and Reform: Reading across the Fifteenth Century* (Columbus, OH: Ohio State University Press, 2011).

Genet, Jean-Philippe, 'New Politics or New Language? The Words of Politics in Yorkist and Early Tudor England', in *The End of the Middle Ages? England in the Fifteenth and Sixteenth Centuries*, ed. by John L. Watts (Stroud: Sutton, 1998), pp. 23–64.

Gill, Louise, 'William Caxton and the Rebellion of 1483', *English Historical Review*, 114 (1997), 105–18.

Gillespie, Alexandra, 'Caxton and After', in *A Companion to Middle English Prose*, ed. by A. S. G. Edwards (Cambridge: Brewer, 2004), pp. 307–25.

Gillespie, Alexandra, *Print Culture and the Medieval Author: Chaucer, Lydgate, and Their Books, 1473–1557* (Oxford: Oxford University Press, 2006).

Goodman, Anthony, *The Wars of the Roses: Military Activity and English Society, 1452–97* (London: Routledge, 1981).

Goodman, Jennifer R., 'Caxton's Continent', in *Caxton's Trace: Studies in the History of English Printing*, ed. by William Kuskin (Notre Dame: University of Notre Dame Press, 2006), pp. 101–23.

Goodman, Jennifer R., *Chivalry and Exploration, 1298–1630* (Woodbridge: Boydell, 1998).

Goodman, Jennifer R., 'Malory and Caxton's Chivalric Series, 1481–85', in *Studies in Malory*, ed. by James W. Spisak (Kalamazoo: Medieval Institute Publications, 1985), pp. 257–74.

Goodman, Jennifer R., *Malory and William Caxton's Prose Romances of 1485* (New York: Garland, 1987).

Gordon, Ian A., *The Movement of English Prose* (London: Longmans, 1966).

Gray, Douglas, *Later Medieval English Literature* (Oxford: Oxford University Press, 2008).

Green, Richard Firth, *A Crisis of Truth: Literature and Law in Ricardian England* (Philadelphia: University of Pennsylvania Press, 1999).

Green, Richard Firth, 'Palamon's Appeal of Treason in the *Knight's Tale*', in *The Letter of the Law: Legal Practice and Literary Production in Medieval England*, ed. by Emily Steiner and Candace Barrington (Ithaca, NY: Cornell University Press, 2002), pp. 105–14.

Green, Richard Firth, *Poets and Princepleasers: Literature and the English Court in the Late Middle Ages* (Toronto: University of Toronto Press, 1980).

Green, Richard Firth, 'The Short Version of *The Arrival of Edward IV*', *Speculum*, 56.2 (1981), 324–36.

Griffiths, R. A., 'Duke Richard of York's Intentions in 1450 and the Origins of the Wars of the Roses', *Journal of Medieval History*, 1 (1975), 187–209.

Gross, Anthony, *The Dissolution of the Lancastrian Kingship: Sir John Fortescue and the Crisis of Monarchy in Fifteenth-Century England* (Stamford: Watkins, 1996).

Grummitt, David, 'Deconstructing Cade's Rebellion: Discourse and Politics in the Mid Fifteenth Century', in *Identity and Insurgency in the Late Middle Ages*, ed. by Linda Clark (Woodbridge: Boydell, 2006), pp. 107–22.

Gunn, Steven, 'Chivalry and the Politics of the Early Tudor Court', in *Chivalry and the Renaissance*, ed. by Sydney Anglo (Woodbridge: Boydell, 1990), pp. 107–28.

Gunn, Steven, *Early Tudor Government, 1485–1558* (Basingstoke: Macmillan, 1995).

Hammond, Eleanor Prescott, *English Verse between Chaucer and Surrey* (Durham, NC: Duke University Press, 1927).

Hanks, D. Thomas Jr, 'Epilogue: Malory's *Morte Darthur* and "the Place of the Voice"', *Arthuriana*, 13.4 (2003), 119–33.

Hanks, D. Thomas Jr, 'William Caxton, Wynkyn de Worde and the Editing of Malory's *Morte Darthur*', in *Arthurian Literature XXIII*, ed. by Keith Busby and Roger Dalrymple (Cambridge: Brewer, 2006), pp. 46–67.

Hanna, Ralph, *London Literature, 1300–1380*, Cambridge Studies in Medieval Literature, LVII (Cambridge: Cambridge University Press, 2005).

Harris, E. Kay, 'Evidence against Lancelot and Guinevere in Malory's *Morte Darthur*: Treason by Imagination', *Exemplaria*, 7.1 (1995), 179–208.

Harris, Kate, 'John Gower's *Confessio Amantis*: The Virtues of Bad Texts', in *Manuscripts and Readers in Fifteenth-Century England: The Literary Implications of Manuscript Study*, ed. by Derek Pearsall (Cambridge: Brewer, 1983), pp. 27–40.

Harriss, G. L., 'Political Society and the Growth of Government in Late Medieval England', *Past and Present*, 138 (1993), 28–57.

Hasler, Antony J., *Court Poetry in Late Medieval England and Scotland: Allegories of Authority*, Cambridge Studies in Medieval Literature, LXXX (Cambridge: Cambridge University Press, 2011).

Hays, Michael L., *Shakespearean Tragedy as Chivalric Romance: Rethinking Macbeth, Hamlet, Othello, and King Lear*, Studies in Renaissance Literature, XII (Cambridge: Brewer, 2003).

Hellinga, Lotte, 'Caxton and the Bibliophiles', *Onzième congrès international de bibliophilie*, ed. by P. Culot and E. Rouir (Brussels: Société royale des bibliophiles et iconophiles de Belgique, 1981), pp. 11–38.

Herman, Peter C., ed., *Rethinking the Henrician Era: Essays on Early Tudor Texts and Contexts* (Chicago: University of Illinois Press, 1994).

Hiatt, Alfred, *The Making of Medieval Forgeries: False Documents in Fifteenth-Century England* (London: British Library, 2004).

Hicks, Michael, *Edward IV* (London: Arnold, 2004).

Hicks, Michael, *English Political Culture in the Fifteenth Century* (New York: Routledge, 2002).

Hicks, Michael, 'From Megaphone to Microscope: The Correspondence of Richard Duke of York with Henry VI in 1450 Revisited', *Journal of Medieval History*, 25.3 (1999), 243–56.

Hicks, Michael, *The Wars of the Roses* (New Haven: Yale University Press, 2010).

Hodges, Kenneth, *Forging Chivalric Communities in Malory's 'Le Morte Darthur'* (New York: Palgrave Macmillan, 2005).

Hornsby, Joseph Allen, *Chaucer and the Law* (Norman, OK: Pilgrim, 1988).

Horrox, Rosemary, *Richard III: A Study of Service* (Cambridge: Cambridge University Press, 1989).

Horrox, Rosemary, 'Service', in *Fifteenth-Century Attitudes: Perceptions of Society in Late Medieval England*, ed. by Rosemary Horrox (Cambridge: Cambridge University Press, 1994), pp. 61–78.

Howes, Laura L., and Sarah McCollum, '"Reducing into English": Translation as Alchemy in the Prologues and Epilogues of William Caxton', *Notes and Queries*, 57.3 (2010), 321–5.

Huber, Emily Rebekah, '"Delyver Me My Dwarff!": Gareth's Dwarf and Chivalric Identity', *Arthuriana*, 16.2 (2006), 49–53.

Jauss, Hans Robert, *Toward an Aesthetic of Reception*, trans. by Timothy Bahti (Brighton: Harvester, 1982).

Johns, Adrian, *The Nature of the Book: Print and Knowledge in the Making* (Chicago: University of Chicago Press, 1998).

Jones, William R., 'Sanctuary, Exile, and Law: The Fugitive and Public Authority in Medieval England and Modern America', in *Essays on English Law and the American Experience*, ed. by Elizabeth A. Cawthon and David E. Narrett (Texas: Texas A&M University Press, 1994), pp. 19–41.

Jusserand, J. J., *English Wayfaring Life in the Middle Ages*, trans. by Lucy Toulmin Smith, 4th edn (1889; London: Benn, 1950).

Kaeuper, Richard W., *Chivalry and Violence in Medieval Europe* (Oxford: Oxford University Press, 1999).

Kaeuper, Richard W., *War, Justice and Public Order: England and France in the Later Middle Ages* (Oxford: Clarendon Press, 1988).

Kantorowicz, Ernst H., *The King's Two Bodies: A Study in Mediaeval Political Theology* (Princeton: Princeton University Press, 1957).

Keen, M. H., *Chivalry* (New Haven: Yale University Press, 1984).

Keen, M. H., *The Laws of War in the Late Middle Ages* (London: Routledge, 1965).

Keen, M. H., 'Treason Trials under the Law of Arms', *Transactions of the Royal Historical Society*, Fifth Series, 12 (1962), 85–103.

Kekewich, Margaret, 'The Attainder of the Yorkists in 1459: Two Contemporary Accounts', *Bulletin of the Institute of Historical Research*, 55.1 (1982), 25–34.

Kekewich, Margaret, 'Edward IV, William Caxton, and Literary Patronage in Yorkist England', *Modern Language Review*, 66 (1971), 481–7.

Kekewich, Margaret, 'George Ashby's *The Active Policy of a Prince*: An Additional Source', *Review of English Studies*, NS, 41 (1990), 533–5.

Kelly, Henry Ansgar, *Divine Providence in the England of Shakespeare's Histories* (Cambridge, MA: Harvard University Press, 1970).

Kelly, Robert L., 'Malory and the Common Law: *Hasty Jougement* in the *Tale of the Death of King Arthur*', *Medievalia et Humanistica*, NS, 22 (1995), 111–40.

Kendall, Elliot, *Lordship and Literature: John Gower and the Politics of the Great Household* (Oxford: Clarendon Press, 2008).

Kennedy, Beverly, *Knighthood in the Morte Darthur*, Arthurian Studies, XI (Cambridge: Brewer, 1985).

Kennedy, Edward Donald, 'John Hardyng and the Holy Grail', in *Arthurian Literature VIII*, ed. by Richard Barber (Cambridge: Brewer, 1989), pp. 185–206.

Kennedy, Edward Donald, 'Malory and his English Sources', in *Aspects of Malory*, ed. by Toshiyuki Takamiya and Derek Brewer, Arthurian Studies, I (Cambridge: Brewer, 1981), pp. 27–55.

Kennedy, Edward Donald, 'Malory's *Morte Darthur*: A Politically Neutral English Adaptation of the Arthurian Story', in *Arthurian Literature XX*, ed. by Keith Busby and Roger Dalrymple (Cambridge: Brewer, 2003), 145–69.

Kennedy, Edward Donald, 'Malory's Use of Hardyng's Chronicle', *Notes and Queries*, 16.5 (1969), 167–70.

Kennedy, Edward Donald, 'Mordred's Sons', in *The Arthurian Way of Death: The English Tradition*, ed. by Karen Cherewatuk and Kevin Sean Whetter (Cambridge: Brewer, 2009), pp. 33–49.

Kim, Hyonjin, *The Knight Without the Sword: A Social Landscape of Malorian Chivalry*, Arthurian Studies, XLV (Cambridge: Brewer, 2000).

King, Pamela M., 'Contemporary Cultural Models for the Trial Plays in the York Cycle', in *Drama and Community: People and Plays in Medieval Europe*, ed. by Alan Hindley (Turnhout, Belgium: Brepols, 1999), pp. 200–16.

Kingsford, C. L., 'The First Version of Hardyng's Chronicle', *English Historical Review*, 27 (1912), 462–82; 740–53.

Kipling, Gordon, *The Triumph of Honour: Burgundian Origins of the Elizabethan Renaissance* (Leiden: Leiden University Press, 1977).

Kittay, Jeffrey, and Wlad Godzich, *The Emergence of Prose: An Essay in Prosaics* (Minneapolis: University of Minnesota Press, 1987).

Korrel, Peter, *An Arthurian Triangle: A Study of the Origin, Development and Characterization of Arthur, Guinevere and Modred* (Leiden: Brill, 1984).

Kratins, Ojars, 'Treason in Middle English Metrical Romances,' *Philological Quarterly*, 45.4 (1966), 668–87.

Kuskin, William, 'Introduction: Following Caxton's Trace', in *Caxton's Trace: Studies in the History of English Printing*, ed. by William Kuskin (Notre Dame: University of Notre Dame Press, 2006), pp. 1–31.

Kuskin, William, *Symbolic Caxton: Literary Culture and Print Capitalism* (Notre Dame: University of Notre Dame Press, 2008).

La Farge, Catherine, 'Conversation in Malory's *Morte Darthur*', *Medium Aevum*, 56 (1987), 225–38.

Lambert, Mark, *Malory: Style and Vision in 'Le Morte Darthur'* (New Haven: Yale University Press, 1975).

Lander, J. R., *Government and Community: England, 1450–1509* (London: Arnold, 1980).

Larrington, Carolyne, *King Arthur's Enchantresses: Morgan and Her Sisters in Arthurian Tradition* (London: Tauris, 2006).

Lawton, David, 'Dullness and the Fifteenth Century', *English Literary History*, 54.4 (1987), 761–99.

Lester, G. A., *Sir John Paston's 'Grete Boke': A Descriptive Catalogue, with an Introduction, of British Library MS Lansdowne 285* (Cambridge: Brewer, 1984).

Lexton, Ruth, 'Kingship in Malory's *Morte Darthur*', *Journal of English and Germanic Philology*, 110.2 (2011), 173–201.

Lexton, Ruth, 'The Political Imagination of Malory's *Morte Darthur*' (unpublished doctoral dissertation, Columbia University, New York, 2010).

Liebler, Naomi Conn, 'Introduction', in *Early Modern Prose Fiction: The Cultural Politics of Reading*, ed. by Naomi Conn Liebler (New York: Routledge, 2007).

Lipton, Emma, 'Language on Trial: Performing the Law in the N-Town Trial Play', in *The Letter of the Law: Legal Practice and Literary Production in Medieval England*, ed. by Emily Steiner and Candace Barrington (Ithaca, NY: Cornell University Press, 2002), pp. 115–35.

Lyall, R. J., 'Politics and Poetry in Fifteenth and Sixteenth Century Scotland', *Scottish Literary Journal*, 5 (1976), 5–29.

Lynch, Andrew, *Malory's Book of Arms: The Narrative of Combat in 'Le Morte Darthur'*, Arthurian Studies, XXXIX (Cambridge: Brewer, 1997).

Lynch, Andrew, 'A Tale of "Simple" Malory and the Critics', *Arthuriana*, 16.2 (2006), 10–15.

McCarthy, Terence, 'Malory and his Sources', in *A Companion to Malory*, ed. by Elizabeth Archibald and A. S. G. Edwards, Arthurian Studies, XXXVII (Cambridge: Brewer, 1996), pp. 75–95.

MacDonald, Nicola, 'A Polemical Introduction', in *Pulp Fictions of Medieval England: Essays in Popular Romance*, ed. by Nicola MacDonald (Manchester: Manchester University Press, 2004).

McKitterick, David, *Print, Manuscript and the Search for Order, 1450–1830* (Cambridge: Cambridge University Press, 2003).

McLaren, Mary-Rose, *London Chronicles of the Fifteenth Century: A Revolution in English Writing* (Cambridge: Brewer, 2002).

Maddern, Philippa, '"Best Trusted Friends": Concepts and Practices of Friendship among Fifteenth-Century Norfolk Gentry', in *England in the Fifteenth Century: Proceedings of the 1992 Harlaxton Symposium*, ed. by Nicholas Rogers (Stamford: Watkins, 1994), pp. 100–17.

Man, Paul de, 'The Rhetoric of Temporality', in *Blindness and Insight: Essays in the Rhetoric of Contemporary Criticism*, 2nd edn (1971; London: Methuen, 1983), pp. 187–228.

Mann, Jill, 'Malory: Knightly Combat in *Le Morte Darthur*', in *The New Pelican Guide to English Literature*, ed. by Boris Ford, 9 vols (Harmondsworth: Penguin, 1982–8), I, Part I, 331–9.

Mason, Roger, 'Kingship, Tyranny and the Right to Resist in Fifteenth Century Scotland', *Scottish Historical Review*, 66.2 (1987), 125–51.

Matheson, Lister M., *The Prose Brut: The Development of a Middle English Chronicle* (Tempe, AZ: Medieval & Renaissance Texts & Studies, 1998).

Meale, Carol M., 'Caxton, de Worde, and the Publication of Romance in Late Medieval England', *The Library: Transactions of the Bibliographical Society*, Sixth Series, 14.4 (1992), 283–98.

Meale, Carol M., ' "The Hoole Book": Editing and the Creation of Meaning in Malory's Text', in *A Companion to Malory*, ed. by Elizabeth Archibald and A. S. G. Edwards, Arthurian Studies, XXXVII (Cambridge: Brewer, 1996), pp. 3–17.

Mitchell, J. Allan, *Ethics and Exemplary Narrative in Chaucer and Gower*, Chaucer Studies, XXXIII (Cambridge: Brewer, 2004).

Morse, Ruth, 'Historical Fiction in Fifteenth-Century Burgundy', *Modern Language Review*, 75.1 (1980), 48–64.

Morse, Ruth, 'Problems of Early Fiction: Raoul Lefèvre's "Histoire de Jason"', *Modern Language Review*, 78.1 (1983), 34–45.

Mortimer, Nigel, *John Lydgate's 'Fall of Princes': Narrative Tragedy in its Literary and Political Contexts* (Oxford: Oxford University Press, 2005).

Muckerheide, Ryan, 'The English Law of Treason in Malory's *Le Morte Darthur*', *Arthuriana*, 20.4 (2010), 48–77.

Murray, Kylie, 'Kingship in Malory's *Morte Darthur* and the Scots *Lancelot of the Laik*', *Medieval Forum* (San Francisco State University, 2007: http://www.sfsu.edu/~medieval/Volume6/murray.html#5).

Nall, Catherine, 'Malory's *Morte Darthur* and the Rhetoric of War', *Medium Aevum*, 79.2 (2010), 207–24.

Nall, Catherine, *Reading and War in Fifteenth-Century England: From Lydgate to Malory* (Cambridge: Brewer, 2012).

Neville, Cynthia J., *Violence, Custom, and Law: The Anglo-Scottish Border Lands in the Later Middle Ages* (Edinburgh: Edinburgh University Press, 1998).

Nolan, Maura, *John Lydgate and the Making of Public Culture*, Cambridge Studies in Medieval Literature, LVIII (Cambridge: Cambridge University Press, 2005).

Norris, Ralph, *Malory's Library: The Sources of the 'Morte Darthur'*, Arthurian Studies, LXXI (Cambridge: Brewer, 2008).

Nuttall, Jenni, *The Creation of Lancastrian Kingship: Literature, Language and Politics in Late Medieval England*, Cambridge Studies in Medieval Literature, LXVII (Cambridge: Cambridge University Press, 2007).

Painter, George D., *William Caxton: A Quincentenary Biography of England's First Printer* (London: Chatto, 1976).

Pearsall, Derek, 'The English Romance in the Fifteenth Century', *Essays and Studies*, 29 (1976), 56–83.

Pearsall, Derek, *John Lydgate* (London: Routledge, 1970).

Pearsall, Derek, *John Lydgate (1371–1449): A Bio-bibliography* (Victoria: University of Victoria, 1997).

Pearsall, Derek, 'Texts, Textual Criticism, and Fifteenth Century Manuscript Production', in *Fifteenth-Century Studies: Recent Essays*, ed. by Robert F. Yeager (Hamden, CT: Archon, 1984), pp. 121–36.

Peterson, Clifford, 'John Hardyng and Geoffrey of Monmouth: Two Unrecorded Poems and a Manuscript', *Notes and Queries*, 27.3 (1980), 202–4.

Peverley, Sarah L., 'Political Consciousness and the Literary Mind in Late Medieval England: Men "Brought up of Nought" in Vale, Hardyng, *Mankind*, and Malory', *Studies in Philology*, 105.1 (2008), 1–29.

Phillips, Joshua, *English Fictions of Communal Identity, 1485–1603* (Aldershot: Ashgate, 2010).

Pincombe, Mike, ed., *The Anatomy of Tudor Literature* (Aldershot: Ashgate, 2001).

Pincombe, Mike, and Cathy Shrank, 'Prologue: The Travails of Tudor Literature', in *The Oxford Handbook of Tudor Literature, 1485–1603*, ed. by Mike Pincombe and Cathy Shrank (Oxford: Oxford University Press, 2009), pp. 1–17.

Piroyansky, Danna, *Martyrs in the Making: Political Martyrdom in Late Medieval England* (Basingstoke: Palgrave MacMillan, 2008).

Pochoda, Elizabeth T., *Arthurian Propaganda: 'Le Morte Darthur' as an Historical Ideal of Life* (Chapel Hill: University of North Carolina Press, 1971).

Pocock, J. G. A., 'Texts as Events: Reflections on the History of Political Thought', in *The Politics of Discourse: The Literature and History of Seventeenth-Century England*, ed. by Kevin Sharpe and Steven N. Zwicker (Berkeley: University of California Press, 1987), pp. 21–34.

Powell, Edward, 'Law and Justice', in *Fifteenth-Century Attitudes: Perceptions of Society in Late Medieval England*, ed. by Rosemary Horrox (Cambridge: Cambridge University Press, 1994), pp. 29–41.

Powell, Edward, 'The Strange Death of Sir John Mortimer: Politics and the Law of Treason in Lancastrian England', in *Rulers and Ruled in Late Medieval England*, ed. by Rowena E. Archer and Simon Walker (London: Hambledon, 1995), pp. 83–97.

Putter, Ad, 'A Historical Introduction', in *The Spirit of Medieval English Popular Romance*, ed. by Ad Putter and Jane Gilbert (Harlow: Longman, 2000), pp. 1–15.

Radulescu, Raluca L., *The Gentry Context for Malory's 'Morte Darthur'*, Arthurian Studies, LV (Cambridge: Brewer, 2003).

Radulescu, Raluca L., '*John Vale's Book* and Sir Thomas Malory's *Le Morte Darthur*: A Political Agenda', *Arthuriana*, 9.4 (1999), 69–80.

Radulescu, Raluca L., *Romance and its Contexts in Fifteenth-Century England: Politics, Piety, and Penitence* (Cambridge: Brewer, 2013).

Reames, Sherry L., *The 'Legenda aurea': A Reexamination of its Paradoxical History* (Madison: University of Wisconsin Press, 1985).

Rees Jones, Sarah, 'Thomas More's *Utopia* and Medieval London', in *Pragmatic Utopias: Ideals and Communities, 1200–1630*, ed. by Rosemary Horrox and Sarah Rees Jones (Cambridge: Cambridge University Press, 2001), pp. 117–35.

Richmond, Colin, 'Identity and Morality: Power and Politics during the Wars of the Roses', in *Power and Identity in the Middle Ages*, ed. by Huw Pryce and John Watts (Oxford: Oxford University Press, 2007), pp. 226–41.

Richmond, Colin, *The Paston Family in the Fifteenth Century: Fastolf's Will* (Cambridge: Cambridge University Press, 1996).

Richmond, Colin, 'Thomas Malory and the Pastons', in *Readings in Medieval English Romance*, ed. by Carol M. Meale (Cambridge: Brewer, 1994), pp. 195–208.

Richmond, Colin, and Margaret Lucille Kekewich, 'The Search for Stability, 1461–1483', in *The Politics of Fifteenth-Century England: John Vale's Book*, ed. by Margaret Lucille Kekewich and others (Stroud: Sutton, 1995), pp. 43–72.

Riddy, Felicity, 'Contextualizing *Le Morte Darthur*: Empire and Civil War', in *A Companion to Malory*, ed. by Elizabeth Archibald and A. S. G. Edwards, Arthurian Studies, XXXVII (Cambridge: Brewer, 1996), pp. 55–73.

Riddy, Felicity, 'John Hardyng's Chronicle and the Wars of the Roses', in *Arthurian Literature XII*, ed. by James P. Carley and Felicity Riddy (Cambridge: Brewer, 1993), pp. 91–108.

Riddy, Felicity, *Sir Thomas Malory* (Leiden: Brill, 1987).

Rollison, David, *A Commonwealth of the People: Popular Politics and England's Long Social Revolution, 1066–1649* (Cambridge: Cambridge University Press, 2010).

Rose, Mischa Jayne, 'Malory's *Morte Darthur* and the Idea of Treason' (unpublished doctoral thesis, University of Wales, Bangor, 1992).

Ross, Charles, *Edward IV* (1974; New Haven: Yale University Press, 1997).

Ross, Charles, 'The Reign of Edward IV', in *Fifteenth-Century England, 1399–1509: Studies in Politics and Society*, ed. by S. B. Chrimes, C. D. Ross, and R. A. Griffiths (Manchester: Manchester University Press, 1972), pp. 49–66.

Ross, Charles, 'Rumour, Propaganda and Popular Opinion during the Wars of the Roses', in *Patronage, the Crown and the Provinces in Later Medieval England*, ed. by Ralph A. Griffiths (Gloucester: Sutton, 1981), pp. 5–29.

Ross, Charles, *The Wars of the Roses: A Concise History* (London: Thames and Hudson, 1976).

Rothwell, William, 'Language and Government in Medieval England', *Zeitschrift für französische Sprache und Literatur*, 93 (1983), 258–70.

Royan, Nicola, 'The Fine Art of Faint Praise in Older Scots Historiography', in *The Scots and Medieval Arthurian Legend*, ed. by Rhiannon Purdie and Nicola Royan, Arthurian Studies, LXI (Cambridge: Brewer, 2005), pp. 43–54.

Rundle, David, 'Was There a Renaissance Style of Politics in Fifteenth-Century England?', in *Authority and Consent in Tudor England*, ed. by G. W. Bernard and S. J. Gunn (Aldershot: Ashgate, 2002), pp. 15–32.

Rushton, Cory, '"Of an Uncouthe Stede": The Scottish Knight in Middle English Arthurian Romances', in *The Scots and Medieval Arthurian Legend*, ed. by Rhiannon Purdie and Nicola Royan, Arthurian Studies, LXI (Cambridge: Brewer, 2005), pp. 109–19.

Scanlon, Larry, *Narrative, Authority, and Power: The Medieval Exemplum and the Chaucerian Tradition* (Cambridge: Cambridge University Press, 1994).

Scanlon, Larry, and James Simpson, 'Introduction', in *John Lydgate: Poetry, Culture, and Lancastrian England*, ed. by Larry Scanlon and James Simpson (Notre Dame: University of Notre Dame Press, 2006), pp. 1–11.

Scanlon, Paul A., 'Pre-Elizabethan Prose Romances in English', *Cahiers Élisabéthains: Études sur la pré-renaissance et la renaissance anglaises*, 12 (1977), 1–20.

Scase, Wendy, *Literature and Complaint in England, 1272–1553* (Oxford: Oxford University Press, 2007).

Scase, Wendy, '"Strange and Wonderful Bills": Bill-Casting and Political Discourse in Late-Medieval England", *New Medieval Literatures*, 2 (1998), 225–47.

Scase, Wendy, 'Writing and the "Poetics of Spectacle": Political Epiphanies in *The Arrivall of Edward IV* and Some Contemporary Lancastrian and Yorkist Texts', in *Images, Idolatry, and Iconoclasm in Late Medieval England*, ed. by Jeremy Dimmick, James Simpson, and Nicolette Zeeman (Oxford: Oxford University Press, 2002), pp. 172–84.

Scattergood, John, 'The Date and Composition of George Ashby's Poems', *Leeds Studies in English*, NS, 21 (1990), 167–76.

Scattergood, John, *Occasions for Writing: Essays on Medieval and Renaissance Literature, Politics and Society* (Dublin: Four Courts, 2010).

Scattergood, John, *Politics and Poetry in the Fifteenth Century* (London: Blandford, 1971).

Schirmer, Walter F., *John Lydgate: A Study in the Culture of the XVth Century*, trans. by Ann E. Keep (Berkeley: University of California Press, 1961).

Shepherd, Stephen H. A., 'The Middle English *Pseudo-Turpin Chronicle*', *Medium Aevum*, 65.1 (1996), 19–34.

Simms, Norman, 'Hungary and Hungarian Knights in Middle English Literature', *Parergon*, 8.1 (1990), 57–72.

Simpson, James, '"Dysemol Daies and Fatal Houres": Lydgate's *Destruction of Thebes* and Chaucer's *Knight's Tale*', in *The Long Fifteenth Century*, ed. by Helen Cooper and Sally Mapstone (Oxford: Clarendon Press, 1997), pp. 15–33.

Simpson, James, *Reform and Cultural Revolution, 1350–1547* (Oxford: Oxford University Press, 2002).

Skinner, Quentin, *The Foundations of Modern Political Thought*, 2 vols (Cambridge: Cambridge University Press, 1978).

Smith, Kathleen L., 'A Fifteenth-Century Vernacular Manuscript Reconstructed', *Bodleian Library Record*, 7 (1966), 234–41.

Spearing, A. C., 'Lydgate's Canterbury Tale: *The Siege of Thebes* and Fifteenth-Century Chaucerianism', *Fifteenth-Century Studies: Recent Essays*, ed. by Robert F. Yeager (Hamden, CT: Archon, 1984), pp. 333–64.

Spearing, A. C., *Medieval to Renaissance in English Poetry* (Cambridge: Cambridge University Press, 1985).

Spedding, Alison, '"I Shalle Send Word in Writing": Lexical Choices and Legal Acumen in the Letters of Margaret Paston', *Medium Aevum*, 77.2 (2008), 241–59.

Spiegel, Gabrielle M., 'History, Historicism, and the Social Logic of the Text in the Middle Ages', *Speculum*, 65.1 (1990), 59–86.

Stanivukovic, Goran V., 'English Renaissance Romances as Conduct Books for Young Men', in *Early Modern Prose Fiction: The Cultural Politics of Reading*, ed. by Naomi Conn Liebler (New York: Routledge, 2007), pp. 60–78.

Steiner, Emily, *Documentary Culture and the Making of Medieval English Literature* (Cambridge: Cambridge University Press, 2003).

Steiner, Emily, and Candace Barrington, 'Introduction', in *The Letter of the Law: Legal Practice and Literary Production in Medieval England*, ed. by Emily Steiner and Candace Barrington (Ithaca, NY: Cornell University Press, 2002), pp. 1–11.

Storey, R. L., *The End of the House of Lancaster* (London: Barrie & Rockliff, 1966).

Straker, Scott-Morgan, 'Propaganda, Intentionality, and the Lancastrian Lydgate', in *John Lydgate: Poetry, Culture, and Lancastrian England*, ed. by Larry Scanlon and James Simpson (Notre Dame: University of Notre Dame Press, 2006), pp. 98–128.

Strohm, Paul, *England's Empty Throne: Usurpation and the Language of Legitimation, 1399–1422* (New Haven: Yale University Press, 1998).

Strohm, Paul, *Hochon's Arrow: The Social Imagination of Fourteenth-Century Texts* (Princeton: Princeton University Press, 1992).

Strohm, Paul, *Politique: Languages of Statecraft between Chaucer and Shakespeare* (Notre Dame: University of Notre Dame Press, 2005).

Stuhmiller, Jacqueline, 'Iudicium Dei, iudicium fortunae: Trial by Combat in Malory's *Le Morte Darthur*', *Speculum*, 81 (2006), 427–62.

Summers, Joanna, *Late-Medieval Prison Writing and the Politics of Autobiography* (Oxford: Oxford University Press, 2004).

Sutton, Anne F., 'Caxton was a Mercer: His Social Milieu and Friends', in *England in the Fifteenth Century: Proceedings of the 1992 Harlaxton Symposium*, ed. by Nicholas Rogers (Stamford: Watkins, 1994), pp. 118–48.

Sutton, Anne F., 'Malory in Newgate: A New Document', *The Library: The Transactions of the Bibliographical Society*, Seventh Series, 1.3 (2000), 243–62.

Sutton, Anne F., and Livia Visser-Fuchs, 'The Provenance of the Manuscript: The Lives and Archive of Sir Thomas Cook and His Man of Affairs, John Vale', in *The Politics of Fifteenth-Century England: John Vale's Book*, ed. by Margaret Lucille Kekewich and others (Stroud: Sutton, 1995), pp. 73–123.

Thompson, Benjamin, 'Introduction: The Place of Henry VII in English History', in *The Reign of Henry VII*, ed. by Benjamin Thompson (Stamford: Watkins, 1995), pp. 1–10.

Thompson, J. A. F., '"The Arrivall of Edward IV": The Development of the Text', *Speculum*, 46.1 (1971), 84–93.

Virgoe, Roger, 'The Death of William de la Pole, Duke of Suffolk', *Bulletin of the John Rylands Library*, 47.2 (1964–5), 489–502.

Visser-Fuchs, Livia, 'Edward IV's "Memoir on Paper" to Charles, Duke of Burgundy: The So-called "Short Version of the Arrivall"', *Nottingham Medieval Studies*, 36 (1992), 167–227.

Wakelin, Daniel, *Humanism, Reading, and English Literature, 1430–1530* (Oxford: Oxford University Press, 2007).

Wakelin, Daniel, 'The Occasion, Author and Readers of *Knyghthode and Bataile*', *Medium Aevum*, 73.2 (2004), 260–72.

Wakelin, Daniel, 'Stephen Hawes and Courtly Education', in *The Oxford Handbook of Tudor Literature, 1485–1603*, ed. by Mike Pincombe and Cathy Shrank (Oxford: Oxford University Press, 2009), pp. 53–68.

Walker, Greg, 'When Did "the Medieval" End?: Retrospection, Foresight, and the End(s) of the English Middle Ages', in *The Oxford Handbook of Medieval Literature in English*, ed. by Elaine Treharne, Greg Walker, and William Green (Oxford: Oxford University Press, 2010), pp. 725–38.

Wallace, David, 'Dante in Somerset: Ghosts, Historiography, Periodization', *New Medieval Literatures*, 3 (1999), 9–38.

Wallace, David, 'Oxford English Literary History', *Journal of Medieval and Early Modern Studies*, 35.1 (2005), 13–24.

Wallace, David, *Premodern Places: Calais to Surinam, Chaucer to Aphra Behn* (Oxford: Blackwell, 2004).

Wang, Yu-Chiao, 'English Romance in Print from 1473 to 1535: Reception and the History of the Book' (unpublished doctoral thesis, University of Cambridge, 2008).

Watts, John, *Henry VI and the Politics of Kingship* (Cambridge: Cambridge University Press, 1996).

Watts, John, 'Ideas, Principles, and Politics', in *The Wars of the Roses*, ed. by A. J. Pollard (Basingstoke: Macmillan, 1995), pp. 110–33.

Watts, John, 'Introduction: History, the Fifteenth Century and the Renaissance', in *The End of the Middle Ages? England in the Fifteenth and Sixteenth Centuries*, ed. by John L. Watts (Stroud: Sutton, 1998), pp. 1–22.

Watts, John, *The Making of Polities: Europe, 1300–1500* (Cambridge: Cambridge University Press, 2009).

Watts, John, 'Polemic and Politics in the 1450s', in *The Politics of Fifteenth-Century England: John Vale's Book*, ed. by Margaret Lucille Kekewich and others (Stroud: Sutton, 1995), pp. 3–42.

Watts, John, '*The Policie in Christen Remes*: Bishop Russell's Parliamentary Sermons of 1483–84', in *Authority and Consent in Tudor England*, ed. by G. W. Bernard and S. J. Gunn (Aldershot: Ashgate, 2002), pp. 33–59.

Watts, John, 'The Pressure of the Public on Later Medieval Politics', in *Political Culture in Late Medieval Britain*, ed. by Linda Clark and Christine Carpenter (Woodbridge: Boydell, 2004), pp. 159–80.

Watts, John, 'Public or Plebs: The Changing Meaning of "The Commons", 1381–1549', in *Power and Identity in the Middle Ages*, ed. by Huw Pryce and John Watts (Oxford: Oxford University Press, 2007), pp. 242–60.

Watts, John, 'When Did Henry VI's Minority End?', in *Trade, Devotion and Governance: Papers in Later Medieval History*, ed. by Dorothy J. Clayton and others (Stroud: Sutton, 1994), pp. 116–39.

Whetter, K. S., 'On Misunderstanding Malory's Balyn', in *Re-viewing 'Le Morte Darthur': Texts and Contexts, Characters and Themes*, ed. by K. S. Whetter and Raluca L. Radulescu, Arthurian Studies, LX (Cambridge: Brewer, 2005), pp. 149–62.

Whetter, K. S., *Understanding Genre and Medieval Romance* (Aldershot: Ashgate, 2008).

Williams, Deanne, 'Medievalism in English Renaissance Literature', in *A Companion to Tudor Literature*, ed. by Kent Cartwright (Oxford: Wiley-Blackwell, 2010), pp. 213–27.

Williams, Elizabeth, 'England, Ireland and Iberia in *Olyuer of Castylle*: The View from Burgundy', in *Boundaries in Medieval Romance*, ed. by Neil Cartlidge, Studies in Medieval Romance, VI (Cambridge: Brewer, 2008), pp. 93–102.

Wilson, Robert H., 'More Borrowings by Malory from Hardyng's Chronicle', *Notes and Queries*, 17.6 (1970), 208–10.

Withrington, John, 'Caxton, Malory, and the Roman War in the *Morte Darthur*', *Studies in Philology*, 89.3 (1992), 350–66.

Wittgenstein, Ludwig, *Philosophical Investigations*, trans. by G. E. M. Anscombe (Oxford: Blackwell, 1953).

Wolffe, B. P., 'The Personal Rule of Henry VI', in *Fifteenth-Century England, 1399–1509: Studies in Politics and Society*, ed. by S. B. Chrimes, C. D. Ross, and R. A. Griffiths (Manchester: Manchester University Press, 1972), pp. 29–48.

Wood, Juliette, 'Where Does Britain End? The Reception of Geoffrey of Monmouth in Scotland and Wales', in *The Scots and Medieval Arthurian Legend*, ed. by Rhiannon Purdie and Nicola Royan, Arthurian Studies, LXI (Cambridge: Brewer, 2005), pp. 9–23.

Workman, Samuel K., *Fifteenth Century Translation as an Influence on English Prose*, Princeton Studies in English, XVIII (Princeton: Princeton University Press, 1940).

Wormald, Jenny, 'National Pride, Decentralised Nation: The Political Culture of Fifteenth-Century Scotland', in *Political Culture in Late Medieval Britain*, ed. by Linda Clark and Christine Carpenter (Woodbridge: Boydell, 2004), pp. 181–94.

Wright, N. A. R., 'The *Tree of Battles* of Honoré Bouvet and the Laws of War', in *War, Literature, and Politics in the Late Middle Ages*, ed. by C. T. Allmand (Liverpool: Liverpool University Press, 1976), pp. 12–31.

Yeager, R. F., 'Literary Theory at the Close of the Middle Ages: William Caxton and William Thynne', *Studies in the Age of Chaucer*, 6 (1984), 135–64.

WORKS OF REFERENCE

Boffey, Julia, and A. S. G. Edwards, *A New Index of Middle English Verse* (London: British Library, 2005).

Briquet, C. M., *Les Filigranes*, 4 vols (Amsterdam: Paper Publications Society, 1968).

Kato, Tomomi, *A Concordance to the Works of Sir Thomas Malory* (Tokyo: University of Tokyo Press, 1974).

Kinneavy, Gerald Byron, ed., *A Concordance to the Towneley Plays* (New York: Garland, 1990).

Kinneavy, Gerald Byron, ed., *A Concordance to the York Plays* (New York: Garland, 1986).

Kurath, Hans, and others, eds, *The Middle English Dictionary* (Ann Arbor: University of Michigan Press, 1952–2001).

A Manual of the Writings in Middle English, 1050–1500, ed. by J. B. Severs and others (New Haven: Connecticut Academy of Arts and Sciences, 1967–).

Mizobata, Kiyokazu, ed., *A Concordance to Caxton's Morte Darthur (1485)* (Osaka: Osaka Books, 2009).

Old French–English Dictionary, ed. by Alan Hindley, Frederick W. Langley, and Brian J. Levy (Cambridge: Cambridge University Press, 2000).

Pfleiderer, Jean D., and Michael J. Preston, eds, *A Complete Concordance to the Chester Mystery Plays* (New York: Garland, 1981).

Pollard, A. W., and G. R. Redgrave, *A Short-Title Catalogue of Books Printed in England, Scotland, and Ireland and of English Books Printed Abroad, 1475–1640*, 2nd edn, 3 vols (London: British Library, 1976–91).

Simpson, John A., and E. S. C. Weiner, eds, *The Oxford English Dictionary*, 2nd edn, 20 vols (Oxford: Clarendon Press, 1989).

Woledge, Brian, *Bibliographie des romans et nouvelles en prose française antérieurs à 1500*, 2 vols (Genève: Droz, 1954–75).

Index